INDIA AND EMERGING ASIA

INDIA AND EMERGING ASIA

EDITOR
R.R. SHARMA

WITH A FOREWORD BY I.K. GUJRAL

SAGE Publications
New Delhi/Thousand Oaks/London

First published in 2005 by

Sage Publications India Pvt Ltd
B-42, Panchsheel Enclave
New Delhi 110 017
www.indiasage.com

Sage Publications Inc
2455 Teller Road
Thousand Oaks, California 91320

Sage Publications Ltd
1 Oliver's Yard, 55 City Road
London EC1Y 1SP

Published by Tejeshwar Singh for Sage Publications India Pvt Ltd, typeset in 10/12 LifeBT at Excellent Laser Typesetters, New Delhi, and printed at Chaman Enterprises, New Delhi

Library of Congress Cataloging-in-Publication Data

India and emerging Asia / editor, R.R. Sharma.
    p. cm.
    Includes bibliographical references and index.
    1. Civil society—Asia. 2. Asia—Social policy. 3. Asia—Economic policy. 4. Asia—Politics and government. 5. National security—Asia. 6. Asia—Foreign relations—India. 7. India—Foreign relations—Asia. I. Sharma, Ram Rattan.

JQ36.I53   303.48'25—dc22   2005   2005021700

ISBN: 0–7619–3426–X (HB)   81–7829–567–9 (India–HB)

Sage Production Team: Madhuparna Banerjee, Anindita Pandey, Girish Sharma and Santosh Rawat

CONTENTS

FOREWORD

The recently held Bandung Conference of 40 leaders of Africa and
Asia was indeed a landmark in the history of the two continents.
As the host, President of Indonesia said, 'It took 50 long years for
this conference to happen, but Asia and Africa have finally assembled
here again. Today, the sons and daughters of Asia and Africa stand
together in this hall as equals. We stand tall, proud and free. In 2005,
we have to sound a different battle-cry. In 1955, the battle-cry of
the day was freedom which made perfect sense given the persistence
of colonialism back then. But now that Asia and Africa are free,
we must take on the next phase and this is the battle for human
dignity.'

All the same let there be no doubt that the world and more
specifically a large part of Asia is in serious trouble. Country after
country is destabilised by the 'Jihadis' who attack at will any civil
society unmindful of religious beliefs of the victims. While the spectre
of September 11 continues to haunt, the diplomacies of the world
have not yet buried its ghost. Remnants of the Taliban are not letting
the Karzai regime stabilise in Afghanistan. History tells us that a
disturbed Afghanistan had always affected the peace and stability of
the adjoining countries in Central and South Asia and now the
Central Eurasia. The process of nation-building in Afghanistan is so
muddled that even the coalition forces are still unable to tackle it
effectively, while deployment of the American forces in Central Asia
has added a new dynamic to the region. A crucial question, from the
standpoint of the security environment, is how long would the US
and the NATO forces remain there, and for how long can Russia and
China tolerate their presence in their strategic backyards.

Instability in the region is nurturing the growth of Islamist fundamentalism in Xinjiang and Uighur autonomous regions of China. Media reports state that over 10,000 Uighurs were given military cum religious training in Pakistan and Afghanistan.

The Central Asian Republics, as we know, were born out of Soviet Union's collapse. They are yet to emerge as viable nation states with muscle to resist the internal insurgencies and external onslaughts of the Islamist revivalists. While economic stagnation is adding to their instability, the authoritarian rulers do not appreciate that oppressive governance is adding fuel to the fire. The SCO (Shanghai Cooperation Organization) of the six powers was well perceived, but it is yet to effectively counter the widely spread fundamentalist militancy.

My ears have heard the sweet music of 'Twenty-first century being the century of Asia' at the BOAO Forum in China. This may happen. But we must not ignore some flash points that are unfortunately located in Asia. In West Asia, we have the bleeding sores of Palestine and Iraq. In East Asia, we see simmering tensions over the Taiwan issue, and the grave new threat of nuclearisation of the Korean peninsula. Finally, in India, the Kashmir issue has led to a perpetual state of hostility with Pakistan that continues to cause anxiety. Though the post Musharraf visit scenario makes me optimistic, all the same, the history of these disputes continue to linger. What does bear emphasis is the presence of a major non-Asian power in Asia's security equations, and the role that this has played in perpetuating, and in some cases, escalating these tensions.

Expedient policies always have a way of returning to haunt their creators. Today, the products of its own past policies have returned to torment America. The policy makers there seem to have forsaken any claim to caution and idealism to formulate a new and aggressive foreign policy doctrine reliant on military force, and a self-proclaimed right to intervene anywhere in any region of the world that its self-interest demands.

The objectives of this new strategy were recently elaborated in the US National Security Strategy document that underlined an ostensible containment of WMD, defeating global terrorism, and promoting democratic values. These objectives while noble in themselves have in actual practice come to cloak a more sinister design.

The stated objective of reducing the threat from the proliferation of weapons of mass destruction is laudable. In Iraq, however, no such weapons of mass destruction have been found till now. It is now clear that the threat of Iraq's weapons of mass destruction were exaggerated and not truthful.

In the absence of any discovery of the weapons of mass destruction, the coalition leaders now say that the war was justified to defeat the threat of global terrorism. This is a pathetic attempt at a post-facto rationalisation of the war. We had no sympathy with the authoritarianism of Saddam Hussein or the others. But it is well known that Iraq's secular regime, in marked contrast to some of its neighbours, was laying emphasis on shunning religious extremism, while giving women equal status and protecting the rights of its Christian and other minorities. The more reasonable inference is that the neo-conservative elites within the US administration saw the tragedy of the attack of September 11 as an opportunity to destroy the only government in the region that was strong enough to challenge the Western policies, particularly as they related to Israel and the Palestine question.

When noble objectives are distorted and used as a cloak to hide dishonourable motives, it is bad enough. Even more objectionable, however, are the means with which the coalition powers had chosen to pursue those objectives.

The unfolding tragedy in Iraq has seemingly given new life and sustenance to the terrorists' cause. In the preceding months, we have witnessed their deadly attacks in Indonesia, Saudi Arabia, Morocco, while in Afghanistan, a newly rejuvenated Taliban is attacking and inflicting losses on the armed forces of the new Afghanis government. I am deliberately not mentioning the horrors of terror that we in India continue to experience on a daily basis.

For sometime now, questions have been raised as to the likelihood of an American aggression on Iran. While nobody should make the mistake of underestimating America's willingness to engage in military operations even when America's own national security is not directly involved, I doubt very much whether the Pentagon will attack Iran, three times the population and four times the landmass of Iraq. But, military operations short of a full-scale invasion cannot be finally ruled out. Given the internal political situation in Iran and the tension between those who want reforms and those who oppose them, America might try to destabilise that country by threatening military invasion.

Here may I put forward certain ideas, which I feel are essential to any process of stabilising Asia. The first must be retaining of the primacy of the United Nations as the global multilateral forum, which embodies the collective will of its member states and the rule of law. It has been sometimes argued that the United Nations process is cumbersome and time-consuming, and requires such improvements as would make it more democratic and representative. It certainly does not follow that the United Nations system and the democratic values it enshrines may be cast aside. Despite all its perceived faults, the multilateral world order has kept the world free from major wars over the past half century, and so fulfilled its primary objective of saving future generations from 'the scourge of war'. The democratic basis on which international relations have been run so far has contributed to the participation of all nations, howsoever large or small, in the management of global affairs, imbibing thereby a sense of global community. Human Rights have been central in this message. The United Nations has encouraged both the notion of peace and prosperity as a global birthright, and the democratic means to attain.

We must conceive of an Asian security order which comprises primarily all the states of Asia. The trilateral consultations at the foreign minister's level between Russia, China and India provide a basis for such an Asian forum. Tripartite consultations should gradually be progressively enlarged to include Southeast Asia and West Asia with a view to eventually unite all of Asia within this forum. An Asian forum will reflect Asian values such as consensus, conciliation, and a peaceful resolution of all disputes. Restoring these values is central to the maintenance of Asian stability.

It is time for Asians who had suffered three centuries of Imperial rule to collectively meet challenges of destabilisation lurking before Asia in general and South, West and Central Asia in particular. In a situation when the South Asian subcontinent and the areas adjacent to it are facing grave threats of destabilisation, it is all the more important to strengthen in every possible manner the bilateral and regional initiatives to meet these situations. Instead of looking to Washington or London for mediation or interventions to stabilise the region, the Asian states must themselves come forward with creative initiatives to build an effective structure of Asian peace and stability in the spirit of the UN Charter which endorses regional security systems. The three survivors in the East Asia economic crisis of the nineties—India, Russia and China—have an important obligation to help forge a system of Asian security and cooperation which will go a long way to revive the global economy that is presently ridden with a deep crisis.

I endorse Prof. Sharma's words:

This is also implicit from the fact that the US is rightsizing its forces in Europe, and diverting some of the resources of US Pacific Command to North Indian Ocean. Indian Ocean is, in fact, re-emerging as a strategic area of concern. The Indian Ocean region encompasses a fifty-six countries, eighteen of which are land-locked. Quite a few of these countries, particularly in Central Asia, and West Asia, have huge reservoirs of hydrocarbon resources. Therefore, there is a larger emphasis on the issue of energy security. The proposal for declaring the Indian Ocean as a 'Zone of Peace' is still being debated. However, there are not many takers. Significantly, there are several other multilateral security initiatives, as the countries of the region grapple with their economic and security compulsion. These initiatives are invariably leading towards multilateral economic agreements and confidence-building measures. Over and above there are, however, several other challenges, which are:

Maintenance of stability, owing to poor governance and de-mocracy deficit, ethnic disputes and sectarian strife, rising terror-ism. These are potentially dangerous areas, which stroke the embers of conflicts, internal dislocations and social unrest.

For fair management of water and energy resources, it is important for India, China and other regional power to seriously examine the non-traditional threats to regional security. Obviously this is a complex task, which, however cannot be pushed under the carpet.

The Bandung Conference has reiterated that the spirit of Bandung, the core principles of which are solidarity, friendship and coopera-tion, continues to be a solid, relevant and effective foundation for fostering better relations among Asian and African countries and resolving global issues of common concern. The 1955 Bandung Conference remains as a beacon in guiding the future progress of Asia and Africa. This volume edited by Prof. Sharma on *India and Emerging Asia* is a serious and timely contribution in understanding the complex profile of Asia.

I.K. Gujral
(Former Prime Minister, India)

16 May 2005

INTRODUCTION

R.R. Sharma

Understanding Asia in the New Millennium

This volume explores new perspectives on Asia. The leading issues which have been explored at length are: the political, cultural and geo-strategic identity of Asia; the security/insecurity environment and related issues; regional cooperation and multilateral arrangements; and finally, the options available to India as a significant player in Asia. Some of the questions which were uppermost in our minds were: what is the nature of society, particularly, civil society in Asia? what is the nature of domestic politics, or the nature of governance? what are the major sources of insecurity? are these regional or global, or both? what is the strength of Asia, and what are its intrinsic weaknesses? how can they be obviated? and, what are the available policy options? In short, our endeavour was directed at one goal—to understand the emerging Asia and its leading problems. Several chapters in this volume suggest that Asia needs to be understood in dynamic terms as a *project in process*.

There is a view shared in many circles that the 'twenty-first century belongs to Asia'. The leaders of both India and China—the two most influential powers in Asia—put this across in the recent past. There is now a larger consensus that Asia's importance has grown manifold in the global arena. Obviously, it plays a strategic and more assertive role in both regional and global politics. Its economic and strategic environment has been transformed in a fundamental sense, particularly in the last decade. And this process is likely to unfold even more vigorously for several decades to come, contributing to its dynamic strength. Any number of indicators pinpoints to the emerging reality that Asia is the most dynamic region of the world in the twenty-first century. The emerging 'Asian Economic Community', which encompasses ASEAN, China, Japan, India and South Korea, is gradually developing as the 'centre of gravity' of the global economy. Evidently, the growing economic importance of Asia is reflected in the fact that its developing nations have registered a continuous economic growth, and political stability. Their economies registered in 2004 an average rise of 7.8 per cent as against 4.6 for Latin America, 4.5 for Africa, and 6.6 for developing economies as a whole.

The geographical spread of Asia is indicative of its importance in global affairs. Asia occupies a little more than one-third of the landmass of the world's territorial spread. It is populated by more than half of the world's homo sapiens. It is blessed with the world's largest energy resources, and this ensures that it would enjoy formidable clout in the global affairs. Writing in *Foreign Affairs*, American analysts William Crow and Alan Romberg observed: 'The qualities that define Asia are enduring; it is huge, diverse, dynamic and, frequently, dangerous.'[1] Asia's endurance has been tested time and again. It has faced serious challenges of economic and political turbulence. In spite of these problems, contemporary Asia is changing, and in many ways, it is quite different from that which existed previously in the first part of the last century. Asia presently, as stated earlier, is incomparably far more developed than at any stage of its development. Shri I.K. Gujral, the former prime minister, aptly points out:

> In Asia, during the course of the past fifty years, millions have been lifted from the very edge of subsistence and hunger to the secure prosperity of the middle class. If we add up the totals for Asia, we will find well over a billion people have made the fundamental transition in their economic and social standing.

He argues that it happened because Asia has had the benefit of 'an egalitarian social structure.... Egalitarianism is one of Asia's great strengths leading to social cohesion. A natural inclination towards education, learning, industriousness, enterprise, and family values—

these are Asia's strength, and the foundation of its prosperity.'[2] Gujral, apparently, seeks to define Asia not only as what it is, but also what it has been in the past—a nursery, a home of great civilisations. Evidently, a cogent idea of progress associated with the mainstream of Asian development is rooted in the emphasis on civilisation.

The point being argued is that Asia has made its mark on the world stage because of its several 'enduring qualities'. Notwithstanding its vastness and diversity, it is moving towards what K. Subramanyam calls, 'Asian security in strategic unity'. The traditional rivalries among the Asian nations are increasingly becoming muted, though these have not yet disappeared. There is now a robust geo-political framework in Asia. Highlighting the emerging scenario, the former US Ambassador in India, Robert Blackwell argued: 'Asia's century is now under way...Asia is poised to become the strategic center of gravity in international politics.'[3]

Obviously, Asia has attracted considerable attention, as suggested earlier, on account of its rapid economic growth over the past decades. Of course, China and India are very convincing examples of this trend. More significantly, the 'Asian Economic Community' is in the making. The perception of this community is closely related to the new dynamics in Asia, and the existing synergies. While Prime Minister Manmohan Singh called it as an 'arch of advantage', Japanese Prime Minister Koizumi termed it as an 'arch of prosperity'. There is a broad recognition that the formation of the community would ensure enormous advantage and benefits owing to closer integration. Several Asian countries such as Singapore, Malaysia, South Korea, Taiwan, Thailand and Indonesia have grown at the rate of 6–7 per cent in the recent past.[4] Thus, nearly all the major economies in Asia-Pacific seem to be quite robust. There are indicators that Japan has finally moved out of 'a decade long recession'. While its economy grew at the rate of 2.7 per cent in 2003, its projected growth rate in 2004–05 is 3.5 per cent. There are other estimates which put it even higher at 4.4 per cent. Chinese economy, apparently, is most healthy in the region. Its reported rate of growth in the year 2003 was nearly 10 per cent. In fact, China has been growing at the average growth rate of about 9 per cent per year since 1980, and it is estimated to maintain its growth rate of 9 per cent and more in the years to come.[5] China is already the fourth largest economy in the world, and it is growing 'three to four times the rate of the first three'. It will soon be 'one of the largest exporters of capital, buying companies across the globe'.[6] The economic success 'of our age is rise of Asia', argued John Major, the former British prime minister. Significantly, economic strength brings in its wake, in due course, political, military, and cultural influence. It is evident that 'political authority is the child of economic success'.

Some analysts argue that the Asian Economic Community could be 'built in a gradual manner to begin with Japan, ASEAN, China, India and Korea (JACIK)'. JACIK has the 'potential to emerge as one of the major regional economic grouping'—as large as EU in terms of income, as large as NAFTA in terms of trade.[7] Significantly, there is now a widespread realisation within several parts of Asia on the imperative need and relevance of a broad overarching framework to consolidate various sub-regional and bilateral initiatives into viable regional regimes. Regionalism (and multilateralism), under the overarching umbrella of Asian Economic Community, has the potential to exploit the synergies between several Asian countries. The proposed East Asian Summit to be held in November 2005 in Malaysia is projected to give an impetus to broader regionalism in Asia. The *socio-economic bonding will ultimately define and consolidate the identity of Asia* and the Asian Economic Community.

The Asian Relations Conference held in Delhi in 1947, at the instance of Jawaharlal Nehru, was the first major exercise in, what he called, 'bringing together for a larger ideal'. This led him to plead for an 'Eastern federation', which could include, among others, 'China, India, Burma, Ceylon, Nepal, Afghanistan, Malaya, Iran'. Nehru was thus the first and the foremost Asian leader of his time who seriously addressed himself to the problems of Asian identity, development, and security. He visualised the prospect of a 'close union' of countries bordering on the Indian Ocean both for 'defence and trade purpose, a system of defence stretching from the Middle East to South East Asia'. He was conscious of the fact that both India and China were destined to play a key role in Asia in the years to come. In geo-strategic terms, China is located at the very heart of Asia. It is the only country that abuts nearly all the regions of Asia. One of the contributors to this volume aptly says that 'China defines Asia; there can be no Asia without China'. China has obviously burst into far-reaching prominence. The resurgent Asia, as argued earlier, is led by China, and is likely to transform and reshape not only Asia, but also the global landscape; its pre-eminence as an economic and military power in world politics is a foregone conclusion.

Likewise, India forms the core of South Asia. Its geography imparts a vantage position to her in the geo-politics of Asia. Because of its 'strategic position', as Nehru puts it, India is also destined to play 'a significant role' in shaping the emerging profile of Asia. It was this vision which led Nehru to declare at the Asian Relations Conference that India is the natural centre and focal point of many forces at work in Asia. That is why India deserved a 'special role' in restructuring Asia. Several years later, the noted historian E.P. Thompson, one of the finest minds of the twentieth century, arrived at a similar assessment stating that 'India is not an important country, but perhaps the most important country for the future of the world'. India is growing with impressive determination, and thus adds huge weight to the Asian balance. However, its development and security is closely intertwined with other sub-regions of Asia. Her potential is enormous, not only in IT, biotechnology, or molecular biology, but also in manufacturing and engineering. It is already in the 'midst of an explosion of ambition'. Obviously, it foreshadows a far larger role for India. In the latter half of the last century, US, Japan and EU were at the forefront of world growth. In the years to come, China and India (and Russia) will join them. As a result, as John Major observes, 'growth in the world economy will be better balanced... and political power will be more widespread.'

The Other Face of Asia

The new Asia, however, has a complex personality. While the profile of its growing strength is pleasing, its intrinsic weakness is daunting. There are several dimensions of its obvious weakness. Some of these are of critical nature, and impinge upon the socio-political stability and security of the Asian countries. The foremost of these is the democracy deficit. In political discourse, the genealogy of democracy in Asia is fairly well researched. The political regimes in many parts of Asia are, by and large, devoid of legitimacy as well as long-term political and strategic vision. The domestic politics and the systems of governance impose severe limitations on the efficacy of political institutions and structures. Quite a few of these countries have had military regimes which were invariably interested in holding on to power. The fragile character of the political system thus, in many countries of Asia, is largely due to 'façade democracies' which have been largely imposed from above. These have been instituted in accordance with the minimal principles of democracy, namely, the so-called 'free' formal elections. In several countries of Asia, the incumbent political elites have built authoritarian models of façade democracy, eliminating nearly all means for the popular will to be expressed through political pluralism. The self-absorbed elite has thus created a political and social environment which fosters social tensions and conflicts. Consequently, the organs of the state resort to coercive means. The end result is popular discontent, leading to radical and underground moments.

In theoretical terms, the façade democracies do not engender a healthy and functional framework of 'elite-mass linkage'. The lack of elite-mass linkage not only prevents the development of socio-political dialogue but also encourages traditionalist–conservative formations. The façade democracy is invariably static and fragile, and it obviously creates wide-ranging instability and insecurity for itself, and most of all for its neighbours. Thus, one of the key problems for many countries in Asia is the total absence of linkages between the people at large, and their governments. This is true of nearly all countries in West and Central Asia, which are the two most volatile regions in Asia. Consequently, the formation of a healthy civil society in Asia has been held in check.

Prof Ernest Gellner, a noted political scientist, has rightly pointed out that the concept of civil society had 'no living resonance or evocativeness' until the middle of the eighties. It was distinctly 'covered in dust'. It then emerged as a highly valued tool of political analysis. Gellner noted that what the term civil society denoted was absent in extensive parts of the world, including Asia. He wrote:

> The absence was felt acutely in societies which had strongly centralized all aspects of life, and where a single political-economic ideological hierarchy tolerated no rivals...this caused the rest of society to approximate an atomized condition, and dissent then became a work of heresy....[8]

Gellner was actually speaking about the socialist countries of East Europe, but his observations, by and large, approximate the political conditions in several parts of Asia, which lack the participatory democracy that allows some space for the development of civil society.

In West Asia, as well as in Central Asia, the political elite does not pretend to have any democratic ambition. It has consciously stalled or backtracked democratic political reform. Likewise, Southeast Asia until 1995 was, in the words of Emerson, 'world's most recalcitrant' region.[9] It waded off all kinds of pressure for democratisation. Myanmar and Pakistan are stuck into military regimes; Indonesia and Philippines had to live under the dictatorship of Suharto and Marcos for a long period. Both Malaysia and Singapore prefer a single party system. The whole of Indo-China had similar regimes. Thailand is also deficient in strong democratic institutions.

It is thus obvious that the emerging fledgling democracies in Southeast Asia have yet to create strong democratic institutions, and a healthy civil society. And, if the security environment is adversely affected by the regional and global politics in future, the 'newly minted' democracies can reverse the process of democratisation. These are, as yet, basically fragile democracies. The substantial threat to Asian security does not come only from without, but from the nature of things, i.e., from within.

In addition to internal factors, which contribute to democracy deficit in various sub-regions of Asia, there are several external factors, which have a strategic bearing on the problem. Most important of these is the Western meddling, particularly that of the US. These external powers have invariably plotted to secure friendly regimes, against the will of the people. There are several examples of this, more particularly in the Middle East. The US, even now, continues to prop up dictators, or human right abusing corrupt regimes. The obvious contradiction between the proclaimed US commitment to democracy and the real action is clearly reflected in several cases of close US cooperation with worst kind of dictatorship. The rhetoric only serves the American short-term interests. The other variant of this kind of politics is to implant formalist democracies, which are only half-genuine, half-imported. Huntington claims that these were the 'third wave' of democracies, which were created 'top down'.[10] Forced democratisation from top down ultimately led to façade democratisation in which case the external patron accepts a pseudo-democratisation.

Global Politics and Security Issues

In terms of global politics, the US has emerged as the pre-eminent player in Asia. Because of a major paradigm shift in the US foreign policy in the wake of events of September 11, the continent of Asia is in imminent danger of becoming more unstable and less secure. Its policies have transformed the strategic space of Asia. Its security policy arsenal now includes the doctrines of 'preemption' and 'hegemony'. These are supplemented by the so-called 'war on terror'. These have been designed to secure and protect American interests in global politics. Consequently, the US has a huge military presence in several regions of Asia. Guided by neo-conservative politics, the US strategy, apparently, is to set up a system of global governance, and force other nations into compliance.

President Bush proclaimed the so-called 'doctrine of the war on terror' in the post-September 11 period. There was a wider consensus that terrorism has emerged as a huge issue in global politics. And therefore, there was a need to wage a global war on terrorism. It was not only a military challenge, but also an ideological challenge. The doctrine of war on terror is, in fact, more relevant to Asia, because the arena of war on terror is Asia. The entire Asia, from West Asia to Northeast Asia, has become the 'theatre of war'. There was no serious consultation with the Asian countries on the issue of terrorism. Rather than seeking to work with the Asian countries, particularly in West Asia, the US proceeded to invade and occupy Iraq, which posed no threat to the US, and had no connection with Al Qaeda, or some other formidable terrorist groups. Richard Clarke rightly observes that Iraqi link to Al Qaeda was a 'minor footnote' in comparison to 'links with other regimes' which are on friendly terms with the US.[11] Rather than seek a unified global consensus to destroy the 'ideological roots of terrorism', the US lashed out unilaterally as a 'super-bully', disdaining multilateral mechanisms and institutions. The nascent consensus against terrorism has thus been shattered by an over-reaching US intervention. Several countries in Asia, rather Eurasia, have vulnerabilities to terrorism, and there was the possibility or the unique opportunity to address their concerns with allies around the world. This is lost, and Asia has become less secure. In fact, the whole of Eurasia, as Brzezinski points out, has now emerged as 'the principal arena of future power politics'.

At this stage one must pause to raise certain questions. What is the appropriate US military role in Asia? What are the American security objectives? In the light of growing economic strength of a number of Asian countries, what sort of US presence in the region is necessarily desirable?

There are several countries in Asia which regard US as a stabilising force in the region. The degrees to which nations hold this view vary. However, this is a perspective shared by quite a few leading players such as Japan, Korea, Philippines, etc. The obvious salient issue is not whether the US should maintain its presence in Asia, but how, at what level, and on what conditions. In the foremost case, US role in Asia has to be one of stabilising presence, more than anything else. Russians have hinted that the US interests in the region can be better served through multilateral security arrangements. However, the current American administration has invariably rejected such ideas on the plea that this would undermine the security relations in Asia. While the security of the region essentially depends on the close cooperation between the Asian nations, major global powers have to be involved. Obviously, the US cannot be excluded from such a strategic framework.

The US has already evolved viable bilateral relations with all major Asian nations—China, Japan, Korea, India and Russia. This is in the wider interest of the US to help maintain the benign environment in the region. A new-look American presence in Asia, with a stronger commitment to Asian regionalism and multilateralism, will serve everyone well for many years to come. Undoubtedly, this will require a more dynamic policy, one that is more 'forward looking', and that seeks to help 'shape the inevitable changes' in Asia. There is a security axiom called 'reassurance', which implies that the security of a country would be sustained by ensuring adequate sense of security of others, including hostile states. There are practically very few states in the region which are hostile to US.

However, Asia is learning to fall back upon its own wisdom and resources. The silver lining is that there are several multilateral organisations which are working over time to build mutual trust and cooperation in economic, political, security, and socio-cultural fields. The most notable of these are ASEAN, ASEAN+3, ARF, SCO and SAARC. As pointed out earlier, ASEAN summits held in the recent past have given a good deal of impetus to regionalism in Asia with the proposed launch of an East Asian Community. This is an important development of major significance, particularly for India. Prime Minister Manmohan Singh has clearly indicated the importance India attaches to her integration with east Asia. India's 'look east' policy has a strong 'economic rationale'. A stronger connectivity with east Asia will not only create productive links in the region, but also foster greater security and prosperity. East Asia was regarded as the theatre of competition between India and China. Times are changing. India-China relations are no longer looked at from an adversarial prism.

Likewise, Russian proposal for triangular strategic cooperation between Russia, China and India is gaining some legitimacy. The three Asian nations are contiguous with almost all other countries in the region and therefore, cooperation between them could lead to stability, peace and security for all. It could also give an impetus to a multi-layered cooperative dialogue. The ground reality has changed to the extent that there is a large consensus, now, in favour of a more cooperative strategic and security paradigm in the region. Thus, there are serious efforts made to put in place the economic and political architecture, which is 'conducive to Asia's emergence as a pre-eminent region.... This can make the 21st century the Asian century in the truest sense'.[12]

To sum up, it needs to be emphasised that the economic, political, and security situation has undergone a paradigm shift in Asia. The ideological battles have receded into the background. While the ideological conflict domain has narrowed down, the challenge of terrorism and religious fundamentalism has moved to the forefront. The events of September 11 have brought about a vast shift in the security concerns. However, the US agenda of the 'war against terrorism' is much broader than eliminating the terrorist groups or states. This, and several other developments, has led Asian affairs to dominate regional and global politics in the opening decade of the twenty-first century. Strategic equations, globally and regionally, are fast changing, and consequently, the salience of world affairs has shifted to Asia.

This is also implicit from the fact that the US is rightsizing its forces in Europe, and diverting some of the resources of the US Pacific Command to north Indian Ocean. Indian Ocean is, in fact, re-emerging as a strategic area of concern. The Indian Ocean region encompasses 56 countries, 18 of which are landlocked. Quite a few of these countries, particularly in Central Asia, and West Asia, have huge reservoirs of hydrocarbon resources. Therefore, there is a larger emphasis on the issue of energy security. The proposal for declaring the Indian Ocean as a 'Zone of Peace' is still being debated. However, there are not many takers. Significantly, there are several other multilateral security initiatives, as the countries of the region grapple with their economic and security compulsions. These initiatives are invariably leading towards multilateral economic agreements, and confidence-building measures. Over and above, there are, however, several other challenges.

(*a*) Maintenance of stability—Owing to poor governance and democracy deficit, ethnic disputes and sectarian strife has led to rising terrorism. These are potentially dangerous areas, which strike the embers of conflicts, internal dislocations and social unrest.

(*b*) Fair management of water and energy resources—It is fairly important for India, China and other regional powers, to seriously examine the non-traditional threats to regional security. Obviously, this is a complex task, which, however, cannot be pushed under the carpet.

The Contributions

S.D. Muni and C. Raja Mohan explore the full range of new foreign policy options that have become available to India in a rapidly changing Asia. The authors go back to Nehru's vision for Asian solidarity in the founding years of the Indian Republic and argue that the dream, which was shattered during the Cold War, might now indeed be realisable. The changed conditions in Asia and India's own growing economic weight and military capabilities have generated the prospect of a much larger role for India in Asian international relations in the coming years. The importance of that role, Muni and Raja Mohan suggest, will depend upon how successfully India will manage its strategic autonomy in a world dominated by one superpower. Besides making the case for simultaneous improvement of India's relations with all the great powers, the authors insist that India must take the leadership in promoting regional economic integration in South Asia. They call for unilateral measures, where necessary, by India to intensify the trends towards regionalism in the subcontinent. Muni and Raja Mohan also call for leveraging India's new capabilities for enhancing its presence in all the abutting regions around the subcontinent—from West Asia to Southeast Asia through the Persian Gulf and Central Asia. They also call for better synergy between the different instruments of India's strategic policy—defence, diplomacy and commerce.

Varun Sahni asserts that Asia is not yet a region, but rather a continent consisting of several regions. In the first part of the chapter, the various key players in Asia—the US, China, India, Pakistan, Indonesia, Iran, Japan and Australia—and the regions in which they are embedded are analysed in order to arrive at a clearer understanding of security in Asia today. In the section that follows, the various security configurations that could emerge on the Asian continent (or more broadly in the Asia-Pacific) are explored, and their respective implications for India examined. Three alternative security arrangements could be envisaged for Asia—a region of opposing axes and balances, a region managed by a *directoire* of great powers, or a region enmeshed in a cooperative security arrangement. Unlike the first two options, which could prove dangerous for India in the long run, cooperative security in Asia would appear to be in India's interests. An 'Asian Helsinki process' could potentially reduce the size of arsenals in Asia, enmesh Chinese and American capabilities in Asia within larger cooperative process, lead to the evolution of a new and authentic Asian identity, build habits of cooperative behaviour on the Asian continent, and perhaps even play a role in the democratisation of China. He concludes with the assertion that there can be fewer tasks more challenging and worthwhile—both in a normative sense and in terms of India's concrete interests—than for Indian diplomacy to begin the groundwork for the construction of a cooperative mechanism of Asian security.

Manoj Joshi explains that it is basically Pakistan's worldview of India, which is the source of problems between the two countries. This worldview is the legacy of the pre-Partition period. In the post-Partition period, the Pakistan army gradually emerged as the dominant force. Joshi argues that the pre-Partition worldview was progressively militarised in a four-tier strategy. The first of these was to earmark a larger portion of budget on defence. Then it tried to enter into several military alignments, both for the purpose of strengthening its own security, as well as to pressurise India. Next, it launched its nuclear programme with a view to building nuclear weapons. Lastly, Pakistan offered its support to separatist movements in India. The other dimension of this was to launch terrorist acts against India. In both cases, the underlying assumption was the destabilisation of the country. Joshi explicates the weakness of Pakistan's strategy.

According to him, these policies skewed Pakistan's economy, foreign relations and domestic politics towards a strategy of unsustainable competition with India. It did create some problems for India, but led to more serious problems for Pakistan itself. However in the post-September 11 period, Pakistan is reviewing the whole gamut of issues related to its domestic politics, relations with India, and global politics. The outcome is uncertain, but bound to impact the future of Asia.

Mahapatra argues that the US considers Japan, China and India as the three major Asian powers. While the understandable desire of the US policy makers has been to maintain unhindered predominance of American influence in Asia, it has not been able to stop the emergence of powerful centres of power in the continent. Japan emerged as a threatening power centre in the eighties, especially in the economic area. It was a time of relative decline in American influence across the globe. Washington thus viewed the growth of Japanese economy in the eighties with envy and suspicion. Fear of a rising Japan dominated the US foreign policy debate. The unprecedented Chinese economic growth and sustained growth of the Chinese military capabilities in the nineties fuelled similar suspicion and apprehension. In contrast, the surfacing of India as a nuclear power with a growing economy in the early twenty-first century has not led to speculations over an emerging Indian threat. Outsourcing of IT jobs has become only a minor irritant in the growing relationship.

He further explains that currently, the US enjoys friendly ties and deep economic relations with all the three Asian powers. But in the area of defence and security, Washington views these three countries differently. Japan is the closest strategic ally. China is generally viewed as a contender for power and influence in Asia. The US has been cultivating India as a new strategic partner. The two post-Cold War era American Presidents—Bill Clinton and George Bush (Jr.)— have carefully managed the country's relationship with the Asian powers to prevent the rise of an anti-American power in the Asian continent.

Girijesh Pant argues that regions are getting de-territorialised by the globalisation processes. In West Asia polarised development of inclusive and exclusive processes is manifesting in the form of reform and resurgence. The participants in the inclusive processes of globalisations are making structural changes by integrating markets at global and regional levels. Resurgence, on the other hand, is surfacing in the form of protest from the marginalised segments of the society. The contention of his paper is that the trajectory of change in West Asia is determined by the unfolding contradictions of weak reforms and strong discontent (resurgence). He says that during the last 50 years, the two principal factors determining the evolutionary process of the region have been the Palestinian–Israel conflict and the global stakes in its oil. However, for the last decade the region has been under pressure from external powers to undertake reforms, which is changing the power structure of the stakeholders. Besides, the external nature of reforms is facing resistance and posing serious problem of legitimacy. On the other hand, resurgence of discontent in West Asia, has spilled over beyond its boundaries, and reached Washington in the most violent form on 11 September 2001, underlining thereby the scale of drift that it has undergone. From the perspective of trans-localisation of subaltern policy of West Asia, 11 September marks the beginning of a new phase. The doctrine of preemption has further aggravated it. The unipolar–globalising world has yet to demonstrate its sensitivities in adequate measure towards the discontent it is creating in West Asia.

According to Pant, resurgence and reform in the emerging West Asia has implications for India. The region is seen by India as its extended neighbourhood. The drift and despair of discontent from the region has been impinging on Indian security. Its energy security is susceptible to the region's energy flows. The stakes are huge, both material as well as ideological.

Ajay Patnaik's paper 'Central Asia's Security: The Role of Asian Powers', looks at the positive role that some of the Asian countries like China, India and Iran have played in the security and stability in Central Asia. He points out that Central Asia's security dimensions have evolved through three phases. The first phase was till the midnineties, before the coming of the Taliban to power in Afghanistan when the Central Asian countries followed an open door policy with their Islamic neighbours. Soon it was clear that these powers were interested in spreading their own brand of ideology to obtain hegemony that hardly helped in ensuring security or development in Central Asia. The second phase heralded with the Taliban coming to power in Kabul. Though Russia became the mainstay of Central Asia's security during this period, China, India and Iran were intensely engaged in the region. The settlement of the Sino-Central Asian border issues and the creation of the Shanghai Five, Iran's role in bringing the Tajik Civil War to an end, and India's help to the Northern Alliance in the war against the Taliban, symbolised the positive role and growing relevance of these Asian powers in the security of Central Asia.

Since the US-led war against the Taliban, Russia and the United States are the main security providers in the region with their respective bases and troop presence. However, Patnaik concludes that through confidence-building measures along the borders, using ethno-cultural affinity to resolve inter-ethnic conflicts, and collaborating in the fight against terrorism, technical and technological assistance, etc., the above three Asian powers will continue to play meaningful roles in the security scenario in Central Asia.

Anuradha Chenoy points out that the history of most Asian states shows a recurrence of armed conflicts ranging from territorial, eth-nic, religious, class and caste issues. These conflicts have been viewed within the traditional security discourse, and states involved have attempted to manage these through the concerns of national security. She analyses these conflicts to show that the roots of these conflicts are primarily rights based. It is argued that the human security and feminist critiques provide a new approach to conflict and their resolution. It is further argued that the human security assumes that women would be protected and guaranteed equity and justice within the broad premise of human rights. She argues that woman's rights need to be specially valorised since patriarchal structures that domi-nate, especially in conflict and post-conflict situations, do not guar-antee women's rights even under the broader concept of human security. Thus, human security needs to be gendered, and Asian states need to accept the concept of human security.

Gulshan Sachdeva tries to pinpoint contemporary economic trends in the Central Asian region. Despite having a very complex legacy, the region has made some progress in market reforms. Due to certain specific features (natural resources, strategic location, political sys-tem and background of political elite), the region has used both standard as well as non-conventional strategies of economic transfor-mation. The Soviet era leaders in more or less non-competitive regimes have tried to pursue economic stability while securing their own dominance in the new political system. They have also tried to learn a few lessons from the Chinese model of development. Most of the regional economic arrangements in the region are either grouping to recreate lost linkages among the former Soviet republics, or initiating multilateral organisations to strengthen regional linkages in the areas of trade, energy, water resource, infrastructure and communications. He argues that although Russia is still an important economic partner, countries in the region have tried to strengthen their relationship with many Asian countries particularly with China, Iran, South Korea and Japan. India's economic relationship with the Central Asian region has declined considerably in the post-socialist period. The main reasons have been lack of information, connectivity, economic decline of the region, and lack of economic and financial sector reforms in some of the countries. As these economies have picked up in the last few years, this is the right time to give a big boost to economic relations. India is also totally absent from any of the regional economic initiatives. India should now seriously pursue extending SAARC to Afghanistan and the Central Asian region. Because of the past record of the SAARC, if Central Asia is not interested in this grouping, India may seriously consider creating another independent organisation involving India and some of the countries in the region.

Rajesh Rajagopalan focuses on the international systemic influences on Asian security. Much of the previous works on regional security see questions of security as bound within the parameters of bilateral policy. From such perspectives, international phenomenon is the sum of the behaviour of states. International insecurity, then, is the consequence of bad policies that states undertake, a reflection of the foolishness of political elites, the obduracy of militaries and the rigidity of bureaucracies. That there might be larger factors at work that condition such behaviour is usually ignored. In Asia, as in other parts of the world, it is important to focus on how the nature of the great power system influences state behaviour and choices; how, for example, does unipolarity affect the choices that states face in promoting their own interest and greater stability in Asia. The author predicts that American dominance, and China's rise present both opportunities and challenges for Asian stability by both suggesting new options and constraining existing ones.

Notes and References

1. William J. Crow and Alan D. Romberg, 'Rethinking Security in the Pacific', *Foreign Affairs*, Spring, 1992.

2. I.K. Gujral, 'India and Asia in the New Millennium', *The Hindu*, 31 October 1998.
3. Robert Blackwell, Lecture delivered at the IDSA 5th Conference on Asian Security, 27 January 2003.
4. Nagesh Kumar, 'Emerging New Asia', *New Asia Monitor*, vol. 1, no. 1, March 2004, p. 1.
5. Ibid.
6. Fareed Zakaria, 'What Bush & Kerry Missed', *The Indian Express*, 21 October 2004, p. 9.
7. N. Kumar, 'Asian Economic Outlook', *New Asia Monitor*, vol. 1, no. 2, July 2004, p. 1.
8. E. Gellner, *Conditions of Liberty: Civil Society & its Rivals*. New York, 1994, p. 68.
9. D.K. Emerson, 'Region and Recalcitrance', *Pacific Review*, vol. 8, no. 2, 1995, pp. 223–48.
10. S.P. Huntington, *The Third Wave: Democratization in the Late Twentieth Century*, Norman, Oklahoma University Press, 1991, pp. 183–84.
11. Richard A. Clark, *Against All Enemies*, New York, London, Free Press, 2004, p. 270.
12. Foreign Minister Natwar Singh's Inaugural Address to 7th Asian Security Conference organised by the Institute of Defence Studies and Analysis (IDSA) on 27 January 2005.

1

ASIA'S QUEST FOR IDENTITY AND SECURITY

R.R. Sharma

The geographical spread of Asia is indicative of its importance in world affairs. Asia occupies a little more than one-third of the landmass of our earth. It is populated by more than half of the world's *Homo sapiens*. The continent has within it a diverse variety of political and economic structures. The resource endowment of Asia is indeed extraordinarily rich. More significantly, a very large area of Asia falls within the vast landmass of Eurasia, and is thus closely connected with Eurasian strategic environment. However, how do we perceive and define the larger political, cultural, economic identity of Asia? This is a complex task, which poses several problems. Jawaharlal Nehru, the first prime minister of India, was probably the first political leader of the emerging Asia to grapple with the complexities of Asian identity, development and security. It is not that he found all the appropriate answers. Nevertheless, his innovative mind came out with a vision, and an appropriate response to the emerging challenges in Asia. Now, when the paramount issue of Asian security and stability has emerged as a leading issue in global politics, it is worthwhile to recall Nehru's pioneering effort to project and articulate the concept of 'collective Asian Security', which could be, as he felt, a significant input into the maintenance of world order.

It also serves a purpose to recall the first Asian Relations Conference held in Delhi in March 1947 at the instance of Nehru, who

passionately articulated the vision of Asian unity, solidarity and
identity. In his inaugural address, Nehru said:

> We stand at the end of an era and on the threshold of a new period
> of history...we can look back on our long past, and look forward
> to the future that is taking shape before our eyes...the time has
> come for us, peoples of Asia, to meet together, to hold together
> and to advance together. It was not only a vague desire, but a
> compulsion....[1]

With considerable clarity, he pinpointed the strategic role of Asia in
global politics in, what he called, the 'atomic age':

> In this atomic age Asia will have to function effectively.... Indeed,
> there can be no peace unless Asia plays her part. There is today
> conflict in many countries, and all of us in Asia are full of our own
> problems. Nevertheless, the emergence of Asia in world affairs
> could be a powerful influence for world peace.[2]

Nehru, therefore, pleaded for a 'close Union of countries bordering on the Indian Ocean, both for defence and trade purposes', a
system of defence, stretching from the West to Southeast Asia in
which 'India because of her intrinsic importance and her strategic
position was to play a significant role'. He desired that 'the coordination of various countries in Middle East, India and the Southeast
Asia is not only possible, but undoubtedly certain in the future.' He
indicated that the question of 'Asiatic Federation' was necessary, both
for defence and trade purposes.

However, the practical outcome of the historic Asian Relations
Conference was minimal. The political impact was likewise limited,
though not altogether insignificant. The conference did not give birth
to any effective mechanism for multilateral cooperation and coordination among the Asian nations. What survived was the vision of
Asian solidarity and the message of the conference, i.e., multilateralism.
The conference pushed Asia outside the community of nations as a
factor of the continental policy.

Emerging Asian Identity

While the search for Asian identity continues, it faces a serious
challenge of political turbulence and destabilisation. It has been, and

continues to be, an arena of acute conflict. Asia has several reasons
to address itself to the problem of security, and the problems of peace
and tranquillity in its vast region. The prevalent insecurity is tied up
with the state of instability, which, however, flows out of the internal
identity crises in several Asian countries. This is amply reflected in
the fact that now internal conflicts have a preponderance over the
international wars and conflicts in the region. One has, therefore, to
examine the several dimensions of the problem of identity. In spite
of these problems, modern Asia is changing, and in many ways, it
is quite different from that which previously existed in the early part
of the second half of the last century. Asia is incomparably far more
developed than at any other stage of its development. In fact, Asia
has been lauded for its fast economic progress and growth over the
past decades. Both China and India are displaying tremendous growth
momentum. Over and above, there is a greater regional economic
integration. Thus, the new transformation is indeed significant. It
now enjoys unparalleled prospects of growth and economic development. The nature of new Asia, however, remains somewhat am-
biguous. Its mode of governance is far from satisfactory. The existing
disjunctures are easily traceable to an earlier period, and thus underline the contemporary Asian dilemmas.

A geographical Asia is not difficult to define in broad terms. But
Asia is not just a 'geographical expression'. Asia is, therefore, defined
in several ways and more particularly, not just what it is, but also
what it has been in the past—a nursery, a home of great civilisations.
Nevertheless, a cogent idea of progress associated with the mainstream of Asian development has by now come to prevail over the
cultural elitism implied by the emphasis on civilisation. The plan to
refashion Asia, or create it anew, has not really taken off substantially.
It remains fragmented because there is no consensus as to what Asia
stands for. Practically, most people in Asian countries seldom see
themselves as Asians, as, for example, the Europeans do. They
primarily identify themselves as citizens of the appropriate nation
state. It is not far fetched to conclude that, as of now, most Asians
do not acknowledge any Asian identity. It is only in the political
discourse that the issue of identity figures as a desirable value and
a long-term objective. Thus, contemporary Asia is, as in earlier times,
divided on several counts and reflects the continuing existence of
several major identities. Invariably, groups of people have several
overlapping or nested identities at the same time. And apparently,

there is a hierarchy of different identities, with privileged groups having preferential access to the resources, and others largely excluded from them. This, and quite a few other factors, leave the prospect of a broader Asian Union and solidarity as a distant project. However, the regional economic integration as a strategy of development is generating synergies, which could be helpful in the long run. It has the potential to engender socio-economic bonding, which is the pre-requisite imperative for the consolidation of Asian identity.

Searching for Democratic Culture and Values

Many Asian states are searching for domestic tranquillity, which remains more as a hope than reality. It is largely due to the fact that a large number of these societies are, by and large, politically dysfunctional. An overwhelming number of people feel that they are often left at the margins, and are excluded. The governing political elite is invariably unresponsive and oppressive. The missing link is the sense of participation. The failure of the leadership is most marked at least in two key areas, namely, governance and economy. The governance is, of course, poor. Over and above, the political elites in several countries of Asia have opted for a kind of façade (authoritarian) democracies, wherein a systematic effort is made to prevent the expression of popular will through institutionalised pluralism. In the economic area, there is deepening poverty, an extensive unemployment, stifling corruption, a patronage system, designed to benefit a small 'self-absorbed elite'. There is a general lack of desired linkages between the political elite and the population. In a variety of cases, the cooperation of the people is sought through coercive means. This obviously leads to a large-scale popular discontent, which in turn, gets channelled into destabilising movements.

The fragile character of democratic systems in many countries of Asia is not entirely due to the domestic politics and its socio-economic dynamics. It needs to be emphasised that democracy is not just an internal, domestic issue in Asia. It is transnational. The emergence and acceptance of democracy is, first of all, the function of the international system. After the Second World War, forced democratisation has invariably been a governing trend. Because of their structural and conjunctural weakness, the Third World countries were forced 'to accept the model of Western democracy that has been the fundamental precondition for their acceptance in the international system'.[3]

The role of US in the first wave of forced democratisation has been cogently argued by Samuel Huntington:

> The single biggest extension of democratic liberties in the history of world came at the end of the World War II, when stable democratic regimes were inaugurated in defeated Axis countries: Germany, Japan, Italy, Austria.... The imposition of democracy on these countries was almost entirely the work of the United States.... As a result of American determination and power, the former Axis countries were 'forced to be free'.

Huntington quotes here from John D. Montgomery, *Forced to be Free: The Artificial Revolution in Germany and Japan*.[4] The same treatment was meted out to the so-called 'penetrated societies' of southern Europe, and later on, to Asian and other Third World countries.

The post-war-forced-democratisation or 'imposed democracies' were accepted by the Asian countries. However, they acted in accordance with their respective historical traditions and idiosyncrasies. The political outcome has been a mixed-one. The implanted democracies have turned out to be 'half genuine, half imported'. The political actors have put on their masks, which bear the 'imprint of forced democratization and cover the real, domestic nature of politics'.[5] The forced democratisation in many parts of Asia has ultimately led to façade democratisation, in which case, 'the external patron accepts a pseudo or superficial democratization'. There are several examples of this.

The process of forcing democracies on other countries has not come to an end, but has acquired a new content in contemporary global politics, and the US is at the forefront of this.

While the hegemonists in Bush administration were united in dismissing Powell's views, they disagreed among themselves over a key question: To what extent should the United States use its power to promote America's ideals? A minority, led by Wolfowitz and Richard Perle was, what the Press often referred to as neoconservatives, but they might be more accurately called democratic

imperialists, argued that the US should actively deploy its overwhelming military, economic and political might to remake the
world in its image.... They were less worried about the dangers
of nation-building, and more willing to commit the nation's
resources...to creating democracies in their wake.[6]

We also learn that the so-called 'democratic imperialists' and 'assertive nationalists'—Rice and Cheney—are deeply skeptical of nation-
building, and 'scornful that American power should create what
others were unable to build for themselves'. Rice, in fact, explained,
'America's pursuit of the national interest will create conditions that
promote freedom, markets and peace. The pursuit of national interests after World War II led to more prosperous and democratic
world'.[7] Obviously, the façade democracies which were forced on the
Third World were in pursuit of the national interests of the US.

Façade democracies have been instituted in accordance with
the minimal principles of democracy, or its 'most fragile features',
namely, the so-called 'free elections'. Consequently, several variants
of façade democracy have taken roots in the political culture of Asian
countries. Forced democratisation in many countries of Asia has
led to façade democratisation where the 'external patron' grants
legitimacy to pseudo or superficial democratisation by building
'an external façade for the given polity', which has an apparent look
of democratic structure from outside. This façade democracy is
'static and fragile, and in most cases it brings instability and insecurity' for itself and most of all for its neighbours.[8] L. Whitehead
suggests that the European definitions of democracy 'seem to give
more stress on social and economic participation, whereas Americans give almost exclusive emphasis to electoral aspect.'[9] Let us
have a look at the different variants of democracies in the Asian
countries.

In political discourse, democracy is invariably projected as the
foremost universal value. There are, in fact, two democratic values,
which stand as *'twin pillars'* in the democratic value system: *'Competition and Participation'*. The noted political scientist, Robert Dahl,
categorises them as the 'two theoretical dimensions of democratisation'. He discusses the historical precedents and deviations of
democratisation as the lack of these combined values namely, 'competitive oligarchies, closed hegemonies, and inclusive hegemonies'.[10]
By competition, he means, 'competition of elites' and participation

refers to the 'participation of whole population in the political processes'. Dahl argues that participation and competition as basic democratic values have been invariably incorporated in the constitutions and institution of all democratic countries. However, there is a 'huge gap between the declared democratic values of the constitutions and socio-political realities' in many countries. Now, if we extend Dahl's twin model of democratic values to Asian countries, we get the following 'ideal type' of democratic system in Asia:

(a) *Formalist Democracies:* In this type of democracies, there is no actual counter elite in the form of an organised and institutionalised opposition that could offer a fundamentally different political alternative. Consequently, the 'misinformed or often intimidated electorate freely re-elect the same ruling elite, may be with large pseudo participation'. (Pakistan is a typical example of this type and falls into the category of façade democracy).

(b) *Elitist Democracies:* In these types of democracies, there do exist some competitive elites. However, they are comparatively small and share power alternatively among themselves. They invariably exclude the mass of the people from real political activities as well as the decision-making processes. Therefore, it leads to a political situation where politics turns into 'a remote realm' for the common man. (A large chunk of Asian countries falls in this category. India is haltingly moving away from this model into a substantive democracy).

(c) *Partyist Democracies:* This is the type in which political parties are the foremost political actors. They invariably seek to exclude other political and social actors from political life by monopolising the decision-making process at the parliamentary level. Implicitly, 'high politics becomes a chamber-dream of the party oligarchy'. (Japan fits into this category).

(d) *Tyrannical Democracies:* These are the clever distortions of majortian type democracies. The tiny political elite obtains parliamentary majority and refers to it for their electoral legitimation. The elites invariably act as tyrants and refuse the necessary compromise in political and social life. They refuse to establish 'consensual democracy for the purpose of fundamental change'. Some analysts have characterised them as an 'infantile disorder'. (All Central and West Asian countries easily fall into this type. They are the best examples of a façade democracy).[11]

From this broad typology of democracy in the Asian countries, it is obvious that there is great deal of 'democracy deficit' in these countries. Quite a few of them have had military regimes, which are devoid of legitimacy as well as long-term vision. While some Asian countries are totally façade democracies, the others are at the halfway point between the façade and real, substantial democracies. Significantly, this has serious implications for regional and sub-regional security and stability. It has also limited the efficiency and efficacy of the political structures. The lack of elite-mass linkages and socio-political dialogue—as 'a dialogue of the deaf'—not only retards socio-economic development, but also encourages traditionalist–conservative formations. It certainly pushes back the formation of a healthy civil society. In order to create stable and accountable democracies, we have to enable civil society to grow and flourish. Democratic development is invariably linked to a vibrant civil society. If we are thinking in terms of creating a valid security order in Asia, we must in that case move in the direction of substantial democratisation, in the first place. The substantial threat for security and stability does not come from without, but from the 'nature of things', i.e., from within.

Quest for Security

The year 1989 was the year of the twentieth century. Some hail it as the 'year of miracles'. This was the year which witnessed the collapse of socialism, and the whole bipolar world. More significantly, this was the year when the Old World Order (OWO) collapsed, and the 'whole logic of the previous world system turned upside down'. The 'pacted peace' with mutually stable alliance systems and 'enemy images' was central to OWO.

In a certain sense, the Old World Order was well organised and regulated. It took care of the international security matters. The New World Order (NWO) which seeks to replace the OWO is in its formative and hazy stage. What, however, is certain is that it is logically aligned to globalisation. From this specific standpoint, NWO has to be based on the 'concept of widest meaning of economic, political, cultural and communicational security in an uncertain global system. It is almost unquantifiable as an aggregate of many factors, so is the behaviour of great number of smaller and bigger, global, national and sub-national actors'.[12] The NWO is conceptually explained within the parameters of 'Chaos Theory', which deals essentially with the concept of 'order within disorder'. The 'world of chaos' will increasingly transform a number of Asian countries to manage a kind of permanent internal crisis due, at least partly, to their increasingly unfavourable conditions in the global polity and economy.

This is largely because of the emerging globalisation, which has enhanced the role of nation states, which seek to secure external and internal condition of economic growth. Now each state strives to create a favourable external economic environment and maintain it against all kinds of odds and changes in world economy. In this effort, all the advantage rests with the developed Western countries, particularly with the US. In fact, efforts to establish American hegemony would eventually mean an 'American globalisation' in the world economy, politics, security and culture in contrast to 'global globalisation'. I will discuss the US policy of hegemony and its implications for Asia at a later stage. For now, it suffices to point out that globalisation poses a major threat to Asian states, which are increasingly marginalised by globalisation. There is a growing recognition that the 'globalisation has shown to be unresponsive and oppressive to human needs and equity of participation. Interdependence suggests that security is connected to new ways of relating to our global community based on inclusion, participation, and access to meeting basic needs'.[13]

The concepts of security have been in the melting pot for nearly two decades. The events of 11 September 2001, however, brought about a lasting change in the perception of security. The Europeans have been preoccupied for over a decade with the new concept of security, within the framework of NATO, pointing out that the narrow military meaning of security has become outdated. The traditional understanding of security had been tied to the idea of defending the sovereignty of the nation states. The danger to the security of a country was assumed to emanate from across the border by the invading 'enemy'. The enemy within the country did not enter into our perception of threats. Towards the end of eighties, it was pointed out that our security concerns must also include not only military security, but also political, economic and social security. The sources of insecurity are indeed many dimensional. Therefore, there is an obvious need to identify the deeper sources of insecurity.

The political security signifies that the state makes every effort to raise the basic strength of its society with a view to protecting it from extremist factors. Likewise, economic security implies that a country has unhindered access, without outside coercion, to its need of raw materials, energy, etc., by means of free trade, etc. Social security obviously refers to the availability of required welfare schemes in a given country so as to maintain a degree of social peace. Obviously, the new dimensions of security are not easily available in the context of Asia for various reasons, which include both domestic as well as international compulsions and constraints. As pointed out earlier, in the aftermath of 11 September 2001, it became even more obvious that bigger and more powerful weapons do not necessarily create greater security. Security was no longer tied to weapons alone. It is aptly argued that social, political and economic exclusion of people are the 'soils where insecurity is bred...' Security is closely associated with religious and ethnic harmony. The various ethnic and religious groups have to respect each other through a spirit of coexistence, and the state on its part has to ensure the protection of minority rights.

A host of security problems can be obviated by promoting multilateral and regional regimes. Undoubtedly, multilateralism and regionalism constitute a practical and viable foundation of security in Asia. In recent years, multilateral regional arrangements have found favour with several Asian countries. The multilateral regimes such as APEC, ASEAN, ARF, SCO illustrate this trend. Both India and China have come out openly in support of multilateral cooperation.

Doctrines of Hegemony and Preemption

The global order is becoming increasingly uncertain and unregulated. It is a 'World of Chaos'. Of course, beholders of 'Chaos Theory' argue that there is an 'order within disorder'. However, much of the contemporary international system is crumbling beneath the burden of unregulated global mechanisms, and the emerging institutions which are programmed and regulated by the global powers and their projected values. Significantly, while democracy is projected as a cherished value, there is, however, a global democracy deficit. There is enormous concentration of power from the economic realm to the cultural sphere. There is no worthwhile mechanism to counterbalance these globally. Decidedly, this has given rise to huge dissatisfaction in the world public opinion.

Taking note of the contemporary anarchy in international relations, political analysts seek to introduce the notion 'hegemon' as a stabilising factor. Quite a few, in fact, are inclined to argue that the US has finally emerged as 'the ultimate hegemon' in the global system. Throughout the recent history of international relations, the US has played broadly three different kind of strategic roles: *limited partner, security manager, hegemon*.

Of these, what role should the United States play invariably depends on its perception of national interest in a region or country. Both in Europe and in Asia, the US has a clearly defined footprint, which is maintained through a web of alliance relationships. Through its political involvement and military presence, it has acquired the requisite muscle to plant its flag in Asia. The American administration took a conscious decision at the dawn of twenty-first century to shift US security policy away from the collective security order to a unilateral policy, which apparently is focused on a more bellicose military posture. Consequently, the Asian security order, already under stress, is entering into a period of turbulent change and more instability.

Evidently, unilateralism has its roots in 'a strain of political thinking best labelled hegemonist'. The strategy of hegemony has passed through several phases of its realisation. And finally, it has arrived as a dangerous doctrine. The hegemonist strain of thinking had always argued, 'America's immense power and the willingness to wield it... is the key to securing America's interests in the world'. The idea is by no means new. 'The worldview that drove it existed long before jet planes plowed into the Twin Towers and the Pentagon... what September 11 provided was the rationale and opportunity to carry out his revolution'.[14] Hegemonist arguments were updated in the early nineties after the demise of the Soviet Union. An initial contribution was a 1992 Pentagon study prepared by Dick Cheney and Paul Wolfowitz. It maintained that US national security policy after the Cold War should seek to 'transform the unipolar moment into a unipolar era' by precluding the emergence of any potential future global competitor.

The US policy of hegemonism rests on a few major propositions. The foremost is that power, especially military power, 'matters'. If 'power matters, great powers matter most of all', argued Rice.[15] Therefore, the US primacy was 'both real and usable'. However, it is not just capability, but also 'the will' to use power that must become a part of the new policy. The power must be 'exercised solely in terms of American interests'. Rice was sufficiently critical of those who advocated, 'that the United States is exercising power legitimately only when it is doing so on behalf of someone or something else'.[16]

Another leading assumption underlying the new hegemonist worldview states that multilateral agreements and institutions are neither essential nor necessarily conducive to American interests. President Bush and his advisors articulated 'a distinctly instrumental view of formal multilateral efforts—they were fine, if they served immediate and concrete American interests'.[17] It is worthwhile to recall that the 1992 draft Pentagon planning document argued that the US 'should be postured to act independently', because 'future coalitions would be ad hoc assemblies often not lasting beyond the crises being confronted, and in many cases carrying only general agreement over the objectives to be accomplished'.[18] If the Asian nations were to follow the above proposition or the reasoning, their security and stability would be totally and permanently compromised.

More significantly, the hegemonists in Bush administration held on to the belief that the US is a 'unique power and others see it as such'. In fact, practically most Americans, who have come to believe that this is self-evident, hold this kind of view extensively. President Bush and his advisors 'accepted this billiard ball view of the world where the United States was the biggest (and most virtuous) ball on the table and could move every other ball when and where it wanted. The only exception was Collin Powell....'[19] Rice puts it across without mincing words. 'America's pursuit of national interests will create conditions that promote freedom, markets and peace. Its pursuit of national interests after World War II led to more prosperous and democratic world. This can happen again'.[20] Since the US possessed unrivalled power, it therefore had the right to set the international agenda.

In the new national security strategy of the United States, previous policies, which were designed to promote multilateralism, howsoever limited, have been rejected in favour of preemptive strikes and of- fensive counter-proliferation strategies. More specifically, the US is now planning to 'restore nuclear weapons to the centre stage of national security policy'.[21] The US Nuclear Policy Review (2002) identifies seven countries against which nuclear weapons may be used in the national interest in certain circumstances. Significantly, six of these, namely, China, Iran, Iraq, Libya, North Korea and Syria, are Asian powers. The remaining country, Russia, is a Eurasian power. The question which is frequently asked is after Afghanistan and Iraq, 'who is the next'. There are still two remaining members of the axis of evil—Iran and North Korea. Additionally, there are a few other so-called 'rogue states', which were described by John Bolton, US Undersecretary of State, as the 'junior varsity axis of evil'. These were identified as Syria, Libya and Cuba. It was proclaimed that they would be confronted. Richard Perle declared that the US would like to 'deliver a short message, a two word message; you are next'.[22] After the Iraq war, this message has in fact been delivered to Syria, North Korea and Iran. Iran has already emerged as the next focus of US concerns.

The point being argued is because of a major paradigm shift in the US foreign policy, the region of Asia is in an imminent danger of becoming more unstable and less secure. Since the US is potentially the most influential power in Asia, its policies have transformed the strategic environment. It will not be out of context to examine the US 'doctrine of preemption' and its strategic likely impact on Asia.

It was, in fact, President Bush who clarified that the US has a 'new doctrine called preemption', which signified a major departure for US foreign policy. The doctrine was explained at length in the National Security Strategy document released by the White House on 20 September 2002. It argued that the US 'will consistently strive to enlist the support of international community, we will not hesitate to act alone, if necessary, to exercise our right of self-defence by acting preemptively'.[23] Evidently, President Bush was of the firm view that preemption was not a mere option, but what Mick R. Gordon of *New York Times* called 'a cardinal principle of his foreign policy'.[24] Logically, preemption is the twin sister of hegemonism. Central to both is the belief in America's unprecedented power, which has to be used to 'remake the world in America's image'.

Preemption strategy does not imply only the use of power against terrorists and tyrants who were determined to seek technologies of mass destruction. It also signified the use of force to remove 'obstacles and threats to liberty and freedom that existed throughout

the world'. Therefore, the US has the right as well as the power 'to
change the status quo'. This may be achieved by bringing about, if
required, a change of regime in the so-called rogue or undesirable
states. The US policy of toppling other governments, particularly in
Asia, is not new. It has propped up dictators, or human rights abusing
corrupt regimes. However, it has never been an openly declared
option of US policy. 'It is not clear to me what advantage there
is in declaring it publicly.... By making it public, we also tend to
add to the world's perception that we are arrogant and unilateral',
lamented Brent Scowcroft, a former security advisor to the first
Bush administration.[25] Unilateralism is of course both the stated
and unstated principle of the American policy. In a short while,
after assuming office, President Bush withdrew from five major
multilateral international agreements including, the ABM Treaty, the
Kyoto Protocol, and the Treaty establishing International Criminal
Court. In the light of the available evidence, it is quite obvious that
'the regime change was 'the gist of both the Afghanistan and Iraq
wars'.[26]

The preemption doctrine, as expected, has had a demonstration
effect. India assumed that it was a universal doctrine. The then
finance minister of India, Mr Jaswant Singh, publicly declared during
his visit to the US that 'every nation has that right.... It is not the
prerogative of any one country. Preemption is the right of any nation
to prevent injury to itself'. Russia, likewise, incorporated it in its
latest military doctrine of 2003.[27] The doctrine appears attractive
to several other countries. However, it stands to reason that it, as
Henry Kissinger aptly asserted, 'cannot be in either the American
national interest or the world's interest to develop principles that
grant every nation an unfettered right to preemption against its
own definition of threats to its security'.[28] There is, obviously, a very
thin line which separates preemption from unlawful aggression.
Any endeavour to legitimise the doctrine/strategy of preemption in
the unstable environment of Asia is shortsighted and fraught with
exceedingly dangerous consequences.

Doctrine of War on Terror and Asia

The 'Doctrine of the War on Terror' was proclaimed by President
Bush in the wake of events of 11 September 2001. This doctrine has

a genetical affinity with the doctrines of hegemony and preemption. In a certain sense, it is a logical extension of these, and is equally pernicious. Moreover, the so-called doctrine of the war on terror is more directly relevant to Asia because the arena of war on terror is Asia. As stated earlier, the entire Asia from West Asia to Northeast Asia has now emerged as the 'theatre of war'. It started with Afghanistan and Central Asia with immediate consequences for South Asia. Subsequently, there was the so-called 'second front' in Philippines in Southeast Asia. The ongoing intensified wars in West Asia/Middle East are as much part of the war on terror. While these wars are regional, they are, however, global in scope. Consequently, there is resurgence of military factor both in Asian, as well as international relations.

The war on terror was declared as a 'civilisation's fight'. It was deemed as an attack on freedom, and any nation not joining the war on the side of the US was supporting the terrorists—'either you are with US, or you are with the terrorists', argued President Bush. There was no choice for a nation. It was almost like a directive, a command. However, it was never made clear as to what was the nature of the war. And towards whom the so-called war was precisely directed. That is why Stanley Hoffman asked:

> Whom are we fighting?.... To proclaim a war on terrorism in general...is ambition, indeed, for we need to distinguish among types of terrorists? A determined project of ridding the world of all rogues and terrorists is a dream that would be seen abroad as a demonstration of rabid imperialism.[29]

In his State of the Union address on 29 January 2002, President Bush referred to expansion of war on terror: 'While the most visible military action is in Afghanistan, America is acting elsewhere. We have troops in Philippines. Our soldiers are working with the Bosnian government. Our Navy is patrolling the coast of Africa'. If one were to read this along with his famous declaration of war against the 'axis of evil', then the whole of Asian region from West Asia to Northeast Asia, through Central, South and Southeast Asia would obviously be converted into the theatre of US war on terror. The war on terror (or terrorism) is not only, as Raphael Perl puts it, 'a misnomer', but 'an open-ended war', which is extremely dangerous, and a continuing threat to global, and particularly Asian, peace.

Southeast Asia

The so-called 'second front' of war on terror was disproportionate
to the evidence on terrorism in Southeast Asia. There is little doubt
that there are some Islamic fundamentalist groups, which are fairly
active in Malaysia, Singapore, Philippines and Indonesia. They are
apparently well organised and armed. However, there is no convincing evidence to suggest that they are definitely linked to international
terrorism, and terrorist groups like the Al Qaeda. In fact, *Far Eastern
Economic Review* reported: 'Many people in the region are now
saying that US efforts to combat global terrorism in the region are
in danger of doing as much harm as good'.[30]

It is no secret that the US has considerable strategic interest in
Southeast Asia. There are at least three major studies undertaken
in the recent past by the US Council on Foreign Relations, RAND,
and Heritage Foundation, which have pointed to the region's
strategic geopolitical significance to US interests, and how these
should be addressed. The reports invariably point out that the region
'sits aside some of the world's most critical sea lanes'. More than
1.5 trillion worth merchandise trade passed through the Straits of
Malacca in the year 2000, which was nearly half of world's trade,
including crucial oil supplies from the Persian Gulf to Japan, China
and South Korea. Any dislocation of energy supplies would have an
immediate and 'devastating impact on the economies of East Asia,
and would have significant secondary effects on the US economy
as well'. Highlighting the vast significance of Malacca Strait,
Bodansky, the Director of the US Congressional Task Force on
Terrorism argues: 'The global strategic growth and expansion of
aspiring powers can be contained and regulated through the mere
control over the movement of their naval forces through the Strait
of Malacca'.[31]

Obviously, the three reports mentioned above suggested that 'the
highest American priority should be assigned to maintaining regional
security through the prevention of intra-regional conflict and domination by an outside power or coalition. Therefore, the US administration should preserve a credible military presence....' It is indeed
imperative to ensure regional security. However, the very idea of its
domination by an outside power—'the US, which should have a credible military presence'—has a negating consequence. Significantly,

the Heritage Foundation study had no compunction in asserting that
the war on terror would 'ultimately be pursued in Southeast Asia with
or without the express approval of local governments'.[32] On the face
of it, the US policy is more indicative of reinforcing its expansive
military presence in the region than dealing with the problem of
terrorism, and many other major regional issues.

Despite the constraints of global politics, multilateralism in Southeast Asia has grown and picked up remarkable speed through regional and extra regional cooperation. ASEAN has shown a
commendable political flexibility by including extra regional countries with which 'complementarities based on shared geography' are
evident in a variety of areas, including security, economic and cultural fields. There is a well-considered effort to develop land and
cross-border connectivity through infrastructure development, both
within and across with neighbours. More significantly, ASEAN and
ARF are working on a policy design to create multilateral regimes.
In fact, there are several schemes of economic integration which are
taking shape in Asia at the regional level. China, India and Japan are
engaged in comprehensive economic cooperation pacts with several
ASEAN countries. Likewise, SCO is critically important for the
region of Central Asia. This has the potential to generate a greater
cohesion among Asian countries, and maintain the security of sea-
lanes in the region.

Central Asia

Unlike Southeast Asia, there are several critical questions about
Central Asia. The Central Asia is fairly important because of its
proximity to Afghanistan and South Asia. The Russian withdrawal
from Central Asia after the break-up of the Soviet Union gave rise to
a variety of security problems. The region was left without a security
manager. Intra-regional feuds and rivalries eroded the possibilities of
regionwide cooperation and consolidation. The 'Commonwealth of
Independent States' did not live up to its expectations for a number
of reasons. The Central Asian republics had therefore to content with
domestic insurgencies, cross-border terrorism, growth of militant
Islam, drug and gun running, etc. The republics witnessed the
emergence of authoritarian regimes, poor governance and extensive

corruption. Because of political and security vacuum, the region has gradually emerged as a hotbed of factional and big power rivalries.

In 1997, the Deputy Secretary of State Strobe Talbot, gave a major address outlining the US approach to Central Asia. He argued that the US has no compelling interest in the region. The region was in no way of critical, strategic importance to the US. 'It has been fashionable to proclaim, or at least predict, a replay of "great game" in Caucasus and Central Asia. The implication of course is that the driving dynamics of the region, fuelled and lubricated by oil, will be the competition of the great powers. Our goal is to avoid and actively discourage....' However, if 'internal and cross-border conflicts simmer and flare, the region could become a breeding ground of terrorism, hotbed of religious and political extremism and battle-ground for outright war'.[33] Strobe Talbot was, however, telling only a half-truth.

The strategic importance of the region grew manifold after September 11. Central Asia which was for some American analysts 'a strategic quicksand' or a 'mission too far' became mission imme-diate and urgent. To begin with, the US decided to be 'Central Asia's security manager'.[34] However, Eugene Rumer makes a bold obser-vation, which is at the heart of the issue. He says:

> In the aftermath of September 11, though it would be shortsighted to define US interests in Central Asia merely in terms of opera-tional counter terrorism requirements and ongoing military op-erations in Afghanistan. The tragedy of the terrorist attacks has given a new and very different meaning to the notion first articu-lated by US policy makers in nineties...the absence of geopolitical competition....[35]

This was officially confirmed by Elizabeth Jones, Assistant Sec-retary of State for Eurasian Affairs, in a testimony before the US Senate Sub-Committee in December 2001. Jones testified that US had no intention of abandoning Central Asia after the Afghan War. She outlined four US priorities in the region: *combating terrorism, reform, the rule of law,* and *Caspian Sea energy resources.* Collin Powel also confirmed that Kazakhstan's oil was of 'critical impor-tance' to the US. Military presence is essential for the US to control Caspian Sea and Caspian energy resources. Apparently, this is a 'sub-text of the war' in Afghanistan.

The US cannot however maintain its footprint in Central Asia without the active cooperation of most important regional powers, namely, Russia, China and Iran. Each of these nations has a huge stake in the region. These nations have offered their cooperation, so far, in the interest of regional stability and security. However, their concern for stability and security does not 'outweigh fears of US preponderance'. Tensions are bound to rise, and resolving the growing tensions, obviously, would be a formidable task. The former Russian Defence Minister Sergei Iranov, in fact, reminded the US that it had promised to close down military bases in Uzbekistan and Kyrgyzstan after the completion of its military operation in Afghanistan. 'We did not object to the bases, but set a condition that they operate only as long as it takes to stabilise the situation in Afghanistan', Iranov informed a NATO Conference in Colorado Springs. He went on to assert that the 'CIS is an extremely important security zone for Russia...we have boosted and will further boost our presence in the Commonwealth of Independent States'. Russia is thus showing a new assertiveness towards the CIS as a part of a broader revision of its 'defence doctrine post-Nine-Eleven'. There is thus a clear signal to the US to accept Russia's dominant role in Central Asia.

While sharply disagreeing with the US on its policy of unilateralism and a host of other issues, President Putin has been steadily expanding the cooperative agenda with the US. Therefore, he will have to walk the razor's edge in promoting Russia's national interests, particularly in Central Asia. He has thus come out with what apparently is a useful concept of building an 'arch of stability' stretching from Europe through the Caucasus and Central Asia to China and Southeast Asia. This is a kind of a counter-paradigm to 'the arch of instability', which the US argued extends from the Caribbean Basin through Africa to South and Central Asia and across to North Korea. This justified the role of the US as a global hegemon. President Putin clarified that the arch of stability must be based on 'entwined regional security arrangements' that should preclude domination either by the US or China.[36] Russia has thus worked out both military alliances as well as bilateral and multilateral agreements with the Central Asian states and China. Russia is also actively pursuing the project of Moscow–Delhi–Beijing triangle, which in its perception could emerge as a pillar of stability in Asia.

Looking globally, international relations are passing through a
turbulent phase. There exists a worldview which seeks to undermine
the credibility of important multilateral institutions, globally as well
as at the regional level. Efforts are being made to erode the well-
meaning patterns of cooperation. Fareed Zakaria aptly summed up
the situation in his *Newsweek* column:

> At this crucial moment in world history, the influential hardliners
> in the Bush administration stand in theological opposition to the
> very idea of international cooperation. Even when the administra-
> tion comes to multilateralism...it does so grudgingly and half-
> heartedly. President Bush's excellent Television address...is quickly
> countered by Vice-President Dick Cheney's combative and dis-
> honest performance.

The security and political landscape in Asia has been changed
largely by the US policies, more particularly in the post-September
11 period. The war on terror has 'accelerated the process of militarisation of Asia'. There is now an intensified arms race in Asia. 'In
a way during the past decade after the end of Cold War, the Asian
region did not witness an arms race worth mentioning. Now all
countries big and small across Asia including China, India, Pakistan
Indonesia, Philippines, Singapore, and Malaysia are...acquiring
weapons'[37], argues Ninan Koshy. The US war on terror has, in fact,
resulted in further escalation of conflicts in Eurasia, in West Asia,
South Asia and Southeast Asian countries such as Philippines and
Indonesia. It is estimated that 'eight of twenty-three high intensity
conflicts are located in the Asian region, which caused over the years
death of at least 25,000 people. The total death toll of the eight
conflicts in the Asian region amount to 1,64,700 people'.[38]

Thus to conclude, under the new dispensation of things, one finds
vast areas of the Asian continent extending from the Caspian Sea and
the Persian Gulf to the Malacca Straits, including the whole of South
Asia in the middle, face a serious challenge of political turbulence
and destabilisation. The ouster of the Taliban from power in Afghanistan and the establishment of an internationally supported Karzai
government in Kabul, the overthrow of the Saddam regime in Iraq
have not brought peace and stability to West and Southwest Asia. The
war in Iraq and Afghanistan has turned into counter-insurgency
operation.

The spillover effect of developments in Afghanistan has had its impact on the stability of regimes in Pakistan and Central Asian republics. The instability in regions directly neighbouring China is likely to affect the situation in the Xinjiang and the Tibetan region. The situation in India—the hub of South Asian subcontinent—has also not remained unaffected by the disquieting developments that have taken place in Pakistan, Nepal, Sri Lanka and Bangladesh. The two neighbouring states of India—Nepal in the north and Sri Lanka in the south—are presently facing a grave challenge to their territorial integrity and stability.

The need of the hour is to take a holistic view of the sources of threat to peace and stability in the West Asian, Central Asian and South Asian regions as a whole and identify their real cause that lies in the 'new imperial' urge behind keeping the present iniquitous and unjust international order intact without seriously addressing the basic faults in the outdated and unworkable international financial, economic and security system. Unilateralism, 'clash of civilisations', war against international terrorism are but a new incarnations of the hegemonistic geopolitical ideas.

Time has come to reject totally these outdated, deleterious concepts and take a new look at the problem of meeting the challenges of destabilisation lurking before Asia in general, and South and Southeast, West and Central Asia in particular. In a situation when the South Asian subcontinent and the areas adjacent to it in West Asia and Central Asia are facing a serious threat of destabilisation, it is all the more important to strengthen in every possible manner, the bilateral and regional initiatives to meet this new threat to the Asian states. Both India and China, the two most important Asian powers, must come forward with creative initiatives to build an effective structure of Asian peace and stability in the spirit of the UN Charter, which endorses regional security system as part of an overall global security system. It is imperative to establish a network of regional institutions to address issues like ethnic relations, cross-border terrorism, reconciliation, transnational crime and illicit trade, environmental degradation, etc. This is likely to stimulate the environment of security and regional integration. The outside powers, the US in the first place, are welcome to such a regional security system as observers and guarantors.

Notes and References

1. *The Indian Annual Register* (IAR), vol. 1, New Delhi, 1947, p. 273.
2. Ibid., p. 275.
3. Attila Agh, 'Basic Democratic Values and Political Realities', *Budapest Papers on Democratic Transition*, no. 70, 1993, p. 10.
4. S.P. Huntington, *American Politics and Promise of Disharmony*. Cambridge, Mass, 1981, p. 249.
5. Attila Agh, 'Basic Democratic Values', p. 11.
6. I.H. Daalder & James M. Lindsay, 'America Unbound: The Bush Revolution in Foreign Policy'. Brookings Institute Press, Washington, 2003, pp. 46–47.
7. Ibid., p. 47.
8. Attila Agh, 'Basic Democratic Values', p. 17.
9. Laurence Whitehead, 'Internal Aspects of Democratization', in G.O. Donnell, et al., *Transition from Authoritarian Rule, Comparative Perspectives*. Baltimore & London, John Hopkins University Press, 1986, pp. 17–18.
10. Robert Dahl, *Oligarchy, Participation and Opposition*. New Heaven & London, Yale University Press, 1971, p. 7.
11. Attila Agh has applied Dahl's conceptual model to analyse the political situation in Eastern and Central Europe. See 'Basic Democratic Values and Political Realities', *Budapest Papers on Democratic Transition*, no. 70, 1993.
12. Attila Agh, 'Basic Democratic Values', p. 5.
13. Monique Makenkamp, P.V. Tongeren, and H.V.D. Veen (eds.), *Searching for Peace in Central and South Asia*. Lynne Rienner Publishers, London, p. 12.
14. I.H. Daalder and James Lindsay, *America Unbound: The Bush Revolution in Foreign Policy*, p. 13.
15. Condoleezza Rice, 'Promoting the National Interest', *Foreign Affairs*, vol. 79, 2000, p. 43.
16. Ibid., p. 62.
17. Daalder and Lindsay, *America Unbound: The Bush Revolution in Foreign Policy*, p. 44.
18. Quoted in Ibid., p. 45.
19. Ibid.
20. Condoleezza Rice, 'Promoting the National Interest', *Foreign Affairs*, vol. 79, 2000, p. 47.
21. Susan Willett, *Costs of Disarmament—Disarming the Costs*. UNIDIR, Geneva, 2003, p. 2.
22. R. Perle, quoted in Daalder and Lindsay, *America Unbound: The Bush Revolution in Foreign Policy*, p. 173.
23. G.W. Bush quoted in David Sanger, 'Bush to Outline Doctrine of Striking Foes First', *New York Times*, 20 September 2002.
24. Mick R. Gordon, 'Serving Notice of a New US, Poised to Hit first and Alone', *New York Times*, 27 January 2003.
25. Brent Scowcroft quoted in Daalder and Lindsay, *America Unbound: The Bush Revolution in Foreign Policy*, p. 126.
26. Daalder and Lindsay, *America Unbound: The Bush Revolution in Foreign Policy*, p. 14. There are two other important analysts, who arrived at a similar

conclusion. See Bob Woodward, *Plan of Attack*, Simon & Schuster, London, 2004; Richard Clarke, *Against All Enemies*. Free Press, New York, 2004.

27. Russian Defence Minister Ivanov, proclaimed that Russia could deliver pre-emptive strikes not only if threatened militarily, but also if faced with attempts to limit Russia access to regions that are essential for its survival, or those that are important from economic or financial point of view, see *The Hindu*, 4 November 2003.

28. Henry Kissinger, 'Consult and Control: Bywords for Battling the New Enemy' in *Washington Post*, 16 September 2002.

29. Stanley Hoffman, *The New York Review of Books*, 1 November 2001.

30. *Far Eastern Economic Review*, 18 January 2003.

31. Yossef Bondansky quoted in Ninan Koshy, *The War on Terror*. Leftward Books, New Delhi, 2003, p. 147.

32. Dana Dillian and Paola Pasicolan, 'South East Asian and War Against Terrorism', Heritage Foundation, October 2001, cited in Ninan Koshy, *The War on Terror*. New Delhi, 2003, p. 153.

33. S. Talbot quoted in *Strategic Forum*, no. 195, December 2002, p. 2. Ninan Koshy, *The War on Terror*. New Delhi, 2003, p. 102.

34. Eugene Rumer, 'Flashman's Revenge: Central Asia after September 11' in *Strategic Forum*, no. 195, December 2002, p. 2.

35. Ibid.

36. Putin quoted by Vladimir Radyuhin, 'Rebuilding Russia's Global Role', *The Hindu*, 27 July 2003.

37. Ninan Koshy, *The War on Terror*. New Delhi, 2003, p. 165.

38. Monique Makenkamp, *Searching for Peace in Central and South Asia*, p. 19.

2

India's Options in a Changing Asia

S.D. Muni
C. Raja Mohan

Introduction

Asia's growing weight in international relations, powered by the rise of China and India, and economic growth across the giant continent, has long been predicted. But few in the world have been prepared for its political and strategic consequences. Within a few years, China is expected to overtake Japan as the world's second largest economy. And if India continues to grow at a reasonable high growth rate of around 7 per cent annually, by the middle of this century, India's economic clout could match that of China. The two nations are set to recapture the places that they held in the world a few centuries ago—as the major producers of goods and services with China as the world's factory and India its back-office. Their economic strength has begun to generate mutually reinforcing growth across the continent.

Along with their growing economic muscle, India and China would naturally want a greater influence in world affairs. Meanwhile, Japan is shedding many of the political inhibitions imposed on it at the end of World War II. History has rarely witnessed the simultaneous rise of three major powers in the same region. Therefore, questions about the peaceful evolution of international relations in Asia, in the coming decades, arise. Equally important is the question—how will international relations and institutions created by the dominance of Europe and North America over the last few centuries be reshaped by the rise of Asia in general, and India and China in particular.[1] While the world begins to consider these questions, the unfolding transformation of Asia is likely to change the dynamics of Indian foreign policy. This paper is an attempt to analyse the opportunities available and the challenges to be encountered by Indian foreign policy in the coming decades.

India's tryst with Asia goes back deep in time. The vision of this engagement was articulated by Nehru both during the freedom struggle and, more forcefully, after Independence. Nehru's vision for Asia has an enduring quality, and some of his conceptions, at least, have become more realisable in the present situation than before. External conditions have never been better for India to contribute to the building of an Asian community that was central to Nehru's vision. If the present day India draws appropriate lessons from Nehru's constraints in building such a community, India can surely make its strategic presence felt in Asia, and also play its legitimate role in shaping the dynamics of the international system as such.

Nehru's vision of a resurgent Asia, and India's critical engagement in reshaping its destiny was based on three basic assumptions. First, that India was geo-strategically central to Asia, for being 'so situated as to be the meeting point of western and northern, and eastern and southeastern Asia'.[2] Second, its historical and cultural roots were deeply embedded in the larger evolution of Asia over the centuries. Nehru was acutely conscious of these roots when he said, 'If you should know India, you have to go to Afghanistan and Western Asia, to Central Asia, to China and Japan and to the countries of Southeast Asia'.[3] The third assumption underlying Nehru's approach to Asia was that the decolonised and newly independent countries of Asia would like to keep themselves away from the great power rivalries and conflicts, and also free themselves forever, from the political and economic bondage of their respective former masters. In this freedom, Nehru saw a constructive and decisive possibility of Asia throwing its legitimate weight in world politics in favour of peace and stability. But for this, Asian solidarity was a precondition, and India was willing to work for it. In so doing, Nehru also underlined the role of regionalism and institutionalisation of cooperation and mutual understanding. He envisaged an 'Eastern Federation':

> If there are to be federations... there should be an Eastern Federation... Such an Eastern Federation must inevitably consist of China and India, Burma and Ceylon, and Nepal and Afghanistan should be included. So should Malaya. There is no reason why Siam and Iran should also not join, as well as some other nations. That would be a powerful combination of free nations joining together for their own good as well as for the world's good.[4]

It was unfortunate that Nehru could not translate his vision of India's role in Asia into a reality. The forces and factors that failed him were many and diverse. Nehru and his India were perhaps not prepared for the challenges thrown up by the turbulent post-Second World War Asian and world politics. The creation of Pakistan raised questions on India's centrality and even primacy in Asia. For, the new state of Pakistan, not only flanked India on its strategic west and east, but also pledged itself to a relentless hostility towards its mother country. Then, Nehru also underestimated the potential for clash of Asian nationalisms. It was a matter of time that the Indian and Chinese nationalisms confronted each other as they sought their own territorial consolidation and competed for influence in the region and the world. After independence from the colonial rulers, the internal contradictions within the developing countries of Asia too became manifest, and provided an opportunity for the major powers and interested neighbours of India like Pakistan and China to exploit these differences.

The intra-Asian rivalries and contradictions were reinforced and exacerbated by the Cold War. Nehru's expectations that India and Asia could avoid the Cold War constraints on the foreign policies of new nations, proved to be naïve and unrealistic.[5] From the beginning, there were deep suspicions in the West of India's own strategic ambitions and there were fears in Washington that New Delhi could be the successor to Tokyo's 'Asiatic imperialism'. India's attempts to mobilise economic and technological support from the West, in the early years of independence, did not succeed because the West wanted strategic compliance, which India was not willing to offer. The West also clearly resisted any coming together of the Asian countries. Some of the immediate and smaller neighbours of India,

not only Pakistan but also Nepal and Sri Lanka, questioned Nehru's
understanding of emerging international forces, to show their preference for the West. India tried to keep itself engaged with critical
Asian issues—in Myanmar (then Burma) and Indonesia, the Suez
canal crisis, the Palestinian struggle, in Indo-China conflict, and even
in the efforts to establish the ASEAN during the late sixties, but the
Cold War divisions that divided Asia and pushed India onto the Soviet
side, would not allow it to make any decisive impact. The perception
of a humiliating military defeat inflicted on India by China in 1962,
and its poor economic performance also eroded much of India's
political clout in Asia.

The vision of Asian solidarity and India's leading role in it, that
Nehru created, was certainly anchored in India's geostrategic reality
and historical-cultural evolution. That this vision could not be realised
was due to the factors related to India's capabilities and the corre-
lation of external forces impinging upon India's perceived role in Asia
and the world. This vision needs to be nursed, reinforced and realised
in the changing context of Asian and world politics, and India's
growing self-confidence and capabilities. Reflecting the essence of
the Nehruvian vision, the then Prime Minister, Vajpayee, had said to
India's military commanders: 'Our security environment ranges from
the Persian Gulf to the Strait of Malacca, across the Indian Ocean,
including Central Asia and Afghanistan in the northwest, China in
the Northeast and Southeast Asia. Our strategic thinking has also
to extend to these horizons'.[6]

The New Situation

The factors and forces that constrained Nehru's India from playing
its legitimate role in Asia have either been mitigated to an extent, or
redefined. The most significant of them is the end of the Cold War
and expansion of the strategic space for India to pursue its national
interests. No less decisive is the fact that both India and Asia have
undergone radical transformation, both internally as well as in relation to the external forces impinging upon them, from their situation during the Cold War years. The characteristic features of the
new situation need to be identified at three levels.

At the global level, the US has emerged as the single most powerful
nation that seems to be committed to put in place not only an

ideological basis for the world order, but is also driven, almost by unilateral messianic zeal, to establish a system of global governance under its overall supervision and command. The will and capabilities of the United States to force peoples and nations into compliance with regard to its envisioned 'New World Order' seem unmatched. At the same time, there is no dearth of protests and challenges to the US assertion, be it in the form of terrorism led by Al Qaeda, or the continuing resistance to its occupation in Iraq and the cry for multilateralism as the rule of global engagement being voiced from the United Nations, Europe, Russia, China, India and many other countries.[7] If the concentration of the military and economic power in the hands of the United States appears unprecedented in the history of international relations, it also has generated the search for strategies among its opponents to conduct an 'asymmetric war' against it.

At the second level, we need to focus on Asia. The debate on whether the twenty-first century belongs to Asia or not is an ongoing one, but there is no denying the fact that Asia has become the principal theatre where contemporary international struggles are playing themselves out. This is likely to remain true for decades to come. The most significant security and economic trends are centred in and around Asia. Two of the most serious areas of global security concerns, namely, terrorism and the proliferation of the weapons of mass destruction are located mostly in Asia. In the name of fighting these two security menaces—the US and 'international community's' presence and their intervention in Asia—are also growing. Asia on its own has joined the push for participating in this US led global governance for security in one form or the other. At the same time, there are anxieties about American unilateralism in the region and a strong undercurrent of Asian preference for a larger role of the United Nations, and the need for effective multilateralism. Asia has its own intra-regional security concerns arising out of the ethnic, sectarian, systemic (related to democracy), and revolutionary conflicts. A number of dangerous forces and activities like arms and drug trafficking, money laundering, propagation of extremist ideologies, etc. are feeding into these conflicts. Further, there are regional flash points, such as the Palestine-Israel conflict, tensions in the Korean peninsula, the Taiwan question and the India–Pakistan hostilities over Kashmir that threaten to undermine peace and stability in Asia.

While being the focus of international security problems, Asia is now the centre of economic growth and commercial dynamism. It has the world's most youthful populations. Asia is the fastest growing continent, with China and India set to emerge as the world's second and third largest economies over the next few decades. China sits on a foreign exchange reserves of nearly 300 billion dollars and in 2002, it 'absorbed $52.7 billion of foreign capital...ranking first in the world'.[8] India, on the other hand, is emerging as the major hub of IT products and services. Its foreign exchange reserves have crossed the $100 billion mark, and exports have recorded a steady growth of 10 per cent in the recent years.[9] Some of the smaller countries like Vietnam and Thailand are also growing very fast, at the rate of more than 6 per cent. The economic dynamism of Asia will be sustained by growing connectivity and infrastructure development. It will also be reinforced by the evident emphasis on integrating markets through free trade arrangements, and restructuring and reforms in individual economies. And all this is happening in spite of SARS and Bird flue scares. Asia is also the principal source of world's energy supply. There are ever new and impressive discoveries of oil and gas not only in the Persian Gulf region but also in India, Bangladesh, Myanmar, Indonesia and Vietnam.

At the third but critical level, India itself has changed significantly in recent years. It has recorded a sustained economic growth of 5–6 per cent and above over the past nearly two decades, leading to the rise of a substantive middle class. In terms of Purchasing Power Parity, it already ranks fourth among the world's economies. Its markets have begun to open up giving new incentives and stimulation to the private entrepreneurs. Economic reforms in India have often been criticised—at home and abroad—for not being rapid enough. Some have described the situation in India as a 'strong consensus in favour of weak reforms'. The successive governments have justified their policies as being determined by the need to take into account the potentially massive social dislocations that will necessarily arise out of economic restructuring. But no one—within India and outside—have doubted the direction and sustainability of reforms. The Indian political class has finally set itself the goal of making India a developed country by 2020. Whether India will get there in that time frame or not, the proclaimed objective of becoming a developed country, in itself, is a big mental leap, given the traditional self-perception as a weak and developing country.[10] The India of early twenty-first century is gaining in self-confidence amidst the demonstration of impressive capabilities in many areas. It successfully addressed the negative fallout from the nuclear tests of May 1998. It handled the Kargil war with utmost responsibility, managed the nuclear factor in the war sensibly, and retrieved the territory that was occupied by Pakistan. Since then a sustained drive to build India's defence capabilities has been launched. In the recent years, India has also emerged out of the spectre of unstable governance, and there are hopes that the blemish of sectarian deviation in its polity, as witnessed in Gujarat, may prove to be a temporary aberration. India has also overcome the sense of strategic isolation it faced immediately after the end of the Cold War. Indian policy has recognised the value of strategic space created by the end of bipolarity and has pursued a productive engagement, with the global powers as well as its Asian neighbours.

India's Approach and Options

India must preserve and expand the strategic space created for its foreign policy in the post-Cold War world. Within a global power structure dominated by the United States, two clear, but extreme, options present themselves at once. One is to bandwagon with the sole superpower to protect national interests in the current situation. The other is to join the willing powers of the second tier to balance the United States. Indian foreign policy articulation has often referred to both the options. There have been occasions when the Indian leadership has described New Delhi and Washington as 'natural allies'. Even more frequently, India has in conjunction with other powers, and in multilateral forums, often pressed the slogan of a 'multipolar world'. But the policy itself appears to have navigated between these two options. There appears to be an instinctive awareness that these extreme options are neither feasible nor desirable. An uncritical alliance with the United States could significantly affect India's credibility as an independent power; the search, on the other hand, for a countervailing alliance to the United States could push India into a fool's errand. With particular reference to Asia, following the US lead and direction in the east could shrink India's strategic space in relation to China and parts of the ASEAN, and in the northwest, it may constrain India's cooperation with Russia, Iran and a number of other Islamic and Persian Gulf countries. At the same time, a hostile or unfriendly relationship with the United States could also curtail many options for India in the region.

India's approach should lie somewhere between the two extremes. Seeking to build a sound bilateral understanding with the US must remain an important Indian objective. But India must recognise there might be limits—arising both in New Delhi and Washington—that circumscribe the potential cooperation between the two nations across the board. On countering terrorism and protecting the sea-lanes, for example, there is room for considerable cooperation. But there are many issues where the perceptions and interests of the two countries might not always coincide. India did not endorse or join the US unilateral intervention in Iraq, nor has it followed the policy of sanctions against Myanmar on the question of its domestic issues of political liberalisation and human rights. India's emphasis must be on issue-based coalitions that will give it flexibility to join different alliances at different times. On some issues, it could have more in common with Russia and China, on others with the United States and Russia, on some others with Russia and Iran, and in some instances with United States and Israel. India has also begun to explore political cooperation with rising powers of the south—Brazil and South Africa. But none of these mechanisms for cooperation should be allowed to become firm alliances that will limit India's political choices. Engagement, *tout azimuth*, should be the main motto for India, for it gives the option of multi-directional engagement with all the major powers as well as the significant regional players like Japan, Australia, Iran, Commonwealth of Independent States and ASEAN. Engagement and issue-based alignments are only instruments; they must serve the objective of making India an indispensable force in the Asian balance of power.

Pursuing Positive Asymmetry in South Asia

Achieving the objective of becoming one of the principal powers of Asia will depend entirely on the ability of India to manage its own immediate neighbourhood. One of the most significant developments in India since 1991 has been radical rethinking about the relevance of a more effective regionalism in the subcontinent and a sea change in the Indian policy towards her smaller neighbours. India has taken important steps to transform her ties with the smaller neighbours from confrontation to cooperation. This change in policy has the potential to transform the political dynamics in the subcontinent in a manner that has not been seen for decades. At the heart of the changing Indian policy towards the neighbours is the so-called 'Gujral doctrine', named after Mr Inder Kumar Gujral who served as the external affairs minister during 1996–97 and as prime minister during 1997–98.[11] Although the doctrine was named after Mr Gujral, given his enthusiastic articulation of it, the broad lines of it were followed by the government of P.V. Narasimha Rao (1991–96), and that of Vajpayee, who followed Gujral. The then External Affairs Minister Yashwant Sinha explicitly acknowledged the debt to his predecessors and the Vajpayee government's commitment to take it forward. He has coined a new expression for the core of 'Gujral Doctrine', namely 'institutionalising positive asymmetry in favour of our neighbours'.[12]

The core objectives in India's approach towards the subcontinental neighbours must be to ensure security and stability of the region, reintegrate the South Asian market, create a web of regional interdependence and preserve India's strategic primacy. Sceptics would indeed argue that the immediate neighbourhood could not fully ensure either India's security, its strategic initiatives or economic aspirations. South Asia and the SAARC region cannot be allowed to become the highest ambition to be pursued by India. But if New Delhi cannot carry its neighbours along, its weight will not be fully felt in other parts of Asia. Strife and antagonism within South Asia will, in the final analysis, be a liability for India's role in Asia and the world. Surely, India alone has not been and will not be held responsible for such strife and antagonism, but its share of responsibility in this respect will be decisive and the largest. No other regional engagement can serve as an alternative to India's engagement with the immediate neighbours. There are clear indications that the policy makers are increasingly aware of the significance of the subcontinent.

Three major factors seem to have shaped the new thrust in India's regional policy. The first is the economic imperative. As the impact of economic globalisation enveloped the subcontinent during the nineties, India found a new force facilitating regional economic cooperation. As each of the South Asian nations sought to integrate with the global market they no longer could avoid cooperating with each other. Until the nineties, regional cooperation was either politically willed or resisted. In the nineties it was driven by larger economic considerations and became inevitable. India now had the opportunity to integrate the regional market under its leadership. For the smaller countries, access to the Indian market became a key to future economic growth. The changing and positive dynamics of India's trade with Sri Lanka and Bangladesh underline this imperative. Sri Lanka is now eager to integrate itself with India in general, and the neighbouring southern states in particular through the proposed 'Comprehensive Economic Partnership Agreement' and a land bridge. Bangladesh is beginning to overcome the political inhibitions on negotiating a Free Trade Agreement with India like Sri Lanka. Bhutan has elevated its income levels by responding to India's energy needs through the harnessing of water resources. That Pakistan too will have no option to shed its traditional reservations about economic cooperation with India has become evident at the Islamabad SAARC summit where it finally agreed to facilitate the South Asian Free Trade Agreement. There are estimates that given proper incentives, Indo-Pakistan trade can reach a $10 billion mark in less than five years. This is the prevailing level of much acclaimed trade between India and ASEAN. It is now up to India to provide the leadership in accelerating the economic integration of the subcontinent.

The second imperative of breaking India's South Asian regional logjam lies in the domestic political dynamics of these neighbours, and the way they impinge on India. Nehruvian preference for democratic and secular polities in the immediate neighbourhood was not a woolly conception. Its relevance has been reinforced in the context of the global thrust in favour of democracy, pluralism and human rights. There are serious internal conflicts in many of India's South Asian neighbours. India's policy preferences in relation to these conflicts have to be inclined towards enduring, broad based forces wedded to constructive nationalism. Lending legitimacy to the extremist forces like the LTTE in Sri Lanka, the radical Islamist forces in Pakistan and Bangladesh and the Maoists in Nepal, or support to the increasingly isolated but assertive monarchy in Nepal, or indifference towards the autocratic governance of President Abdul Gayoom in Maldives, cannot be in India's long-term interests. Political stability in the immediate neighbourhood is indeed desirable but not at the cost of sacrificing the long-term values of pluralism and democracy. Addressing the question of evolving a judicious policy mix of the short-term requirements and long-term interests in these conflict prone situations should be accorded due priority. Sacrificing tomorrow for today is an expensive proposition. Working for longer-term objectives would not be easy, given the steady growth in the strength of the anti-India lobbies in almost all of these countries. India must find ways in the interim to cope up with the prickly nationalism and the tendency to blame New Delhi for all the failures of the local elites. India, under the Gujral Doctrine and beyond, has recognised the importance of resolving long-standing bilateral conflicts with the neighbours by going more than half the distance. In return for a more generous approach, the only condition that New Delhi today insists upon is the commitment from the neighbours not to allow activities hostile to India on their soil.

The third imperative of India's South Asia policy is to preserve its strategic space within the subcontinent in relation to the extra-regional powers. Despite the tough rhetoric of the Nehruvian period and assertion by Indira Gandhi's India, the attempts to insulate the neighbourhood from the influences and interventions of the great powers did not succeed. The steady growth of the political profile of both China and the United States in the neighbourhood has continued even after the end of the Cold War. India's irritants with its smaller neighbours have allowed the external powers to effectively checkmate India within the subcontinent. Pakistan, too, has used New Delhi's problems with the smaller neighbours to expand its anti-India activities. This situation has to be reversed through the advantage of India's changing engagement with these great powers. India cannot afford to subordinate its priorities in the immediate neighbourhood with the initiatives of the US, UK, Europe, China or even Japan. Nor can it keep out the rest of the world amidst a globalisation of South Asian security. The challenge for India is to find appropriate means to preserve its primacy in the region in this complex emerging environment.

Looking East: Phase Two

The 'Look-East policy' launched by India in the beginning of the nineties was a vigorous response towards the extended neighbourhood in the east in the post-Cold War situation. The policy was in fact initiated first with Myanmar, when India began a constructive engagement with the military regime there in the early nineties. The broader Look East policy in the regional context was articulated by the then Prime Minister Narasimha Rao, in his Singapore Address in 1994.[13] Under this policy, India has achieved notable success in securing institutional integration with the ASEAN region, that include not only the membership of ASEAN Regional Forum (ARF), but also the holding of the first ASEAN Plus One Summit in December 2002. India is still not a part of Asia Europe Meeting (ASEM), or of the Asia-Pacific Economic Cooperation (APEC) forum. Participation in APEC may not be indispensable for India at its present stage of development, particularly from the narrow point of view of its economic interests, but this forum can facilitate India's engagement with the major players in the region, beyond ASEAN, like Japan, Australia and Korea. The core strategic objective of India in the ARF has to be that it remains driven by ASEAN without either being overwhelmed by the US, or dominated by China. Within ASEAN, India needs to evolve a differentiated approach towards the older members on the one hand, and the new ones on the other. There are clearly two ASEAN(s) for policy purposes in view of the stark economic, political and strategic differences between the older and the newer members of ASEAN.

By the turn of the century, India began to talk of a second phase of the Look East policy.[14] The second phase of India's Look East policy has focused on developing more intensive economic contacts. The emphasis is on expanding trade, mobilising investments and sourcing energy from this region. The ASEAN occupies a special place in this respect and there, Thailand and Singapore have been, and are expected to play, a critical role. Creating a free trade arrangement with ASEAN as a whole, as well as with selected individual countries, is an important aspect of the strategy of economic integration. India has set a target of a trade turnover of 30 billion dollars with the ASEAN by 2007 and a free trade area by the early years of the next decade.[15] India also aims at developing physical connectivity with Southeast Asia through Myanmar and Thailand. The new phase in the Look East policy is not limited to Southeast Asia alone. It involved the deepening of ties with Australia, Japan and South Korea—all of whom are major economies and effective political factors in the region.

The consolidation of India's economic initiatives will require streamlining of India's approach in three areas. First, a faster and more intensive structural reform in the Indian economy. We have noted that this factor is relevant in the overall pursuance of India's engagement with the whole of Asia and the world, but such reforms will have to be carried out within the parameters of their social and political imperatives at home. Second, a greater strategic vision to drive India's economic diplomacy seems to be an urgent need of the hour, so that decision are not bogged down over concerns about short-term revenue losses and narrow considerations of immediate and reciprocal advantages. Indian diplomacy can profitably evaluate, and learn from the Chinese use of economic tools for advancing their strategic objectives in the region. Third, there is also the need for greater initiative and participation on the part of Indian entrepreneurs and business class to get involved in Southeast Asia. During the regional economic crisis in 1997–99, Indian investors could expand their economic presence in Southeast Asia, but they did not. They appeared largely being hesitant on taking risks, or on looking ahead, or for being too deeply involved in the domestic market.

A vigorous economic Look East policy will not only contribute to India's growth and dynamism but also ensure development and stability of its turbulent and strategically sensitive region of the northeast. Underlining these linkages, the then Prime Minister Vajpayee had said:

> When I look at the north-east, I also naturally look at India's extended neighbourhood in Southeast Asia. This is a region where truly historic socio-economic transformations are taking place. Because of its proximity to Southeast Asian markets, India's northeastern region enjoys a locational advantage of great importance... India is working actively to promote regional and sub-regional trade and economic cooperation. Our north-eastern states can become our economic bridgehead to Southeast Asia. Equally, vibrant commercial exchanges with Southeast Asia can galvanise growth and development in the north-east. I, therefore, urge all the eight states in the region together to prepare the ground to participate vigorously in the emerging opportunities with our Southeast Asian neighbourhood. This also includes tourism, where I see a major synergy between the north-east and ASEAN countries.[16]

In the second phase, India should also expand and reinforce earlier initiatives taken in the field of building defence and security cooperation. The Southeast Asian countries are engaged in a massive defence modernisation and form an attractive market for Indian products and services. In order to harness this market, India has to increase its expertise and involvement at the level of its diplomatic missions in the region (defence attaches), and improve its bargaining and negotiating skills. Care has also to be taken for introducing technologies and weapons systems that may have long-term implications in the region on India's own strategic interests, as well as for peace and stability in the region. The public sector defence units like the HAL are not always the best instruments of diplomacy in defence deals. The private sector has entered the defence field in India and there is a need to integrate them in the pursuit of a policy of defence cooperation with this region. Then there is the question of the credibility of meeting the time-lines and executing already inked deals, including in defence services area. In the past, some of the agreements with the countries like Malaysia, Vietnam and Laos had to be abandoned without implementation. India's credibility as a dependable defence partner needs to be enhanced.

India has considerable capabilities and experience in peacekeeping, anti-piracy, and search and rescue operations. The Indian Ocean region, washing the shores of the Southeast Asian countries, needs these capabilities in view of the large commercial cargo transiting through it. There are also undesirable activities in terms of the transport of illegal arms, drugs and fissile material through the Indian Ocean. Interdiction of such cargo is necessary for peace and security in the region where India can play a very significant role. India's cooperation with the US in patrolling the Malacca Straits during the Operation Enduring Freedom has been an important step forward in raising India's regional naval profile. Such cooperation with other regional countries needs to be explored. Hindering illegal trafficking in arms and drugs through the sea lines of communication will also help in curbing terrorism, insurgencies and internal conflicts in a number of South and Southeast Asian countries. Such a cooperation would also involve securing access rights, joint exercises and regular interaction between Indian and regional navies.

Looking West: In Search of a Forward Policy

During the last few years, Indian policy towards Afghanistan and Central Asia has acquired a new dynamism. If the series of initiatives towards these regions in recent years are put together, a de facto

Look West policy comes into view. But there is also a dark shadow between India's aspirations for a larger role in its West Asian neighbourhood and the realities on the ground. Pakistan, as a political as well as a geographical factor, remains an important obstacle to more productive cooperation with the extended neighbourhood to the West. Nevertheless, the 1990s saw considerable advance in India's engagement with the region; and thanks to the events of September 11 and the consequent American war against terrorism, many new possibilities for India have been opened in the region.

In Afghanistan, the post-September 11 developments have dramatically reversed the fortunes of India and Pakistan in Afghanistan. Under pressure from the United States, Pakistan had to reverse its support to the Taliban and facilitate its demise. And the rebel groups earlier supported by India now occupied key positions in the interim government set up in Kabul with the backing of the international community. For India, it was a victory twice over. The defeat of the Taliban represented a huge gain for India as the Taliban controlled Afghanistan had become a sanctuary along with Pakistan, for extremists operating against it. More fundamentally, September 11 facilitated better understanding of India's concerns regarding terrorism, in the United States and the international community. In turn, it has developed a convergence of interests between India and the international community (led by the US) in waging a comprehensive war against terrorism, and cleansing its breeding grounds in Afghanistan and Pakistan.

Despite this convergence at the level of ideas, many practical problems remain, particularly because India's enhanced presence and role in Afghanistan is not acceptable to Pakistan and the US has tried to keep Pakistan in good humour. The Bush administration, while welcoming India's contribution to the reconstruction of Afghanistan, thought it fit enough to convey Pakistani concerns to India.[17] The US clearly did not want India to get too closely involved in Afghanistan, particularly in the security sector and the training of the new Afghan army. Its apprehensions are rooted in a determination to avoid the impact of Indo-Pak rivalry in Afghanistan. Not being too closely involved with the management of the security situation in Afghanistan might suit India for the moment, and allow it to focus exclusively on the less controversial developmental assistance.

The central obstacle to a larger and more effective Indian involvement in Afghanistan and Central Asia remains the absence of its direct physical access to these Western neighbours. Pakistan has been unwilling to allow the facility of transit trade between Afghanistan and India, despite the fact that such an arrangement would be beneficial to all. India in the meanwhile has signed a preferential trade agreement with Afghanistan and is seeking to develop an alternative route to Afghanistan via Iran.[18] India is cooperating with Iran in developing the Chahbahar port on the Makran coast near the Iran-Pak border. A road exists from there till the border with western Afghanistan. From there India is building a link road to the central circular highway in Afghanistan. This will not only provide India an access to Afghanistan and Central Asia, but also reduce landlocked Afghanistan's historic dependence on Pakistan for access to the Arabian Sea. This has the potential to rework the geopolitics of the region. While exploring the options to skirt around Pakistan, New Delhi is also urging Islamabad to consider the opportunities for cooperation and the prospect that Pakistan could serve as bridge state between India and its western neighbourhood:

> Pakistan, with its unique geographical position at the confluence of the Sub-Continent, the Persian Gulf and Central Asia can play an invaluable bridge role in connecting an energy-hungry India with its booming markets to those of Central Asia, West Asia and the Gulf. If Pakistan can find within itself the strength and wisdom to change its current approach towards India, there are immense benefits that it can derive as a transit route for the movement of energy, goods and people. We could then very well see this entire region rise on the tide of regional cooperation as has happened in the case of ASEAN.[19]

The return of Central Asia to the world, from the innards of the Soviet Union, generated considerable romance in New Delhi about rekindling the historic links between India and Central Asia. As the fragile and newly independent nations of Central Asia, were hardly prepared for independence in 1991, the metaphor of the 'Great Game'—invoking the rivalry between Imperial Russia and Great Britain in the nineteenth century for influence in the region—became the dominant prism of viewing Central Asia. The discovery of large quantities of oil and natural gas in the region reinforced the sense of an ongoing grab for these resources in the region. Unlike the Great Game of the past, the players now would be different and include Russia, the United States, China, India, Pakistan, Iran, Saudi Arabia and Turkey.[20] India was among the first countries to establish diplomatic relations with the five Central Asian Republics—Turkmenistan, Uzbekistan, Tajikistan, Kyrgyzstan and Kazakhstan. India's focus was riveted on these five republics located to the east of the Caspian Sea. India's engagement with Azerbaijan, Armenia and Georgia in the Caucasus was to come later and remain secondary.

India has defined for itself a fourfold objective in Central Asia. First was to gain a political and economic presence in these countries that were joining the global mainstream, and were of considerable strategic significance to India. Second, India is also strongly interested in preserving the moderate religious character of the regimes, most of whom were led by the former Soviet Communist party bosses. Third, Indian interest has been to gain access to the large hydrocarbon resources in the region by leveraging the large Indian market for natural gas and oil. And finally, there has been the unstated objective of limiting Pakistani influence in the region. The results of a decade-long intensive engagement with Central Asia present a mixed picture. While the old goodwill and high level personal contacts of the Soviet period gives India an initial advantage, the lack of connectivity greatly hinders it in pursuing concrete initiatives. Facing the land barrier in the form of Pakistan and Afghanistan, India has sought alternate routes into Central Asia through Iran. But the agreements to create land and rail corridors into the region through Iran never really took off. The inhibiting factors in this respect include Iran's own loss of the traditional trading culture, India's difficulties of financing economic cooperation, and the weak economic performance of the new Republics. India's attempts to circumvent some of these factors through credit lines have also not made much impact because the amounts that India can offer are still very modest and the required infrastructure relating to banking facilities and air travel have not matched the requirements in time and size. On the political front India had little problem in finding common cause with the Central Asian Republics (CARs) in opposing religious extremism and ethnic separatism. Although India and the CARs looked at security cooperation to counter terrorism, it was Moscow, Beijing and Washington that eventually became the players in dealing with these challenges. The former two set up the Shanghai Cooperation Organisation along with the neighbouring CARs to deal with the challenge.

The ouster of the Taliban at the end of 2001 provided India a new set of opportunities. Through an intensive engagement, India has begun to raise its profile in Central Asia in the last few years. The then External Affairs Minister Yashwant Sinha underlined the fact that 'Our cooperation with Central Asia includes cultural, economic, defence and security relations. For us Central Asia is our "immediate and strategic neighbourhood".'[21] The attention drawn by Sinha to the defence and security reinforced the speculation around the world that India has been trying to develop its military presence in the region, including a military base in Tajikistan.[22] While both sides have denied that it is a base for India, there has been confirmation that New Delhi is helping Dushanbe upgrade its air base in Ayni. More important is the fact that India's security and defence interaction with Central Asian countries has steadily expanded in recent years. These included substantive military exchanges, as well as cooperation in counter-terrorism. While there is broad-based expansion of bilateral relations, access remains the principal challenge for India in the region. Underlying the importance of road connection, mentioned earlier, to Afghanistan and Central Asia through Iran, the then Foreign Minister Sinha had said: 'Once this road is complete, it will reduce by 1500 km the distance from India to Central Asia'.

The competition with Pakistan for influence in Afghanistan and Central Asia is a reality. While making all the effort to skirt around Pakistan, New Delhi must also look at the prospects for neutralising or co-opting Islamabad in its search for access and expanded presence in Afghanistan and Central Asia. Such prospects, though look somewhat over-optimistic, yet they need not necessarily be unrealistic. The implementation of a free trade regime in South Asia, the opening up of trade routes between India and Pakistan—all reinforce the logic of economic integration between the subcontinent and Afghanistan. The challenge for India lies in taking the leadership role to facilitate this rather than get caught in a permanent argument with Pakistan over Afghanistan. Leveraging the size of its market, India can effectively work on developing energy corridors to Central Asia that run through Pakistan and Afghanistan.

Finding the Balance in West Asia

The Persian Gulf has also now begun to loom large in India's strategic calculus. Economically, the traditional importance of the Gulf as a destination of India's migrant labour and also a source for India's energy needs has been enhanced manifold due to India's rising economic aspirations and expanding economy. As India's growth rate picked up, it has emerged as one of the world's five largest importers of petroleum products, and therefore, a critical market for hydrocarbons, particularly huge gas reserves, strategically closer to the production centres in the Gulf region. The changing dimensions of India-Gulf energy relationship have now added a security dimension to it. To make this relationship secure and dependable in the long run, India is exploring the prospects of a free trade agreement with the Arab Gulf states. The Gulf Cooperation Council (GCC) has itself moved towards a customs union making its future potential for growth immense. India's partnership with this integrating market can be advantageous to both the sides. For building up this partnership, India had assiduously begun to reach out to conservative Sheikh-doms like Saudi Arabia, as well as moderate Arab Gulf states, without jeopardising its traditional links with the Baathist Iraq.

The security issues in the Gulf have assumed serious and complex dimensions in the aftermath of September 11 events and the US attack on Iraq. The invitation from Washington to New Delhi to participate in the stabilisation force in Iraq after the ouster of Saddam Hussein further sensitised India to the complexities of Gulf security. The countervailing pressures and consideration that did not allow the Government of India to respond positively to the US invitation were 'long-term national interests, our concerns for the people of Iraq, our long standing ties with the Gulf region as a whole as well as our growing dialogue and strengthened ties with the US'.[23] The prevailing chaos in Iraq affirms the prudence of India's caution on the one hand, and poses a challenge to India's diplomacy, to find ways and means of getting itself meaningfully engaged with Iraq.

The prudence and caution in the policy towards the Persian Gulf is also reflected in India's distancing itself from the US approach to Iran. It would not be an exaggeration to say that Iran has become an anchor of India's Gulf policy in the changed strategic context of the region. Iran and India are fast discovering their bilateral economic and political convergences that are rooted in the geopolitical interests of the two countries, and are not tied to the current state of Iran-US relations, or the nature of the regime in Teheran. On the economic front, Iran saw India as the natural export destination for its huge natural gas reserves. Building a natural gas pipeline to India, via Pakistan, became one of the biggest priorities in the subcontinent.

The rise of the Taliban in Afghanistan had drawn India and Iran strategically closer. And the uncertainties in the region and concerns about the direction of American policy, continue to reinforce this strategic convergence between the two countries.

Further beyond, in the larger region of West Asia, India's policy has gone beyond the past comprehensive alignment with the Arab world in its disputes with Israel to a long overdue even-handed approach to the region. This shift, particularly the building of a new bonhomie with Israel, has come in for some strong criticism at home; the new balance in India's policy to West Asia marks a return to the Nehruvian approach. Nehru's India was among the first countries to recognise Israel when it was formed. Although India did not establish full diplomatic relations with Israel, it allowed an Israeli consulate to function in Mumbai, and maintained contact at many levels. It was during the Indira Gandhi years that coincided with the Arab and Third World radicalism, which saw India's policy towards Israel acquiring a stridency and becoming increasingly one-sided. Rajiv Gandhi began the process of correcting this imbalance by engaging the Israelis, as well as their friends, in the United States on an informal basis. It was the Narasimha Rao's government which established full diplomatic relations with Israel.[24] The changed context in West Asia after the Gulf War of 1991 and the initiation of the peace process between the Arabs and Israel provided an opening for India to plug the absence of a relationship with Israel.

For a variety of reasons, India's relationship with Israel acquired a rapid momentum since the late nineties. The old ideological affinity of the BJP leaders with Israel was certainly a factor. During his tenure as foreign minister in 1977–79, Atal Bihari Vajpayee was instrumental in organising an unannounced visit by the Israeli Defence Minister Moshe Dayan to Delhi. During his visit to Israel, in July 2000, the then External Affairs Minister Jaswant Singh let it slip that India's past policy towards Israel was held hostage to the domestic electoral politics, which reflected a strong view not just in the BJP but also the strategic establishment.[25] The recognition of Israel as a source of modern technologies—both civilian and military—that were not available elsewhere, also constituted another element of the deepening relationship. Beyond advanced technologies, Israel had also developed the skill and resources to update old Russian defence equipment. The influence of the Jewish lobby in the United States and the growing coordination between Indian Americans and Jewish

Americans in Washington provided another basis for expanding relations between India and Israel.

While the gains from the relationship with Israel are indeed tangible, they are not a substitute for an expanded engagement with the Arab world. India has no reason to give up its relations with the Arab world where it has huge economic and political stakes. India has, in fact, maintained its traditional voting positions in favour of Palestinians and Arabs on the core disputes with Israel, despite some heavy lobbying by Israel, particularly during the visit of Ariel Sharon, the first by an Israeli Prime Minister to India. New Delhi took a long while to grant high level visits from Israel. Neither the Indian President nor the Prime Minister is yet to make return visits to Israel. Within weeks after the visit of Sharon, Prime Minister Vajpayee travelled to Syria, one of the radical Arab states, to demonstrate the continuing solidarity with the Arab cause.[26] This balancing between its traditional relationship with the Arab world and Israel is a trend that most of the great powers have adapted. India, like other major powers, cannot afford to take one-sided positions in conflicts in any region. But the balancing between competing interests will be permanent imperative and it is not always easy to manage.

Fortunately for India, while there has been some concern in the Arab world at the growing Indo-Israeli relationship, no significant opposition to it has been voiced. The Arab world is certainly concerned about the likelihood of Indo-Israeli defence cooperation altering the military and nuclear balance in West Asia. As the peace process began to break down in recent years, there is also the concern in the Arab capitals that India's policy is too balanced and that New Delhi's voice has been too muted in its criticism of Israel. There is also a view in India that the Arab nations have taken India's position for granted and that there has not been enough sensitivity about New Delhi's security concerns, particularly in the routine resolutions against India that are passed in the Organization of the Islamic Conference (OIC) year after year. This view too has found an echo in West Asia—that the Arabs have themselves to blame for the new Indian relationship with Israel:

Backed with the US, they (the Arabs) wholeheartedly supported Islamabad and the Afghan Mujahideen, taking for granted that India would always be in their grip, due to its need for Arab oil and remittances from Indians working in the Gulf. Even when it was proven in the 1990s that Pakistan took advantage of the Jihad momentum arising from the Afghan war to undermine India's stability, the Arabs did not take notice of the long-term risk of such a policy to their ties with India. Motivated by ideological and emotional pressure, they firmly stood by Pakistan, using the Organisation of Islamic Conference to build support for Islamabad and the Jihadi groups in Kashmir, as though the Kashmir issue was their key national cause or would serve their supreme interests.[27]

Balancing its competing imperatives from its relations with Arabs and Israelis is only one of India's future challenges in West Asia. India has reasons to be concerned that its present exclusive relationship with Israel might not last for long. There have been hints of interest in Pakistan, at the highest political level, in establishing diplomatic relations with Israel. Tel Aviv, too, has a high stake in normalising relations with Pakistan, one of the world's leading Islamic nations. The future of India's low-skilled manpower, which remits large amounts of hard currency, is coming under a cloud as large nations like Saudi Arabia are under pressure to provide employment to sons of the soil. The ideological linkage between extremist groups in West Asia and the Indian subcontinent is real, and India has to find ways to insulate itself from the instability in the region that must be expected to become more acute. As India embarks on a rapid growth path, the dependence on the oil from the region too will rise in the coming decades.

India has also new opportunities in the region to move away from mere purchase of oil to establishing long-term energy security relationships. As the Arab countries seek to modernise their economies, they are looking for economic partnership with India which can emerge as an important foreign investor and a source of badly needed intermediate and advanced technologies. The Arab nations are also beginning to look at regional economic integration among themselves as well as with the United States and Europe. India should prepare itself to take advantage. India has in recent years begun informal consultations with the OIC and its leading players. Some members of the OIC made moves to make India an observer of the organisation, but had to back off amidst resistance from Pakistan. But there has been little debate in New Delhi about the pros and cons of intensifying India's institutional links with the OIC.

India and Asia: The Unfinished Agenda

As India looks ahead to a larger role in an Asia that is being transformed, managing its great power relations remains at the top of its priorities. For the first time in decades India has improved relations with all the great powers in the region. Yet the full potential of its multi-directional engagement remains to be realised. While the Indo-US relations have improved, there are many areas of concern. The commercial ties with the US remain way below those between Washington and China. The areas that India has discovered an advantage, for example, in the outsourcing of back-office functions, have become a political controversy in the US. On the political front, New Delhi and Washington have come some distance in addressing their differences over non-proliferation. While they have identified a new framework,[28] there may be prospects for India to access advanced high technologies from the US. India has also concerns about continuing likelihood of being hyphenated with Pakistan on issues relating to non-proliferation and regional security.

Pakistan also remains an area where there is a 'deficit of trust' in India's current improvement of relations with China. In remarks on Sino-Indian relations, the then External Affairs Minister Yashwant Sinha said:

> Some aspects of China's relations with Pakistan, including their nexus in nuclear and missile proliferation, however, continue to cause serious concern in India as they have a direct and negative bearing on our national security environment. We regard China as a friend and we expect friends to show greater sensitivity to our security concerns.[29]

While there is a blossoming economic relationship, the challenge of addressing the boundary dispute remains. Getting a national consensus in favour of a pragmatic settlement of the boundary dispute as well as getting Beijing to sign on it will not be easy. The very movement towards a realistic discussion of the boundary dispute could bring the problems of Tibet back into the centre-stage of Sino-Indian relations. India's ties with Japan have begun to look up, but there is a long way to go before they reach maturity. The economic ties between India and Japan are stagnant and the political and security ties are yet to develop. India's ties with Russia look good on the surface, but there is a huge problem gathering on the economic front. Trade between the two nations has plummeted and people to people contact has begun to decline. In other words, the unfinished agenda on the bilateral front with the major powers is a large one. But fortunately, the overall environment is conducive to an engagement with all of them. India has unprecedented strategic flexibility in engaging all the major powers at the same time and is under no compulsion to align with either one of the great powers against the others. Nor is it being asked to.

The opportunities for regional economic integration within South Asia and with the other sub-regions of Asia are beckoning India. The notion of an Asian economic community and the talk of a common Asian currency are no longer considered wild ideas. India's economic reforms give it the capacity to be part of this new process in Asia; but is India ready to lead the process? While India has entered into a rash of free trade agreements with many nations and groupings in the region, they remain somewhat hollow—with long time frames for implementation and large negative lists in place. The Indian industry continues to slow down if not resist free trade agreements. And where they have already been agreed to, it has sought to limit their scope. The commerce ministry, with its narrow focus on revenues, is not yet ready to make trade a national strategy. Developing greater coordination between commerce and foreign ministries and giving trade a strategic dimension, remains an important challenge for Indian policy makers.

Developing better coordination between India's defence establishment and the foreign office has become important amidst the changing defence scenario in the region. As the US reconfigures the disposition of its armed forces in Asia, Japan raises its defence profile and China expands its military capabilities, India needs a dynamic strategy that is capable of taking advantage of the new opportunities and limiting the impact of negative developments. The coming years will see increasing demand on India to deploy its forces far beyond its shores in Asia and the Indian Ocean littoral. Amidst the prospect of many states failing in the region and other contingencies, India will have to consider the creation of special expeditionary forces and the development of political criteria under which it will use force in the region. India already has begun defence cooperation with a variety of countries in the region. It conducts military exercises with countries as diverse as China and Vietnam, Iran and the United States. It sends peacekeeping forces to far-away lands. It has begun to sign more significant defence agreements, such as the one with Singapore, which give Indian forces expanded reach. India is also once again talking about defence exports, as well as providing training and other services to friendly nations. Much of this defence diplomacy, however, remains ad hoc and needs a coherent set of goals and institutional capacities at home to make it effective.

India's ability to gain greater economic and political weight in Asia now rests on gaining physical connectivity to large parts of Asia. Unfortunately, the Partition has created two physical land barriers— Pakistan and Bangladesh—on its flanks. Finding ways to overcome these barriers will be the biggest strategic challenges for India. Neither of these neighbours today gives transit facilities for India to reach the other parts of Asia. India has two options—to circumvent these barriers or cut through them. India has embarked on strategic projects in Iran to gain access to Afghanistan and Central Asia in the West and through Myanmar to its own territory in the Northeast as well as Southeast Asia. But long-circuiting Pakistan and Bangladesh cannot be a lasting solution. India must leverage the development of alternative access routes to gain trade and transit rights through Pakistan and Bangladesh. It must also leverage the proposed projects for pipelines from the West to open up Pakistani space for its own interests. It must also find creative ways to overcome the Bangladeshi resistance to economic integration. This could include the potential trans-regional economic cooperation with China. Whether it is China's Kunming initiative from Yunnan or its West Region development strategy focused on globalising Xinjiang and Tibet, India must find ways to fold economic cooperation with China into efforts to remove the political obstacles to economic cooperation in the subcontinent.

An imaginative policy towards the neighbours remains an important instrument to achieve India's larger ambitions in Asia. For the first time in decades, India, today, is engaged simultaneously in purposeful negotiations to resolve its long-standing disputes—the question of Jammu and Kashmir with Pakistan and the boundary dispute with China. The resolution of either of the disputes or both could radically alter the security condition of India and liberate its military and financial resources to play a larger role in Asia. If India moves towards a substantive reform of its security sector and creates an institutional synergy among its tools of diplomacy and statecraft,

India will be well positioned to exploit the many opportunities coming its way in Asia.

Notes and References

1. For a discussion of some of these issues, see James F. Hoge, Jr., 'A global power shift in the making', *Foreign Affairs*. New York, July/August 2004.
2. Text of Nehru's speech at the First Asian Relations Conference held in New Delhi on 23 March 1947. Surjit Mansingh (ed.) *Nehru's Foreign Policy: Fifty Years On*. Appendix A, Mosaic Books, New Delhi, 1998, pp. 149–56.
3. Ibid.
4. Jawaharlal Nehru, *The Unity of India: Collected Writings, 1937–1940*. London, 1941, p. 327. Also cited in ibid., p. 100.
5. For a discussion of Nehru's vision for India in Asia and its limitations, see S.D. Muni, 'Nehru's India in Asia: Anatomy of a Blurred Vision', in Surjeet Mansingh, ed., *Nehru's Foreign Policy, Fifty Years On*. New Delhi: Mosaic Books, 1998, pp. 100–120.
6. 'Shrug Off the Cold War, This is a New World', *Indian Express*. New Delhi, 7 November 2003.
7. For a discussion of the new trends in Washington, see Ivo H. Daalder and James M. Lindsay, *America Unbound: The Bush Revolution in Foreign Policy*. Washington DC, Brookings, 2003.
8. She Ke, 'Asia-Pacific Economies: Wide Gaps in Growth', *Beijing Review*, 27 February 2003.
9. Joanna Slater, 'Asian Economic Outlook: India-Sunny Forecast', *Far Eastern Economic Review*, 28 August 2003.
10. President APJ Abdul Kalam has been at the forefront of popularising this vision of India as a developed nation by 2020. See APJ Abdul Kalam and Y.S. Rajan, *India 2020: A Vision for the New Millennium*. New Delhi, Penguin, 2002. Also see the 'Economic Resolution', adopted at the Meeting of the National Executive of the BJP, Hyderabad, 11–12 January 2004, for the views of the dominant partner in the ruling coalition. The resolution commits the party to make India a great power.
11. The doctrine was articulated in a speech by Mr Gujral at the Royal Institute of International Affairs, reproduced in I.K. Gujral, *A Foreign Policy for India*. New Delhi, Ministry of External Affairs, 1998, pp. 69–81. See also Gujral's *Continuity and Change: India's Foreign Policy*. New Delhi, Macmillan, 2003, pp. 107–74 for a special section dealing with 'Gujral Doctrine'.
12. See '12th SAARC Summit and Beyond', Seventh Dinesh Singh Memorial Lecture by External Affairs Minister Yashwant Sinha, Sapru House 3, February 2004. See also C. Raja Mohan, 'Neighbourhood Policy: Yashwant Doctrine?', *The Hindu*, 13 January 2003. For a background on India's neighbourhood policy after the Cold War, see S.D. Muni, 'India and Its Neighbours: Persisting Dilemmas and New Opportunities', *International Studies*, vol. 30, no. 2, April–June 1993; and also his, 'Problem Areas in India's Neighbourhood Policy', *South Asian Survey*, vol. 10, no. 2, July–December 2003, pp. 185–96.

13. Prime Minister Narasimha Rao's 'Singapore Lecture', Singapore, September 1994, text published by the Institute of Southeast Asian Studies, Singapore. For an update on this theme, also see Prime Minister Atal Bihari Vajpayee's 'Singapore Lecture' on 9 April 2002.

14. 'The first phase of India's "Look East" policy was ASEAN-centred and focused primarily on trade and investment linkages. The new phase of this policy is characterised by an expanded definition of "East", extending from Australia to East Asia, with ASEAN at its core. The new phase also marks a shift from trade to wider economic and security issues, including joint efforts to protect the sea-lanes and coordinate counter-terrorism activities', in 'Resurgent India in Asia', speech by External Affairs Minister Yashwant Sinha at Harvard University, Cambridge, MA, USA, 29 September 2003.

15. Prime Minister Vajpayee's speech at the India-ASEAN Business Summit, Bali, Indonesia, 7 October 2003, cited in *Strategic Digest*. New Delhi, vol. 33, no. 11, 2003, pp. 1155–57.

16. Prime Minister's address to the Second Northeast Business Summit in New Delhi, 20 January 2003. http://pib.nic.in/release/release.asp?relid+754

17. Jyoti Malhotra, 'US to India: Lay off Afghanistan Please', *Indian Express*. New Delhi, 8 December 2002.

18. C. Raja Mohan, ' India's New Road to Afghanistan', *The Hindu*, 7 September 2003. Also S.D. Muni, 'India's Afghan Policy: Emerging from the Cold', in K. Warikoo (ed.), *The Afghan Crisis: Issues and Perspectives*. Bhavana Books, New Delhi, 2002.

19. External Affairs Yashwant Sinha's speech at the SAARC Chambers of Commerce and Industry Symposium in Islamabad, 2 January 2004. Available at www. meadev.nic.in

20. For an assessment of the new Great Game, see Karl Meyer, *Tournament of Shadows: The Great Game and the Race for Empire in Asia*. London, 2001.

21. Sinha's keynote address at the Third India–Central Asia Conference in Tashkent, 6 November 2003. For a background to India's emerging relationship with Central Asia, see S.D. Muni, 'India and Central Asia: Towards a Cooperative Future', Nirmala Joshi (ed.), *Central Asia: The Great Game Replayed*. Delhi, New Century Publications, 2003, pp. 97–141.

22. C. Raja Mohan, 'India's Pamir Knot', *The Hindu*, 10 November 2003; 'Why India attaches importance to Central Asia', *People's Daily*, Beijing, 15 November 2003. http://english.peopledaily.com.cn/200311/15 eng20031115_128321. shtml

23. Government of India, *Statement on the Question of Sending Indian troops to Iraq*, 14 July 2003.

24. For a comprehensive account of India's relations with Israel over the decades, see P.K. Kumaraswamy, *India–Israel Relations: Humble Beginnings, Bright Future*. Washington DC, American Jewish Committee, 2002.

25. 'It was felt injustice should not be done to Muslims...India's Israel policy became captive to domestic policy and therefore an unstated veto'; Jaswant Singh's remarks in Israel quoted in 'Arab diplomats sore with Jaswant, Advani', *Indian Express*, 17 July 2000. This view was backed by J.N. Dixit who said, 'There is an element of truth in what Jaswant Singh said. It is the leadership of some of our political parties which is inclined to use such an argument on

the Muslim vote bank for their own purposes', cited in 'Out of the Closet', *Hindustan Times*, 8 July 2000.

26. In an interview to the *Syria Times* on the eve of his visit to Damascus, Mr Vajpayee reassured the Arab world that it has nothing to fear from the growing defence engagement between India and Israel. 'Our friends in the Arab world should rest assured in this regard. The important point is India has not diluted and will not dilute any aspect of its relationship with the Arab countries', *Indian Express*, 15 November 2003.

27. Abdullah al Madani, 'Indo-Israeli Ties: Arabs Have None but Themselves to Blame', *Gulf News Online*, 14 September 2003. http://www.gulf-news.com/Articles/Opinion.asp?ArticleID=97496

28. The framework goes by the name 'Next Steps in Strategic Partnership'. These were identified in simultaneous statements by President Bush and Prime Minister Vajpayee in January 2004. See the statement by Atal Bihari Vajpayee on 13 January 2004. Available at www.meadev.nic.in

29. Yashwant Sinha, Admiral R.D. Katari Memorial Lecture, New Delhi, 22 November 2003. Available at www.meadev.nic.in

3

A CONTINENT BECOMES A REGION: FUTURE ASIAN SECURITY ARCHITECTURES

Varun Sahni

Asia is not a region; it is a *continent* consisting of several regions. Although we state this proposition as a truism, it can indeed be buttressed conceptually. The 'continent' is essentially a geographical concept:[1] 'One of the main continuous bodies of land on the earth's surface...' is how it has been defined.[2] The concept of the continent has clarity, despite minor debates about whether, for instance, Antarctica is a continent or not. In sharp contrast, the concept of the region remains vague and elusive, as William R. Thompson demonstrated over 30 years ago.[3] From a security perspective, Barry Buzan's notion of the 'regional security complex' is probably the most appropriate, and certainly the most applicable, conceptual tool currently available to give coherence to the troublesome concept of the region. Buzan defines the security complex as 'a set of states whose major security perceptions and concerns are so interlinked that their national security problems cannot reasonably be analysed or resolved apart from one another.'[4] The essential notion at the heart of Buzan's concept is that 'regionally based clusters' are the 'normal pattern of security interdependence in a geographically diverse, anarchic international system.'[5] The essential structure of a security complex is determined by the patterns of friendship and enmity within it, as also the distribution of capabilities among the principal states of which it is composed.[6] The purpose of this chapter is to ask what it would take for Asia to *become* a region, and whether it would be in India's interest to encourage or impede that process of metamorphosis.

There are many critical issues and developments, in the contemporary period and the recent past, that have had an impact on security in Asia and vie for policy and analytical attention. To identify only the most important security concerns on the Asian continent, we could focus our attention on the problems arising out of the military occupation of Iraq, the deadlock in the Israel-Palestine conflict, Afghanistan in flux, the growing presence of external actors in Central Asia, persisting uncertainty on the Korean peninsula, the enduring threat of terrorism in Southeast Asia, nuclear and missile proliferation to/from Pakistan, and the ongoing India-Pakistan détente. While other issues could undoubtedly be added to this large and diverse list, they will not lead us to greater analytical clarity about security in Asia. To the contrary, we must move beyond headline grabbing issues and developments and focus instead upon the underlying power configurations in Asia today, if we are to get to grips with the security *problématique* in contemporary Asia.

The next section analyses the various key states of Asia and the regions in which they are embedded in order to arrive at a clearer understanding of security in Asia today. In the section that follows, the various security configurations that *could* emerge on the Asian continent (or more broadly in the Asia-Pacific) would be explored and their respective implications for India examined.

Security in Asia Today

Today no analysis of the configuration of power in Asia—or indeed any other continent—can even begin without taking account of the preponderance of American power. Not since the high noon of the Victorian period (1860–80) has a single state so dominated world politics in terms of sheer capability. The US today spends more on its military capabilities than the *next 15 countries* on the military spending list *combined*. Even this datum understates US preponderance because several of the countries behind it on the military spending list are its own friends and allies. Furthermore, a much higher proportion of US military spending goes into military research and development. What this means is that an unbridgeable technological gulf has also opened up between the US and *all* the other key states in the international system.

As Table 3.1 shows, the US military presence in the Asia-Pacific is organised around two large regionally-organised 'unified combatant commands': the US Pacific Command (USPACOM) based at Honolulu, Hawaii and the US Central Command (USCENTCOM) based at MacDill Air Force Base in Florida. As would be apparent from the data in Table 3.1, USPACOM has a large naval and airforce component while USCENTCOM is predominantly made up with the army element.

Apart from these regional commands, the US Special Operations Command, also based at MacDill Air Force Base, is heavily involved in parts of Asia. Since the Second World War, the US has maintained significant forces in Alaska and has around 40,000 troops each in Hawaii, Japan and South Korea. The bulk of the US military presence in this part of the world is maintained afloat the Pacific Fleet.

However, apart from these traditional deployments, the most significant American military presence in Asia today is in Iraq, where over 146,000 US troops are tasked with the military occupation of Iraq. We can see in this part of the world US forces performing the entire range of military tasks that 'imperial powers' have done through recorded history: to conquer (Iraq), to deter (the Pacific Fleet, American forces in Japan and South Korea, and American strategic bombers on Guam), to punish (Afghanistan) and to police (Iraq). The policing function, which would require the conversion of a significant part of US military capability into an imperial constabulary, is the only one that the American forces are not doing well. It is, therefore, perfectly logical that Washington is keen to sub-contract this vital military task to other states.

Thus, while the US is the pre-eminent status quo power globally, its role in Asia in the recent past has been to wreak havoc with the status quo. The new American grand strategy of 'muscular dominance' formulated by neo-conservative politics has been shaped around the trinity of military dominance, the war on terrorism and the Middle East, with preemptive action as the new doctrine to attain American interests.[7]

If 'preponderance' is the key word that best describes the US in Asia today, 'centrality' is perhaps the best key word with which to characterise the role of China. Geostrategically, China is at the very heart of Asia. It is the only country that is a part of or abuts all the

Table 3.1
US Military Presence in the Asia-Pacific (2003)

Formation	Nos. Deployed
■ Pacific Command (USPACOM)	285,549
• Army	64,410
• Air Force	39,540
• Navy	15,640
• Marine Corps	25,559
• Pacific Fleet	140,400
▪ Reserves	13,470
▪ Civilians	29,600
■ Central Command (USCENTCOM)	206,310
• Army	183,200
• Air Force	3,780
• Navy	3,130
• Marine Corps	13,800
▪ Marine Expeditionary Unit Fifth Fleet	2,200
• Special Forces	2,400

Location	
❑ Alaska	18,650
❑ Hawaii	39,000
❑ Guam	4,490
◆ Singapore	151
◆ Japan	40,680
◆ South Korea	41,360
◆ Australia	110
◆ Diego Garcia	668
◆ Thailand	69
◆ Afghanistan	8,500
◆ Bahrain	4,500
◆ Djibouti	800
◆ Iraq	146,400
◆ Kuwait	38,160
◆ Oman	270
◆ Pakistan	1,300
◆ Qatar	3,300
◆ Saudi Arabia	~ nil (training)
◆ United Arab Emirates	570
◆ Uzbekistan (UN Operations)	1,050

Source: The International Institute for Strategic Studies, *The Military Balance 2003–2004.* London, Oxford University Press, 2003, pp. 25–28.

regions of Asia apart from West Asia—Central Asia, South Asia, Southeast Asia and East Asia. If Asia the continent is ever to become Asia the region, it would be due to the role played by China, for good or for ill. Thus, it would not be too much of an exaggeration to say that China defines Asia; there can be no Asia without China. This truism will be even truer 20 years from now, by which time China would have become the single largest economic power, and at least, the second largest military power in the world system. Unless China implodes under the weight of its own internal contradictions, which seems a rather remote possibility, or gets severely weakened in a crippling cross-Taiwan straits war, which is just as unlikely, dealing and coping with Chinese power will be the biggest challenge facing not just India but all other Asian states.

With its border questions largely settled, China has embarked upon economic growth in what appears to be a status quo mode at the regional level coupled with a mildly revisionist orientation at the systemic level. As we will see in the section that follows, the historic role that China *could* play is to be the prime mover of a Helsinki-type process in Asia. As far as India itself is concerned, an improved strategic relationship with China must essentially have two, and ideally three, critical elements in it. The two essential elements in a China–India *détente* would be: (*a*) a border settlement which provides 'equal and mutual security' to both states and (*b*) the establishment of a stable deterrence relationship between the two states. The third, the ideal element which would move the China-India relationship from a 'negative security' to a 'positive security' dimension, would involve the two states working together to create a cooperative security arrangement on the Asian continent.

India, seen from an Asian perspective, can best be characterised as an 'emerging power'. To understand what an emerging power is we first need a prior understanding of what a 'middle power' is. We define middle powers as the special category of states that lack the system-shaping capabilities of the great powers, but whose size, resources and role, nonetheless, precludes them from being ignored by the great powers. In other words, middle powers may lack the capacity to challenge the way in which the great powers run the international system, but they are sufficiently powerful to defy any great power attempt to force them to behave in a manner against their choosing.[8] Emerging powers, then, are middle powers on the ascendant: states that have the capability and intention to manoeuvre their way into great power status. India, from this conceptual vantage point, is a quintessential emerging power. It should be pointed out that India's emergence is more likely to be in the realm of international political economy than that of international security. Furthermore, much like China, India will remain a status quo power at the regional level and be mildly revisionist at the level of the international system.

Since the India-Pakistan war of 1971, which led to the creation of Bangladesh, South Asia as a region has remained prey to 'structural insecurity'. The Indo-centric nature of South Asia is a fact of history and geography, a structural element that India cannot avoid and its neighbours cannot afford to ignore. Geographically, India forms the core of South Asia, and its neighbours, the periphery. India shares borders with each of the other countries in the region, while none of its neighbours share a land border with any South Asian country other than India. Indian military power in conventional terms far outweighs the collective power of *all* its regional neighbours. Thus, the only way the other countries of South Asia could contend with Indian power was by resorting to external balancing—seeking extra-regional intervention—which India resolutely opposes. Until Pakistan's nuclear tests in June 1998, there seemed to be no way out of this security dilemma. However, by gaining strategic parity with India, Pakistan has shattered the structural insecurity that has plagued South Asia and opened the possibility of durable peace in the region.

Some Indian analysts contest this sanguine view with the argument that a nuclear Pakistan would be more, and not less, belligerent vis-à-vis India. Pointing to the Kargil war between India and Pakistan in the summer of 1999, they suggest it was possible only because Pakistan had nuclear weapons and could, therefore, infiltrate its forces across the Line of Control (LoC) in Kashmir without the fear of starting a full-fledged war. However, Kargil does *not* disprove the proposition that nuclear deterrence can work in South Asia. (After all, India resisted the temptation of crossing the international border, and Pakistan finally called it a day and pulled out.) What Kargil proves is the fact that nuclear weapons buttress the status quo, and are rather poor tools for a revisionist foreign policy, much less the sort of Pakistani adventurism witnessed in Kargil.

It is undoubtedly true that Pakistani insecurity, vis-à-vis India, lies at the heart of the regional security *problématique* in South Asia. However, a more secure Pakistan is a necessary (but not sufficient) prerequisite for durable peace in South Asia.

It is important to note that India-Pakistan antagonism is distinct from the structural insecurity problem, as outlined earlier. India's conflict with Pakistan has its roots in ideology and identity rather than in an asymmetry of power. Indeed, among important sections of Pakistan's political elite, the obsession of parity with India has a certain hallucinatory quality. The central problem remains that Pakistan was founded on the 'two nation theory', an ideology that conferred distinct national identities on Hindus and Muslims. From the Indian perspective, the passage of time may be the best solution to the India-Pakistan problem. For the post-Partition generation of the Indian elite, Pakistan has *always* been another country, coloured differently on the map in school. For them the equation *'Pakistan = homeland for Indian Muslims'* makes absolutely no sense, since there are as many Indian Muslims today as the *entire* population of Pakistan. As the post-Partition generation reaches positions of power and influence in India in the coming decades, the centrality of Pakistan in India's *Weltanschauung* is likely to diminish considerably. Whether a similar process will take place in Pakistan is an open but crucial question.

Indeed, the key word that can best describe Pakistan today is 'confusion'. The fundamental question facing the rulers and people of Pakistan is the way in which their collective identity is redefined. It is sobering to note that the same military establishment that is now seeking to 'liberalise' Pakistan has been responsible for the 'Islamisation' of the country in the first place. Few countries in the world have had such a revisionist foreign and security policy for such a long time. There was a moment in the early nineties when Pakistan was simultaneously engaged in three asymmetric conflicts: Afghanistan, Punjab and Kashmir. Although recent events have undoubtedly dented Pakistan's self-confidence in this area, the legacy of this history lives on.

Thus, the configuration of relative power in South Asia in the post-Cold War period is characterised by Indian dominance, Pakistani defiance, and overt bilateral nuclearisation leading to strategic parity between the two. While India and Pakistan have officially been at peace since 1971,[9] their armed forces continue to fight each other, particularly in the Siachin Glacier conflict. In the Kashmir Valley and further afield, Pakistan is pursuing a low cost, moderately effective strategy of supporting insurgent groups against New Delhi. India has officially described the Kashmir insurgency as a 'proxy war' or as 'cross-border terrorism', an epithet that successfully captures

Pakistan's role in organising, arming and financing the insurgent groups but belies the endogenous reasons for widespread Kashmiri discontent.[10] It is still too early to assess whether the recent thaw in India-Pakistan relations will substantially alter the negative dynamic described earlier.

Apart from the four states—the US, China, India and Pakistan—considered earlier, there are four others—Iran, Indonesia, Japan and Australia—that rise to the level of key states in the Asia-Pacific. Regarding Iran today, the key word is 'fluidity'. The internal situation in Iran—the struggle between its conservatives on one side and its moderates and reformers on the other—is occupying all its energies, considerably diminishing Iran's external role. The internal struggle in Iran is hugely important for the international system as a whole, inasmuch as it involves the playing out, in full public view, of the civil war between democracy and theocracy that has engulfed much of the Islamic world.

The other key state in Asia that is in the throes of transition is Indonesia; like Iran, the result of that transformational process will reverberate far beyond the borders of the country itself. In recent years, the twin challenges of terrorism by Jemaah Islamiyah and secessionist activities in some of the outlying islands have raised fears about the cohesion of Indonesia. Although the chances of a successful Indonesian democratic transition have enhanced substantially in recent years, Indonesia remains critical to the stability of Asia for all the wrong reasons.

The stress that Indonesia is facing internally has also radiated outward to the other states of Southeast Asia. Till recently, Southeast Asia was increasingly being regarded as a proto-security community, a European Union-in-the-making. However, in recent years, intensified tensions between several regional states—Singapore and Malaysia, Malaysia and Brunei, Thailand and Cambodia—coupled with a range of newer asymmetric threats have led to an increased pace of military modernisation.[11] This is especially evident in the case of the airforces of the region: Myanmar took delivery of ten MiG-29 aircraft in February 2003; in April 2003, Indonesia placed an order for two Su-27SK and Su-30MK fighter aircraft each and also two Mi-35 armed helicopters; Malaysia followed suit in May 2003 with an order for eighteen Su-30MKM fighter aircraft.[12]

Apart from Iran and Indonesia, there are two other significant processes of transition currently underway in the Asia-Pacific that have not received the attention they deserve. Unlike Iran and Indonesia, both these processes pertain to the external behaviour of the states concerned rather than to their internal dynamics. The key word to describe Japan during the Koizumi administration is 'normalisation'. Whether it involves visiting Shinto shrines or despatching forces to Iraq, Japan under the leadership of Junichiro Koizumi is slowly but surely 'normalising' its role in the international order in the strategic sense with the expansion of the scope of its military activities. This process is still in its early stages but is likely to intensify in the coming years due to a host of factors including inter-generational change in Japan, blatant misbehaviour by North Korea both on the nuclear question and on the kidnapping of Japanese citizens, and as well as changing attitudes in Japanese society about the alliance with the US and the presence of American forces on Okinawa.

The final key state that we will consider in this section of the article is Australia, which is best characterised by the key word 'involvement'. Post-Bali, there is a new sense of vulnerability in Australia which has found expression in a fresh bout of Australian engagement in its region. In July 2003 Australia despatched 2,225 military and police personnel to the Solomon Islands due to concerns that the country was on the brink of collapse.[13] Australia's intervention in the Solomon Islands follows its successful involvement in 2002 in the UN-led process that led to the independence of East Timor.[14] As can be seen in Table 3.2, the total strength of Australia's armed forces on active duty is only 53,650, which is by far the smallest size of any of the key states in the Asia-Pacific. However, size is not the only factor that matters in terms of military efficacy. Australia's military has been rightly described as a 'boutique' force—small in size, highly mobile, superbly trained, high tech and lethal in its performance of certain critical niche tasks.

Any listing of the 'key states' on the Asian continent is likely to raise questions about inclusions and omissions. In making the list that follows, we have been guided by the core idea within the concept of 'pivotal states' advanced by Robert Chase, Emily Hill and Paul Kennedy—a state's 'capacity to affect regional and international stability'[15]—while remaining uninfluenced by the list that Chase, Hill and Kennedy themselves propose. An explanation about some notable omissions is, nevertheless, necessary. We do not consider Egypt and Turkey, due to their predominantly African and European locations respectively, as key *Asian* states although they undoubtedly have

Table 3.2
Conventional Military Capabilities of the Key States in Asia Compared

	Australia	China	India	Indonesia	Iran	Japan	Pakistan
Total Population (millions)	19.4	1,299.2	1,040.2	218.5	72.4	127.6	147.5
Total Armed Forces (active)	53,650	2,250,000	1,350,000	302,000	540,000	239,900	620,000
Total Paramilitary Forces	0	1,500,000	1,087,700	195,000	40,000	12,250	294,000
GDP in 2002 (in US Dollars billions)	401	1,300	505	177	111	4,000	68
GDP per capita in 2002 (in US Dollars)	20,585	970	486	810	1,553	31,360	462
Military Expenditure in 2002 (in US Dollars billions)	8.0	51.0	13.8	6.6	5.1	39.5	2.7
Defence Budget in 2003 (in US Dollars billions)	9.9	22.4	16.2	1.8	4.2	41.4	2.8
Main Battle Tanks	71	7,180	3,898	0	1,565	1,020	2,386
Light Tanks	0	1,650	90	365	80	0	0
Armored Reconnaissance Vehicles	0	0	100	142	35	90	0
Armored Infantry Fighting Vehicles	0	2,500	1,600	11	750	70	0
Armored Personnel Carriers	364	2,000	317	481	670	830	1,251
Artillery—towed & self-propelled	385	15,200	4,355	125	2,395	750	1,617
Air Defence Guns	0	23,700	2,424	415	1,700	70	1,900
Surface-to-Air Missiles	48	1,012	2,050	93	250	800	1,190
Principal Surface Combatants (Warships)	11	63	29	17	3	54	8
Patrol & Coastal Combatants	15	368	45	36	56	7	9
Submarines	6	69	19	2	3	16	10
Combat Aircraft	161	2,600	779	90	311	350	380
Armed Helicopters	16	45	90	17	19	102	9
Strategic Airlift Aircraft	0	35	25	0	0	0	0

Source: The International Institute for Strategic Studies, *The Military Balance 2003–2004.* London, Oxford University Press, 2003, pp. 109–10, 136–38, 140–42, 149–50, 152–59.

an impact on power balances and developments in West and Central Asia. We also do not include Saudi Arabia, Kazakhstan, Malaysia or South Korea in our list, although all four could plausibly be considered by other analysts as key Asian states. Following the September 11 attacks on the US and the invasion and occupation of Iraq, the pivotal role of Saudi Arabia has diminished considerably. In the case of Kazakhstan, neither it nor any other Central Asian state is likely to challenge the overweening extra-regional influence of China, Russia and the US; in other words, the stability of Central Asia would continue to depend principally on extra-regional actors.[16] While Malaysia is intrinsically important, its importance as a pivotal state is miniscule in comparison to the overwhelming presence of Indonesia. South Korea, likewise, in our judgement does not rise to the level of a pivotal state in a region consisting of China, Japan and the US, although the overt nuclearisation of North Korea could substantially alter that.[17]

The omission from our list that most needs to be justified is that of Russia, which till the implosion of the Soviet Union was undoubtedly an Asian power, but which has in recent years become increasingly focused on European and North Atlantic developments. The pilfering of an enormous chunk of the Russian economy during the Yeltsin years and its rapidly declining and aging demographic profile are other reasons for doubting Russia's reemergence on the Asian scene.[18] The biggest factor in favour of continuing to regard Russia as a key Asian state is its arms transfer policy, which has an enduring impact on Asian balances of power.[19] As Table 3.3 clearly reveals, there have been some really large arms transfers from Russia to various regions in Asia in just the last four years (1999–2003). As two scholars on arms transfers have noted, 'The Russian arms industry is still characterised by an extreme degree of over-capacity and a strong dependence on exports, both of which are primarily the result of the collapse of domestic arms procurement that began in 1992.'[20] However, the situation is slowly changing under Vladimir Putin: 'As in 2002, the 2003 Russian defence budget has a strong focus on arms procurement, including weapon acquisitions and military R&D.'[21] Nevertheless, arms exports remains a major driver of Russian military industry: military exports in 2002 were US $4.3 billion, and the value of the Russian order book over the next five years has already reached $16 billion.[22] Of these, exports to China and India account for a large proportion of the Russian arms trade.[23]

Table 3.3
Arms and Equipment Transfers from Russia to Asian States (1999–2003)

Region/Country	Type of Equipment
West Asia	
▪ Iran	T-72 MBT (100); BMP-2 AIFV (200); Mi-17 hel (4), Mi-8 hel (30)
▪ Syria	AT-14 ATGW (1,000); S-300 SAM (?); Su-27 FGA (4); MiG-29 FGA (?)
▪ United Arab Emirates	Il-76 tpt (4); Partzyr-S1 SAM (50)
▪ Yemen	Su-27 FGA (14); T-72 MBT (30); MiG-29SMT FGA (24); MiG-29 FGA (31)
Central Asia	
▪ Kazakhstan	Su-27 FGA (16); S-300 SAM (?)
South Asia	
▪ Afghanistan	IL-117 3-D radar (2); Mi-17 hel (4); MiG-29B FGA (8)
▪ India	*Kilo* SSK (1); 2S6 AD (24); Il-78 tkr ac(6); SS-N-25 ASSM; Su-30MKI FGA (172); *Krivak* III FF (3); KA-31 hel (12); SS-N-27 ASSM (?); *Admiral Gorshkov* CV (1); MiG 29-K FGA (24); Mi-18iB hel (40); T-90 MBT (310)
▪ Pakistan	Mi-171 hel (12)
▪ Sri Lanka	Mi-35 cbt hel (2); BTR-80A APC (10); BMP-2 AIFV (36); MiG-27M FGA (4); MiG-23UB FGA (2)
East Asia	
▪ China	S-300 SAM (30); *Kilo* SSK (8); SA-15 SAM (35); Su-27 FGA (200); *Sovremenny* DDG (4); BMD-3 AIFV (?); Ka-28 hel (12); FT-2000 SAM (?); Il-78 tkr ac (4); SSN-24 SSM (24); Su-30 MKK FGA (78); Su-27UBK FGA (28); A-50 AEW (6); Kh-35 ASM (?); Su-30MK2 FGA (28)
▪ North Korea	Mi-17 hel (5)
▪ South Korea	BTR-80 APC (20); BMP-3 AIFV (23); T-80 MBT (33); *Igla* SAM (?); *Metis* ATGW (?); Be-200 tpt (1); Ka-32 hel (41); Ka-32T hel (3); Il-103 trg (15)

Table 3.3 (contd.)

Table 3.3 (contd.)

Region/Country	Type of Equipment
Southeast Asia	
▪ Indonesia	Mi-17 hel (2); Mi-2 hel (8); Su-30 FGA (2); Su-27 FGA (2); Mi-35 hel (2)
▪ Malaysia	MiG-29 FGA (18); Mi-17 hel (10); *Metis*-2 ATGW (?); Su-30MKM FGA (18)
▪ Myanmar	MiG-29 FGA (10); MiG-29UB trg (2)
▪ Singapore	SA-16/SA-18 SAM (?)
▪ Vietnam	Su-27 FGA (6); *Tarantul* 2 corvette (2)

Source: The International Institute for Strategic Studies, *The Military Balance 2003–2004*. London, Oxford University Press, 2003, pp. 280–83, 291–93, 303–09.

AD: air defence guns; AEW: airborne early warning; AIFV: armoured infantry fighting vehicle; APC: armoured personnel carrier; ASM: air-to-surface missile; ATGW: anti-tank guided weapon; cbt hel: combat helicopter; CV: aircraft carrier; DDG: guided missile destroyer; FF: frigate; FGA: fighter/ground attack aircraft; hel: helicopter; MBT: main battle tank; SAM: surface-to-air missile; SSK: submarine; SSM: surface-to-surface missile; tkr ac: tanker aircraft; tpt: transport aircraft; trg: trainer aircraft
Numbers are in parentheses; '?' indicates 'unconfirmed/numbers not known'.

Despite this obvious factor, we have chosen not to include Russia in our list of key Asian states; indeed, we could argue that it shows precisely how one-dimensional Russian influence in Asia now is.

Asian Security Futures

What is the strategic future of Asia likely to be? Could Asia the continent become Asia the region? For the latter to happen, a continent-wide security interdependence that is currently missing would have to emerge. Without seeking to be derivative, we could take a cue from the historical processes that over time wrought a region out of the European continent. Broadly speaking, three security futures could be envisaged for Asia: a region of opposing axes and balances, a region managed by a *directoire* of great powers, or a region enmeshed in a cooperative security arrangement. What would each of these regional configurations look like? What is the relative likelihood of their emerging? What is their relative desirability for India? These are matters which we must examine and ponder over.

Axes and Balances of Power

With the end of bipolarity, scholars groped through most of the nineties to identify a new overarching theme in world politics. In the process of doing so, some rather dramatic visions of the future emerged. For instance, Thomas Fraser Homer-Dixon suggested that resource scarcity would make parts of the world extremely volatile and unstable.[24] In contrast to Homer-Dixon, Francis Fukuyama presented a world in which liberal democracy has permanently triumphed.[25] A decade later, it would appear that both Homer-Dixon and Fukuyama have identified political dynamics that apply to parts of the world removed from Asia: while West Africa seems to be lapsing into pre-modernity[26] and Europe seems to be forging a post-modern future for itself,[27] much of Asia remains firmly in the throes of Westphalian modernity epitomised by the sovereign territorial state.[28] Thus, the political logic of realism, with its power balances and security dilemmas, continues to drive inter-state politics in large parts of Asia. Balance of power politics lies at the heart of all of the regions of Asia with the possible exception of Southeast Asia. The question that is worth examining is whether balance of power politics would rise from the regional to the continental level, thereby transforming all of Asia into a region for the first time since the end of European colonialism on the continent.[29]

The logic of two opposing axes of power in Asia emerges in the context of the rise of China and future attempts by the US to 'contain' Chinese power. It is assumed that if China becomes too powerful and difficult to accommodate, an axis could emerge in Asia for the containment of China running, for example, through Washington-New Delhi-Jakarta-Hanoi-Tokyo. However, it is just as plausible to argue that an alternate axis, running through Teheran-New Delhi-Kuala Lumpur-Beijing, could be formed around 'Asian values' and be aimed against the West.

These hypothetical axes could indeed be part of a much larger global divide. If Samuel Huntington is to be believed, future world politics will be a case of 'the West versus the Rest'.[30] In particular, Huntington asserts, Islam and Confucian civilisations will pose a threat to Western civilisation. Which side of this global fault line would India be on? India would seem to straddle the fault line: in civilisational terms, it is emphatically not a part of the West, but as a state its major adversaries are Pakistan and China or, in Huntington's terminology, Islam and Confucianism. If the twenty-first century does turn out to be even a mild version of the Huntingtonian vision, India will find itself being drawn into civilisational strife, unless it is strong enough to maintain its autonomy and aloofness.

It could be argued that the vision presented earlier, apart from being highly speculative, is also unduly pessimistic and even apocalyptic. Our response would be to point to European inter-state politics during the half century preceding the outbreak of the First World War. The construction of the Triple Alliance and the Triple Entente was a fitful one with many false starts. Yet over time the two opposing axes became so durable and so inter-locked, that in retrospect the outbreak of war in 1914 seems almost inevitable.[31] It was an arrangement designed to give security, and yet its final result was to make Europe more insecure than it had been at any time since the defeat of Napoleon Bonaparte. As Basil Liddell Hart famously remarked about the outbreak of the First World War, 'Fifty years were spent in the process of making Europe explosive. Five days were enough to detonate it.'[32] Extrapolating from the European example, there are thus compelling reasons for India to eschew the path of opposing axes of power in Asia.

Directoire of Great Powers

If opposing axes is not the best way to go about constructing a security architecture for Asia, what about the option of securing guarantees for stability and order from a *directoire* of Asian great powers? Dick Wilson, for example, has floated the idea of a future Asian 'security trinity' consisting of China, India and Japan.[33] Even more interesting is the idea emanating from some Russian policy analysts, such as former Russian Prime Minister Yevgeny Primakov, of a new Big Three Alliance consisting of China, Russia and India to counterbalance an increasingly assertive and offensive NATO. This surely is a possibility worth examining.

The *sheer mass* of China, India and Russia has always led to speculation about what would happen if they were to work together, the underlying idea being that if they were to *act in concert* they could play a world historical role. This idea has impeccable antecedents. Lenin, for instance, had observed in 1923:

> In the last analysis, the outcome of the struggle will be determined by the fact that Russia, India, China, etc, account for the over-whelming majority of the population of the globe. And during the past few years it is this majority that has been drawn into the struggle for emancipation with extraordinary rapidity, so that in this respect there cannot be the slightest doubt what the final outcome of the world struggle will be. In this sense, the complete victory of socialism is fully and absolutely assured.[34]

More recently, a study sponsored by the US Department of Defense has noted that China, India and Russia—dubbed by the study as the three 'Transition States', 'the largest and most important states in Eurasia'—were 'undergoing far-reaching transitions aimed at creating the foundations for regional and even global power', before concluding that they were 'unlikely to join the Western democratic core any time soon, but also unlikely to become full-fledged adversaries' of the Western Alliance.[35] If both Lenin and the Pentagon see some merit in the notion that China, Russia and India together have system-transforming mass, this is clearly an idea to take quite seriously.

What are the factors that are likely to work for or against the idea of an Asian *directoire?*[36] First, there is the question of economic growth rates, competitiveness and cooperation. Three questions, in particular, are germane in this context: is China going to remain the only rising power, or would Russian decline be eventually reversed, and would India start catching up? would Russia and India be forced to 'balance against' a rising China? would greater economic interaction, and the inevitable competition that will follow, lead to instability, or would lead to the discovery of a larger set of mutual interests?

Just as important as economic is the socio-political dimension, pertaining to such issues as social cohesion, national unity and territorial integrity. In terms of ethno-politics, for example in Tibet, Xinjiang, Mongolia, Siberia and the Indian Northeast, the policies of the three states invariably impact on one another, often in very negative ways. Geopolitical issues in the shape of unresolved borders and differentials in economic and demographic growth rates, leading in the latter case to unregulated population movements, both within and across sovereign borders, further complicates the formation of a Big Three Alliance. Finally, and most crucially, is the question of socio-economic cleavages in these large states, raising the question of whether they can survive as cohesive and united sovereign entities.

Going hand in hand with economics and social issues are questions of ideology, politics and stability. China's political system throws up a number of questions: in what direction will Chinese politics evolve, and over what time frame? what would be the nature of political participation in China in the future, and what would be its impact on stability? Likewise, policy coherence in India is also a significant issue. Will a new majoritarian 'party of government' emerge, or will the politics of coalition building become less turbulent over time? Will the Russian state recapture the commanding heights of state power? Finally, thinking out of the box, will a new transnational political ideology emerge—global environmentalism, for example— that would create unprecedented linkages between the three states?

We must also be sensitive to the fact that developments outside China, India and Russia will play a major role in determining the likelihood and feasibility of an Asian *directoire*. To give an example, much would depend on the future of the Atlantic Alliance. If the European Union were to emerge as an autonomous locus of decision making, what impact would that have on Russia? Would it not make Russia even more Eurocentric? Just as important as the future of the European Union would be the future role of Japan. A strategically autonomous Japan could easily upset the apple cart of Asian security. We have been analysing the likelihood and feasibility of an Asian *directoire* of great powers to manage Asian security. But would the establishment of an Asian *directoire* be in India's interest? At first glance, it would seem that India's only concern should be to ensure that it in the *directoire*, which otherwise seems to be a sensible way to manage Asian security. However, the experience of Concert of Europe would suggest otherwise.[37] The problem with a *directoire* is that it either 'freezes up' the security architecture in a manner that does not reflect dynamic changes in capabilities and interests, or alternately that it gets divided internally on the question of change versus stability. Furthermore, Indian policy makers and the country at large would need to reflect whether a continental *gendarme* role of the sort played by British India would be in the interests of contemporary India.[38]

Cooperative Security

If both axes of power and a continental *directoire* would not be in India's interest, what about the construction of a regional security arrangement in Asia? Could this be an alternate route to containing Chinese power, maintaining stability in Asia and minimising the role of the US on the Asian continent? In other words, would an Asian cooperative security mechanism serve India's interests? Unlike the first two options, cooperative security in Asia—an Asian Helsinki process—would appear to be very much in India's interests. What are the various elements that could go into its construction?

As was the case in the first two security architectures, Asia has a lot to gain from the experience of Europe. The Helsinki process had many 'baskets' of issues, some pertaining to inter-state relations, other to matters *within* sovereign boundaries. Thus, mutually balanced force reductions and concerns about human rights violations were both a part of the Helsinki process. In Asia, it is easy to see that the internal aspect of the Helsinki process may be considerably less acceptable to Asian states than it was even to the states of eastern and central Europe. This is for two reasons. First, the states of Asia are, with some notable exceptions, young states, many of them postcolonial. Thus, these states are likely to guard their sovereignty with far greater zeal than did the long consolidated and somewhat tired states of Europe. Second, it is argued in some quarters that Asian cultures prefer the group over the individual, order over liberty and obligations over rights. While the latter argument is clearly a contentious one, we should not be surprised if many states in Asia resist the intrusive nature of the Helsinki process in what they regard as their 'internal affairs'.

We must remember that the original Helsinki process was itself a contentious one. As a scholar has observed, 'The issue was whether the *project* for a European security conference developed over the years, which finally merged into the *process* known as the Conference on Security and Cooperation in Europe, should be built into a permanent inter-systemic *organisation* or not.'[39] Different states also made different uses of it:

> The CSCE process was only possible at all as a part of and expression of East-West détente. What this meant and whether in the long-term it would lead to a kind of convergence of the systems, whether each side would consider it more damaging or more to their advantage, or how the advantages of this kind of antagonistic co-operation were distributed, was discussed in and between Eastern and Western countries extensively, partially in earnest, partially as propaganda, and this on the other hand, partially in supporting the CSCE process and partially as attempts to torpedo it.[40]

In other words, we should not be surprised if the process of creating a cooperative security architecture in Asia is a tortuous and contentious one. It would still be well worth the effort if it were to reduce the size of arsenals in Asia, enmesh Chinese and American capabilities in Asia within a larger cooperative process, lead to the evolution of a new and authentic *Asian* identity, build habits of cooperative behaviour on the Asian continent, and may be even play a role in the democratisation of China. Sadly, the Conference on Security and Cooperation in the Asia-Pacific (CSCAP) is currently a pale shadow of its European counterpart. There can be few tasks more challenging and worthwhile—both in a normative sense and in terms of India's concrete interests—than for Indian diplomacy to begin the groundwork for the construction of a cooperative mechanism of Asian security.

Notes and References

1. That is not to say that the word 'continent' is bereft of strategic meaning. In particular, the concept of the 'continental state' (as opposed to the 'maritime state') has been considered by many scholars as significant in strategic terms. For more on this see Colin S. Gray, 'Seapower and Landpower' in Colin S. Gray and Roger W. Barnett (eds.), *Seapower and Strategy*. Annapolis, United States Naval Institute, 1989, pp. 3–26; and John J. Mearsheimer, *The Tragedy of Great Power Politics*. New York, W.W. Norton, 2001, pp. 83–137.
2. *The Shorter Oxford English Dictionary*, vol. 1, Oxford, Oxford University Press, 1983, p. 412.
3. William R. Thompson, 'The Regional Subsystem: A Conceptual Explication and a Propositional Inventory', *International Studies Quarterly*, vol. 17, no. 1, March 1973, pp. 89–117.
4. Barry Buzan, Ole Wæver and Jaap de Wilde, *Security: A New Framework for Analysis*. Boulder, Lynne Rienner Publishers, 1998, p. 12. This is Buzan's latest definition of a concept he first proposed in 1983.
5. Barry Buzan, Ole Wæver and Jaap de Wilde, *Security: A New Framework for Analysis*. Boulder, 1998, p. 11.
6. Barry Buzan, *People, States and Fear*. Boulder, Lynne Rienner Publishers, 1991, p. 211.
7. A powerful critique of the new American grand strategy can be found in Sherle R. Schwenninger, 'Revamping American Grand Strategy', *World Policy Journal*, vol. 20, no. 3, 2003, pp. 25–44. Perhaps the best analysis of preemptive action is M. Elaine Bunn, 'Preemptive Action: When, How and to What Effect?' *Strategic Forum*, no. 200, July 2003. Institute for National Strategic Studies, National Defense University, Washington, DC.
8. Though middle power concept has not been adequately analysed, the best work on the theme is Carsten Holbraad, *Middle Powers in International Politics*. London, Macmillan, 1984.
9. On the various wars between India and Pakistan, see Šumit Ganguly, *The Origins of War in South Asia: Indo-Pakistani Conflicts Since 1947*. Boulder, Westview Press, 1994.
10. For a solid account of the Kashmir insurgency, see Šumit Ganguly, *The Crisis in Kashmir: Portents of War Hopes of Peace*. Cambridge, Cambridge University Press, 1999.
11. *The Military Balance 2003–2004*. The International Institute for Strategic Studies, London, Oxford University Press, 2003, p. 149.
12. Ibid.
13. *The Military Balance 2003–2004*. The International Institute for Strategic Studies, London, 2003, p. 148. Also see the following paper, which was extremely influential in shaping Australian policy: 'Our Failing Neighbour—

Australia and the Future of Solomon Islands', *ASPI Policy Report*, June 2003, Australian Strategic Policy Institute, Canberra.

14. On this see 'New Neighbour, New Challenge: Australia and the Security of East Timor', *ASPI Policy Report*, May 2002, Australian Strategic Policy Institute, Canberra.

15. Robert S. Chase, Emily B. Hill and Paul Kennedy, 'Pivotal States and US Strategy', *Foreign Affairs*, vol. 75, no. 1, January/February 1996, p. 37.

16. On the newfound American interest in Central Asia, and the likelihood that the US will remain in Central Asia for a considerable period of time, see Charles William Maynes, 'America Discovers Central Asia', *Foreign Affairs*, vol. 82, no. 2, March/April 2003, pp. 120–32.

17. On the last point see Taewoo Kim, 'Living with North Korean Bomb? Current Debates in and Future Options for South Korea', *KIDA Paper*, no. 2, June 2003, Korea Institute for Defense Analyses, Seoul.

18. On Russia's economic collapse and its chances of recovery, see Joseph E. Stiglitz, *Globalization and its Discontents*. New York, W.W. Norton, 2002, pp. 133–65; and Marvin Zonis, Dan Lefkovitz and Sam Wilkin, *The Kimchi Matters: Global Business and Local Politics in a Crisis-Driven World*. Chicago, Agate, 2003, pp. 242–53.

19. I thank Han Hua for sensitising me on this point.

20. Elisabeth Sköns and Reinhilde Weidacher, 'Arms Production', *SIPRI Yearbook 2002: Armaments, Disarmament and International Security*. Oxford, Oxford University Press, 2002, p. 351.

21. *The Military Balance 2003–2004*. The International Institute for Strategic Studies, London, 2003, p. 269.

22. Ibid., pp. 270–71.

23. Ibid., p. 271.

24. See Thomas F. Homer-Dixon, 'On the Threshold: Environmental Changes as Causes of Acute Conflict', *International Security*, vol. 16, no. 2, Fall 1991, pp. 76–116.

25. See Francis Fukuyama, 'The End of History?' *The National Interest*, Summer 1989, pp. 3–18.

26. See Robert D. Kaplan, 'The Coming Anarchy', *The Atlantic Monthly*, vol. 273, no. 2, February 1994, pp. 44–76.

27. See Robert Kagan, *Of Paradise and Power: America and Europe in the New World Order*. New York, Alfred A. Knopf, 2003.

28. See Robert Cooper, 'The Next Empire', *Prospect*, October 2001, pp. 22–26, on how countries like China, India and Pakistan remain modern states primarily concerned with classic balance of power considerations.

29. It could be argued that there was a continentwide balance of power in Asia during the 'Vasco da Gama Epoch', to use K.M. Panikkar's evocative phrase. See K.M. Panikkar, *Asia and Western Dominance*. New York, Collier Books, 1969.

30. See Samuel P. Huntington, 'The Clash of Civilizations?' *Foreign Affairs*, vol. 72, no. 3, Summer 1993, pp. 22–49.

31. See Paul W. Schroeder, 'The Nineteenth Century System: Balance of Power or Political Equilibrium?' *Review of International Studies*, vol. 15, 1989, pp. 135–53.

32. Perhaps the best historical accounts of the process by which the opposing axes of power were built in Europe in the years between the end of the Crimean War (1856) and the outbreak of the First World War (1914) can be found in B.H. Liddell Hart, *History of the First World War*. London, Pan Books, 1970, pp. 1–48; and David Thomson, *Europe Since Napoleon*. Harmondsworth, Penguin, 1966, pp. 459–544.

33. See Dick Wilson, 'The Asian Security Management Challenge: A Future "Trinity" of China, India and Japan', RGICS, no. 10, Rajiv Gandhi Institute for Contemporary Studies, New Delhi, April 1994.

34. V.I. Lenin, 'Better Fewer, But Better', *Pravda*, vol. 49, no. 4, March 1923, in David Skvirsky and George Hanna trans. *Lenin's Collected Works*, vol. 33, Moscow, Progress Publishers, 1965, p. 500. Accessed from: http://www.marxists.org/archive/lenin/works/1923/mar/02.html.

35. *Strategic Assessment 1999: Priorities for a Turbulent World*. Washington, DC, Institute for National Strategic Studies, National Defense University, 2000, p. 205.

36. This analysis flows from some comments I made as the discussant of a conference paper by Kanti Bajpai: 'Confidence building measures between India, China and Russia', at an international conference on 'India, China, Russia: Dynamics of the Asian Triangle' organised by the India International Centre and the Centre de Sciences Humaines, New Delhi, 16 January 2002.

37. Easily the best study of the Concert of Europe remains Henry Kissinger, *A World Restored: Metternich, Castlereagh and the Problems of Peace, 1812–22*. Boston, Houghton Mifflin, 1957; see also David Thomson, *Europe Since Napoleon*. Harmondsworth, Penguin, 1966, pp. 81–98, 129–59; Paul W. Schroeder, 'Did the Vienna Settlement Rest on a Balance of Power?' *The American Historical Review*, vol. 97, no. 3, June 1992, pp. 683–706.

38. In this context, C. Raja Mohan invokes the legacy of Lord George Nathaniel Curzon, First Marquess of Kedleston, tenth Viceroy of India (1898–1905) and British Foreign Secretary (1919–24). See C. Raja Mohan, 'Jaswant and Lord Curzon's Legacy', *The Hindu*, New Delhi, 28 January 2002; also see C. Raja Mohan, *Crossing the Rubicon: The Shaping of India's New Foreign Policy*. New York, Palgrave Macmillan, 2004, pp. 204–36.

39. Wilfried von Bredow, 'The OSCE: Construction and Identity Problems' in *OSCE Yearbook 2000*. Baden-Baden: Nomos Verlagsgesellschaft, 2001, p. 42. Emphases in the original.

40. Ibid.

4

INDIA AND THE FUTURE OF ASIA: ARRANGING A SOFT-LANDING FOR PAKISTAN

Manoj Joshi

India's Recent Past and Asia

India's location gives it a unique geopolitical position in Asia. West, East, Southeast and Central Asia, long-established geopolitical units, are its neighbours. Its relations with the countries of these areas have therefore been shaped by both economic interests and security concerns. But throughout the Cold War years, which also coincided with India's bureaucratised command economy, its approaches were somewhat passive. Central Asia was under the control of the Soviet Union, while Japan and the ASEAN grouping, oriented towards the US, were suspicious of India. Relations with Pakistan and China were hostile at worst, and cold at the best, and its economy was worked on the principle of autarky.

The collapse of the Soviet Union and the end of the licence-quota raj created openings that have since been politically exploited to give India a larger, and qualitatively changed, footprint in the Asian region. India's 'Look East' policy, détente with China, its wooing of the ASEAN, improved relations with Japan, are all part of an attempt to assume a larger Asian identity, based this time not on soaring rhetoric, but practical need. For example, India's Petroleum Minister

Mani Shankar Aiyer's efforts to push for pan-Asian cooperation in the oil front is motivated as much by self-interest, as practical economics. Likewise, India's aid relationship with Japan, overtures to the ASEAN and improved ties with China are aimed at boosting Indian trade and enhancing India's economic growth.

While the historical global cockpit, Europe, remained largely at peace through the Cold War and its aftermath, Asia became the focus of conflicts. But with the end of the Vietnam war and the assimilation of Indo-China into ASEAN, the Russian withdrawal from Afghanistan and the end of the Iran-Iraq war, the era of open conflict has ended, but many faultlines remain—Vietnam and China in the South China Sea, India and Pakistan in Kashmir, China and the US in Taiwan, Israel and the Arab world in Palestine, the US in Iraq and Iran, North Korea and Japan, China and India over their border and so on. The creation of the ASEAN Regional Forum (ARF) has gone some way to moderate conflict, but though it is the principal forum for a security dialogue in Asia, it lacks the coherence that the Conference on Security and Cooperation in Europe (CSCE) had, perhaps because of the bipolar nature of the Cold War. Its membership, currently comprising of the ASEAN, Australia, the US, Russia, EU, China, India, Pakistan and a number of other countries is focused on Asia-Pacific, and its principal work currently is to provide a platform for discussion on issues on a consensual basis.

India, China as the Fulcrum of Asia

A major tectonic shift in Asia has been the dramatically improved Sino-Indian relations, beginning with the visit of India's former Prime Minister Rajiv Gandhi to Beijing in December 1988. It was during this visit that Chinese supreme leader Deng Xiaoping told him, 'The coming of the Asian era in the twenty-first century, if it really comes, will be only after both India and China join the group of advanced economies.' Former Prime Minister Atal Bihari Vajpayee, 15 years later, bounced the comment back at China's party chairman Hu Jintao during a meeting at St. Petersburg in June 2003 noting that 'if the two countries were to cooperate this could even result in the twenty-first century turning into an "Asian century"'. In these 15 years, while the collapse of the Soviet Union eased the strategic strains between the two countries, India and China reached a number of bilateral agreements to put their relations on an even track. The reform of the Indian economy leading to faster growth and the emergence of India as an Information Technology hub, as well as India's nuclear test in 1998, led to a readjustment of Sino-Indian relations on a new plane.

These trends have led the National Intelligence Council, a think-tank associated with the Central Intelligence Agency of the US, to note in a report in early 2005, that China and India will emerge as major global players by 2020, and that their impact will be similar to that of the emergence of the US in the early twentieth century, or Germany in the nineteenth century. According to the report, the combination of high economic growth, expanding military capabilities and large populations 'will be at the root of the expected rise in economic and political power for both countries'. These two countries could well help shape the twenty-first century as the Asian century, just as the twentieth was seen as the American century.[1] As the report notes:

> Barring an abrupt reversal of the process of globalisation or any major upheavals in these countries, the rise of these new powers is a virtual certainty. Yet how China and India exercise their growing power and whether they relate cooperatively or competitively to other powers in the international system are key uncertainties.[2]

The report says that 'the greatest benefits of globalization will accrue to countries and groups that can access and adopt new technologies' and that China and India 'are well positioned to become technology leaders'. But this process will have to be supported by other policies that stress good governance, universal education and market reforms. This could actually allow China and India 'to leapfrog stages of development, skipping phases that other high-tech leaders such as the United States and Europe had to traverse in order to advance'.

Relations between China and India have been improving since the mid-nineties. It was the 2003 visit of former Prime Minister Atal Bihari Vajpayee to Beijing that set the stage for greater economic engagement, even while providing a new framework for discussion on their border. There is every indication that the two Asian giants intend to settle their border dispute and set the stage for engagement across the economic spectrum. One of the major success stories has been the enormous increase in Sino-Indian trade that has grown from a few hundred million dollars in the beginning of the nineties, to over US $13 billion in 2004, where their target was $10 billion for 2005. There has been some talk of Sino-Indian tensions emerging from trade and economic competition, particularly in Southeast Asia. But as External Affairs Minister Natwar Singh pointed out in early 2005:

> While there are differences between us, there is also an increasingly greater realization that there is enough space and opportunity in the region for both India and China to prosper.[3]

The role played by the two countries, both invitees to the 10th ASEAN summit at Vientane, made this clear. Having successfully wooed the ASEAN, India is now set to be part of an extended East Asian community by 2020, with the cooperation of China. While China has already signed a Free Trade Agreement with the ASEAN, India is negotiating one. An East Asian grouping has the potential to rival the other emerging economic entities like Latin America and European Union.

There are, of course, several uncertainties that could become obstacles in the unfolding of this future. While the chances of political conflict between India and China appear to be receding, they have to worry about external factors such as an oil shock, or the fallout of an economic downturn in other regions, or internal problems like water shortage, public health catastrophes and internal political instability. Both also have to be concerned about working out their specific fixations—Taiwan for China and Pakistan for India.

The India–China–Pakistan Triangle

Since the sixties, when Pakistan 'discovered' China, the triangle that the two countries form with India, has been a major factor in South Asia. China pulled Pakistan's chestnuts out of the fire of the war of September 1965, failed to do so in 1971, and thereafter became somewhat circumspect. In the nineties, even while involved in building détente with India, China aided Pakistan's quest to obtain strategic parity with India by supplying nuclear weapons technology and missiles. Chinese conventional weapons transfers, too, have helped Pakistan to maintain an adequate ratio of forces to deter India.

But the Sino-Pak relationship is now changing because, first, Pakistan now has autonomous capability in the missile and nuclear field. Second, India's economic growth and strategic weapons capabilities have compelled China to take into account India's growing nuclear and military capability into its own security calculus, just as India did with regard to China for several decades. Third, China's desire to be seen as a 'responsible' power, too, has persuaded it to moderate, if not end, its proliferation activities. Fourth, China has had to also confront the fact that Pakistani policies in Afghanistan had encouraged the growth of Islamic fundamentalism resulting in a potential security threat to its Xinjiang region. After September 11, China for the first time came out with some details of jihadi activities in its western territories by activists who had been trained and nurtured in jihad establishments in Pakistan and Afghanistan. This change became apparent during the Indo-Pak conflict in Kargil in 1999. The Chinese response was less than supportive, and the result was that Pakistan had to request the US for help.

Sino-Indian problems are shallow compared to the much deeper roots of the India-Pakistan conflict, which harp back to the very founding of the two countries by partitioning British India. In the run up to Partition, the Muslim League's political aims were—to declare itself as the sole representative of the Muslims of India, and to have constitutional mechanisms that would equalize the political power of the numerically fewer Indian Muslims with that of the Hindu majority.

In the post-Independence period, perhaps it was because the army, rather than the Muslim League that held the reins of power, the idea of equalising political power with 'Hindu' India was progressively militarised, and resulted in a four-tier grand strategy of the new state of Pakistan—first, to spend a significant proportion of the country's budget on defence; second, to develop military alignments that could aid in checking India; third, to build nuclear weapons; and fourth, to support separatist movements as well as create a jihadi infrastructure to promote terrorist acts against India with a view of destabilising it and breaking it into manageable units.

A well-known Pakistani defence analyst has pointed out, that all of Pakistan's substantial defence planning has essentially revolved 'only around India which is seen as a powerful state with hegemonic ambitions'. But by the mid-nineties, the majority of the policy-making elite saw this not as a matter of self-defence but also 'hoped to humble India's desire to project itself as a regional power.'[4] In other words, Pakistani policy which she has also characterised elsewhere as 'linear', had gone well beyond the legitimate concerns of self-defence.

These policies skewed Pakistan's economy, foreign relations and domestic politics towards a strategy of unsustainable competition with India. This has created great problems for India, but probably had much more serious consequences for Pakistan—collapse of liberal democracy, rise of sectarianism and growth of poverty. Given this situation, Pakistan is being compelled to alter its half-century-old grand strategy based on confronting, and more recently, even breaking up India.[5] To this end, it has been aided by the September 11 ultimatum that compelled Islamabad to abandon the Taliban, and accept the Indian offer to negotiate a normalisation through the process of a composite dialogue.

In the following sections we will delve into the India–Pakistan equation, going back to the consequences of Partition to see just how difficult or easy it is to achieve first, an Indo-Pakistani détente which can then be built upon to create an entente. Looked at any way, the outcome will have a significant impact on India and the future of Asia.

Partition and its Consequences

Despite the tensions between the Congress and the Muslim League, there was nothing to suggest that the relations between the two new dominions would be as hostile as they turned out to be.[6] An important aspect of Partition was the disruption of the united economy of the subcontinent, with serious consequences for Pakistan.[7] Pakistan inherited rich agricultural lands producing raw materials and foodgrains, while the bulk of the ports, marketing centres and indus-trial areas remained in India. The first and immediate impact came from the vast transfer of populations with attendant murder and destruction of property. In this period, trade links were affected and marketing and industrial links disrupted. Rail and road networks, too, were abruptly severed by the new international boundaries.

The problem was compounded by the fact that its two wings were separated by Indian territory; indeed, surrounded as it was, almost wholly by India, East Pakistan was perhaps more seriously affected.

Calcutta was the dominant metropolis for Bengal with its concentration of industry, managerial talent and educational institutions, and its loss was a grave one for East Pakistan. While Partition did not lead to an immediate departure, forced or otherwise, of the minority Hindus, their steady drift to India left East Pakistan without many professionals.

At some point, this situation could have stabilised and the new nations could have reconstructed their relations on the basis of a new trading regime. However, this did not happen because of the bitterness accompanying Partition and the unresolved Kashmir conflict that froze their relations in a negative mode from the very outset. For Pakistan it became an important point to shun everything Indian and to seek alternative trade partners. As an economic historian has pointed out:

> Pakistan turned quickly to the diversion of trade away from India.... Tariff and non-tariff barriers were quickly erected between India and Pakistan, and mutual trade declined sharply.[8]

The difficulties in conducting direct bilateral trade has had a distorting impact on their economies, but again, because of size, the effect has been greater on Pakistan. A year after independence, 32 per cent of Pakistani imports came from India, which in turn bought 56 per cent of Pakistani exports. In 2000–2001, India's imports were 0.42 per cent of Pakistan's exports and it provided just 0.13 per cent of India's imports. Even if the latter figures do not take into account the illegal and third country trade or the creation of a separate Bangladesh, this is low.

A similar dramatic change came in their security orientation. Initially, there were expectations that the two would retain a common governor-general and the British were particularly keen that they have a united defence system, under their guidance. For a century or so before independence, India had played a major role in British Imperial strategy. Forces sourced from India participated in several imperial expeditions to China, the Horn of Africa and Mesopotamia. As Parthasarthi Gupta has pointed out, during World War II and in its aftermath, the British War office and the Indian Commander-in-Chief, Sir Claude Auchinleck, were 'for retaining the subcontinent as a single unit in terms of defence organisation and defence potential, whatever the nature of political devolution in other spheres'.[9]

The British believed, that given their experiences with the Congress and the Muslim League, that it would be a relatively easier process to reach an accommodation with Pakistan. The initial Indian reluctance to join the Commonwealth was a matter of some concern. However, the assessment was that as long as Pakistan was a member, the British could meet their defence requirements in the region— first, to counter any Russian challenge and second, to have bases that could guard the vital oil lifelines. A meeting of the Chiefs of Staff in May 1947 concluded that there were overwhelming arguments for having Pakistan in the Commonwealth:

> We should obtain important strategic facilities, the port of Karachi, air bases and the support of Moslem manpower in the future.... Be able to increase our prestige throughout the Moslem world.[10]

But it was perhaps inevitable that the two new states soon began to see their defence problems through their own political perspectives. The tensions that preceded Partition, the indeterminate status of Hyderabad and Kashmir, all detracted from the idea of viewing defence issues on a common basis. Both India and Pakistan soon made it clear that the Joint Defence Council was primarily to supervise the division of assets. Any idea of military cooperation after independence evaporated in the holocaust that followed the division of the country. This was followed in quick succession by the Junagadh affair and then the war over Kashmir. By the end of September 1947, the supreme headquarters had been wound up on Indian insistence.

A Faulty Grand Strategy

The British decision to see Pakistan as its most important ally in the region was to have important consequences. First, it resulted in Britain manipulating the UN Security Council on behalf of Pakistan in the aftermath of the invasion of Kashmir by a tribal army encouraged and officered by Pakistan. This has been amply brought out by the studies of Prem Shankar Jha and C. Dasgupta. As Dasgupta has concluded:

> The British archives throw a fascinating light on the ways the British generals (heading the Indian and Pakistani armies) and diplomats in India and Pakistan coordinated their moves to

contain the war and ensure that an Indian advance stopped well
short of the Pakistan border.[11]

Second, it led to Britain brokering the military relationship between
Pakistan and the US. Throughout 1948 and 1949, despite a basic
decision to allow the British to take the lead on the Kashmir issue,
the US maintained an even-handed and neutral stand. But a shift
began in 1952 with the coming of the Republican administration
headed by Gen. Dwight Eisenhower in the US.

American arms aid enabled Pakistan to maintain armed forces well
above its legitimate requirements of self-defence or deterrence, and
encouraged it to adopt military rather than diplomatic and political
approaches to resolve its problems with India. The aid, which first
introduced supersonic jets, modern tanks, self-propelled artillery
and armoured personnel carriers into the South Asian region, may
have been instrumental in 'militarising' Pakistan's attitudes towards
India.[12] By this time, Pakistani polity had, in any case, slipped out of
the hands of politicians and into the control of the civilian and military
bureaucracy.

External alliances were just one leg of the Pakistani strategic
doctrine of seeking effective parity with India. Its second military leg
was not to seek actual parity, but to maintain an adequate ratio of
forces that could deter any Indian attack, and also provide some
offensive potential to the Pakistani forces. After the failure of this
doctrine to prevent the emergence of Bangladesh, two other elements
were added—the building of nuclear weapons as the ultimate military
equaliser, and a covert one seeking to exploit India's domestic
faultlines by supporting separatist movements with a view of breaking
down India into 'manageable' units.

Beginning from the fifties, Pakistan has spent a significantly higher
proportion of its GDP, as compared to India, to maintain, what it
considers, the adequate ratio of forces vis-à-vis India. In the sixties
for example, Pakistan spent over 50 per cent of all its federal expenditure on defence. Even in the eighties, this figure averaged over 30
per cent. In contrast, Indian expenditures never exceeded 25 per cent
in the sixties, and 20 per cent in the eighties. In the nineties, Indian
percentages came down below 15, but Pakistan's expenditure remained over 30 per cent.[13] This led to two consequences.

First, it reduced government ability to fund development programmes, and second, this meant that the government was grabbing an

unconscionable amount of public funds, which the Pakistan Army
needed to generate a self-perception that it was the true guardian of
Pakistani sovereignty. As a leading Pakistani defence analyst, Ayesha
Siddiqa Agha has noted, 'The internal political dynamics of Pakistan
after 1947 compelled the leadership to seek a confrontational relationship that could form a solid justification for a linear policy
approach.'[14]

Whatever may have been the negative consequences for development, this expenditure did enable Pakistan to maintain effective parity
with India in the conventional field. In a RAND report prepared for
the US Army in the mid-nineties, Ashley Tellis pointed out that
India's advantage of numbers only came into play twenty-one days
after the initiation of conflict.[15]

Bean-count assessments do not take into account what a SIPRI
study on military capacity and the risk of war pointed out—that
traditional analyses do not provide an adequate measure of 'military
capacity or effectiveness'; it points towards 'cultural' factors, as well
as the role of organisational and political issues as additional factors.[16]

There does seem to be a certain tendency in Pakistan to take risk
as evidenced by the 1965 Operation Gibraltar and the Kargil war.
Stephen Cohen has noted that given its size, location and terrain,
Pakistani generals are 'attracted' to the doctrine of offensive defence.
'That is, in time of heightening crisis, Pakistan has not hesitated to
be the first to employ the heavy use of force in order to gain a material
advantage'.[17]

While the American link was ostensibly oriented towards fostering
Western interests, there was a greater commonality of interests in the
alliance with China that came in the wake of the Sino-Indian border
war of 1962. This was based on a Chinese need to find a reliable
partner in the Southwest Asian region, as well as a mutual benefit
in containing India. The working of the second requirement became
apparent first, in 1965, when a Chinese ultimatum to India may have
been a crucial factor in India ending the Pakistan-initiated war at a
point when Pakistani military capacity had been seriously degraded.[18]
The second was in the early nineties when the Chinese supply of
nuclear-capable ballistic missiles ensured nuclear parity between
India and Pakistan and may have encouraged the Kargil operation.[19]

The third leg of the strategy was to support separatist movements
in India, even those using terrorism as an instrument of policy. This
began with the support of Sikh militants in Punjab in the early

eighties. Then when the Kashmir uprising took place the focus
shifted, though an effort was made to link the two movements. But
despite its best efforts, Pakistan was unable to convert a popular
uprising in the Valley to its advantage. But Islamabad did get involved
deeper through proxies like the Lashkar-e-Taiba and the Harkat-ul-
Mujahideen, and directly through ISI agents, but to little avail.
Pakistani policy has gone well beyond its stated goal of providing
'political, diplomatic and moral' support for Kashmir; it has sought
to assist the break-up of India or, if this is not an immediate prospect,
to tie down India in a multiplicity of internal conflicts. As Philip
Oldenburg pointed out:

> Pakistani leaders have not understood that, drawing a false inference
> from the emergence of Bangladesh...that Pakistan could only
> protect itself from India by encouraging its dissolution.[20]

From 1990 to the present time, Pakistan has conducted a proxy war
against India in Kashmir with the knowledge that India is unlikely
to respond because of the fear that the situation would degenerate
into a nuclear confrontation. Since at no point had Pakistani forces
physically crossed the Line of Control, India was compelled to fight
a defensive campaign.

The fourth leg of the strategy was to develop nuclear weapons.
The Indian test at Pokhran in 1974 is said to have touched off the
Pakistani programme. But almost all observers believe that the event
was merely a catalyst. Pakistan had much earlier, in the wake of the
loss of its eastern wing, decided to initiate a programme. With the
help of China, Pakistan was able to field a nuclear deterrent by the
mid-eighties and had actually outdone India in such key areas as
missile delivery by the early nineties.

The Crisis in State and Society

After the passing away of Mohammed Ali Jinnah and assassination of
Liaquat Ali Khan, Pakistan has passed through four cycles of Army
rule.[21] Right from the outset, it came under the pressure of religious
leaders wanting to run the state on Islamic principles. This in turn led
to an emasculation of the country's political class and the emergence

of the army as a central institution in the politics of Pakistan.[22] As Stephen Cohen has pointed out, from the very beginning, the Pakistan army had helped to defend its country's borders and established internal order. 'Moreover, it always regarded itself as the special expression of the idea of Pakistan.'[23] But it has also prevented the emergence of a vibrant political class which, with the help of a civilian bureaucracy, ought to have governed the state. Ayesha Siddiqa Agha has noted that while Islamabad's threat perceptions of India have been the 'standard explanation' for Pakistan's arms procurement and build-up, other factors may have played a dominant role, such as inter-services rivalry and civil-military relations.[24]

The Army-dominated political system, however, has been doomed to be a failure, it also brought Pakistan to disaster in 1971 when the eastern half of the country was sheared off to create Bangladesh. But while the trauma helped restore civilian rule under Zulfikar Ali Bhutto and enabled Pakistan to write its Constitution in 1972, it did not change the Army's fundamental views regarding its role in Pakistan. In July 1977, the Army was back in the saddle when Army chief Gen. Zia ul Haq declared martial law. Bhutto was arrested and tried for murder and sentenced to death, and finally executed in April 1979. This period was characterised by a more dangerous trend when, to legitimise his rule, Gen. Zia ul Haq began to 'Islamise' Pakistan. Influenced by the Jamaat-e-Islami, Zia imposed shariat laws in Pakistan, which was essentially to introduce the jurisprudence of one sect of Muslims over the others.[25] This had major consequences for the Shia community, that constituted 20 per cent of Pakistan, as well as in the laws of banking and commerce.

Besides this, Islamic political formations, belonging to the Ahle Hadis and Deobandi sects, got unprecedented power because of the jihad against the Russian invasion of Afghanistan, and the money their madrasas began to get through the zakat funds. Zia used the Army's Inter-Services Intelligence to run the Afghan jihad in the early eighties, an action that required organising, equipping and launching jihadis from Pakistan to fight the Russian and Afghan forces. To gather up the jihadis, the ISI 'sub-contracted' the recruitment to various religious groups and madrasas. The jihad led to the Jamaat-e-Islami and its leader Qazi Hussain Ahmed gaining considerable influence in Pakistani political circles. Since it was the only political party allowed access to the Afghan camps, it developed important links with the Afghan groups like Hizbe-Islami. This was quite an achievement for an outfit whose leader had been sentenced to death for the anti-Qadiani agitations of 1953 and which had been banned in the Ayub period.[26]

Aided by Saudi and ISI money and influenced by the Afghan jihadi leaders, Pakistani zealots belonging to the Jamaat in particular, and the Ahle Hadis and Deobandi sects in general, began to advocate a hard Islam within Pakistan as well. This in turn has had several consequences. First was the promotion of sectarian violence against those perceived to be unIslamic, particularly the Shias and Ahmediyas, but not excluding Sunnis of the Barelvi sect. Second, it led to what Khalid Ahmed calls 'surrender of internal sovereignty' to the militias belonging to these sects.[27]

The lack of basic educational facilities and poverty encouraged poor students, over one million of them at any given time in recent years, to attend madrasas or religious schools. Till recent times, the major output of these madrasas were sent to the Afghan or Kashmir 'fronts'. But with the jihad tap drying up, the presence of these persons, who graduate at the rate of some 7,000 per year, remains a cause of great concern. The consequences of these policies were aptly brought out by Mohammed Amir Rana in his remarkable 2002 survey of the jihadi and sectarian organisations. The survey began with the following paragraph:

> During the course of the last two decades, thirty thousand Pakistani youth have died in Afghanistan and Kashmir, two thousand sectarian clashes have taken place and twelve lakh youth have taken part in the activities of jihadi and religious organisations. This jihadi culture was born of the Afghan war, inspired by the Iranian Revolution and nurtured by the American 'Operation Cyclone'. Osama bin Laden's wealth and his extremist thoughts spearheaded its growth and the Taliban gave it practical shape. In consequence, Pakistan got neither Kabul nor Srinagar, but was itself saddled with terrorism.[28]

Sectarian conflict broke out in the North-West Frontier Province, encouraged by the Zia regime and led to the killings of a large number of Shias in Parachinar and the assassination of Allama Hussaini, a prominent Shia leader in 1988. In Punjab, tensions had been on the rise since the mid-eighties with the founding of the Anjuman-e-Sipah-e-Sahaba by Maulana Haq Nawaz Jhangvi in an area dominated by

Shia landlords. In 1990, at the height of his campaign of 'extreme insult and denigration' against the Shias, Maulana Haq Nawaz was himself murdered. In the ensuing period, there has been violence organised by both sides. Deobandi lashkars have attacked Shias in Gilgit, and in 2003, the violence extended to even Balochistan, coordinated by organisations such as the Jaish-e-Mohammed, Sipah-e-Sahaba, the Lashkar-e-Jhangvi. In response, Shia outfits like the Tehreek-e-Fiqh-e-Jafariya and Sipah-e-Mohammed have not hesitated to murder Sunnis.[29]

With the death of Gen. Zia in an as yet unexplained aircrash in August 1988, civilian rule was restored in Pakistan, but not stability. From this period, there have been several spells of rule by Benazir Bhutto's Pakistan People's Party, followed by the army-inspired Pakistan Muslim League government of Nawaz Sharif. But in October 1999, there was a falling out between Sharif and his Army mentors and the result was another coup that brought the present ruler of Pakistan, Gen. Pervez Musharraf to power. Though formally there is a civilian prime minister of Pakistan, and governments of various parties, including the Islamist parties ruling the states, effective power remains in the hands of the armed forces.

The Economic Crisis

The major consequences of Pakistan's Afghan adventure and decision to maintain effective parity with India became apparent in the nineties. Faced with sanctions after the nuclear test of 1998, Pakistan stood at the brink of default on its foreign debt. Hardly any international donor or creditor, private or public, was prepared to provide financing till the IMF came to its aid in 1999. Pakistan was suddenly face-to-face with an all-round crisis characterised by a deep and protracted economic recession, a sharp increase in poverty and a critical debt-servicing burden. Actually this crisis would have come earlier, in the eighties, but was staved off by the massive economic assistance that was provided to Pakistan to fight the Russians in Afghanistan.

Pakistan is a predominantly agricultural economy that has built up a modest industrial base in steel, textiles, cement, leather goods, plastics, etc. Currently, the share of agriculture to the overall output is 25 per cent, while services have grown up to 50 per cent or so. The share of manufacturing has remained at about 16–17 per cent for the past three decades. Indeed, the growth of manufacturing has actually declined; while it grew at a reasonable 8.2 per cent in the eighties, it slowed down to 4.4 per cent in the early nineties and fell to 2 per cent in the ensuing years. It has picked up since, but this has been more due to capacity addition rather than utilisation. Investment has been declining, more particularly foreign investment, and this combined with Pakistan's historically low rate of domestic savings, currently 12–14 per cent of the GDP, bodes ill for the future.[30]

The poverty pool, according to one estimate, is some 50 million people out of the population of 140 million. Projections are that, if poverty continues to grow at the present rate of 5 per cent, and if population grows at 2 per cent, the number of people living in absolute poverty would be around 84 million, or some 50 per cent of the population, by 2010. While this calculation of poverty was based on caloric food intake, it has wider ramifications in terms of lack of access to education, healthcare, safe drinking water, and employment.

Shahid Javed Burki has pointed out that if Pakistani trends of the late nineties continued, its GNP would increase by 3.25 per cent a year and reach just $544 billion by 2025 while India's GNP could be of the order of $11.6 trillion. Pakistan's per capita income would be $2,530 while that of India could be $8,286 and could actually make Pakistan the poorest country in South Asia. Incidence of poverty could rise to 62 per cent and the absolute numbers of the poor could be 133 million, almost the entire population in 1999.[31]

Ushering Change in Pakistan

Elites in Pakistan, the US, India, and other countries have recognised that the present state of affairs cannot be allowed to continue in Pakistan. The three-pronged crisis of Pakistan—that of a flawed grand strategy, its state and governance, and economy—have, on occasion, fed on each other with negative consequences for itself and its neighbours, India and Afghanistan, as well as the world. There is agreement that Pakistan must become, as Jinnah envisioned, a modern, tolerant and democratic polity.[32] This involves nothing short of a U-turn since it requires a change of its flawed grand strategy

which, as we have noted, is fixated on an unsustainable competition
with India.

But just how is this to be achieved? Pakistan's democratic institutions had collapsed following the military coup of October 1999.
In September 2001, when it was compelled to face an American
ultimatum that demanded not only an end to support of the Taliban
but also positive support to that end in the form of bases, it had
little choice but to comply. Gen. Pervez Musharraf, the Pakistani
dictator, turned on the Taliban and later, under combined Indian and
American pressure, began to change course on supporting jihadis in
Kashmir as well.

This was quite risky as Siddiqa Agha has pointed out, 'Over the
past 50 years, the India factor has gained such prominence in the
national psyche that it is considered politically risky to make changes
in the foreign and defence policies.'[33] But the shift has not been
painless, nor as yet categorical. The October 2002 elections in
Pakistan saw a hung National Assembly with the Islamist parties, like
the various factions of Jamiat-ul-ulema Pakistan and Jamaat-e-Islami,
who oppose American intervention in Afghanistan making their best
ever showing.

Tactical considerations compel both the US and Pakistani leaders
to dilute their policy options, while India has a limited leverage in
nudging Pakistan to change. Given the complexity of the undertak-
ing, it is clear that it cannot be achieved by compulsion alone. The
Pakistani 'soft landing' to a normal state requires subtle, but firm
handling. It also requires, on the part of both India and the US,
considerable engagement, though of differing kinds.

One of the unintended consequences of September 11 has been
the acceleration of trends towards building trust between India and
Pakistan. This may appear to be strange logic. But one should look
at it in this way. Prior to the event and its denouement for Pakistan,
the issue of building confidence and trust remained something that
was ideally achievable, but in some distant future. Musharraf's decision to turn Pakistan's Afghanistan policy on its head was ostensibly
done, as indeed he noted, to 'protect' Pakistan's nuclear option and
Kashmir policy. But they marked a distinct and bold departure from
the past, one that had immediate benefits for India. This trend was
deepened by the December 13 attack on the Parliament House in
New Delhi. The Indian diplomatic offensive, accompanied by the
massing of its forces in the border encouraged the General to take

his next step. This was his January 12 declaration that Pakistan rejected terrorism 'in all its forms and manifestations' and that it would 'not allow its territory to be used for any terrorist activity anywhere in the world'. He banned five radical Islamic groups and arrested some 2,000 suspects.

Twice in this period, India came close to attacking Pakistan, but backed off. The reasons were obvious. A military attack was unlikely to achieve what it sought, and there was no guarantee that the situation would not spiral out of control. The US, too, played an important role and sought and obtained commitments from Pakistani authorities that they would end infiltration across the Line of Control 'permanently'.

The world community now began to accept the Indian position that the Kashmir dispute could not be settled overnight. But Pakistan could begin the process by stopping cross-border infiltration, which would sharply reduce the threat of an Indo-Pakistan conflict. This, in turn, could enable a climate where the two countries could undertake a dialogue to resolve the Kashmir issue.[34]

Indian Policy and Change

Indian policy towards Pakistan has fluctuated between bouts of engagement, concession and indifference. While there was considerable engagement in the early fifties, India turned its back to Pakistan following its alliance with the US, even though it was in this period, that a major subject, the sharing of the Indus waters, was hammered out through an agreement backed by the World Bank. In the sixties in the wake of the defeat in the Sino-Indian border war, Indian policy became defensive and reactive.

However, when India achieved a signal victory over Pakistan in 1971, a conscious decision was taken in New Delhi not to rub Islamabad's nose in the dirt. India agreed to the release of the 90,000 prisoners of war it had, and also agreed to sign the Simla Agreement of 1972 that did not seek to capitalise on its military victory and actually accepted that Kashmir was an issue that needed to be resolved, albeit through dialogue. For some two years or so, there was a short period of 'moderation and rationalism' in Pakistan's approach to India. However, soon relations went back to their former status of hostility and by 1975, according to J.N. Dixit, 'Bhutto had lost interest in building up Indo-Pak normalcy.'[35] There have been several suggestions that India missed an opportunity to resolve the Kashmir issue in the period 1972–82. What does emerge from an analysis of the Simla Agreement and its aftermath is that despite possibly good intentions at the summit, there was little follow-up.

But there was a period of stability in Indo-Pak relations between 1977 and 1984, even if the situation was building up for a confrontation. The resumption of massive military aid to Pakistan by the US, and the simultaneous acceleration of the Pakistani nuclear weapons programme began to put India under pressure. This was compounded by the outbreak of the Sikh militancy in Punjab, with active assistance on the part of Pakistan, which brought relations to a new low, and there was even talk of war at the end of 1984, the year in which Indian forces occupied the Siachen glacier and when the Operation Bluestar fiasco eventually led to the assassination of Indira Gandhi.[36] But there was an effort to normalise ties again during the Rajiv Gandhi era. Talks were held to untangle the new dispute on Siachen, and the process of official exchanges got underway. But relations remained tense, and included a phase when the two countries mobilised forces in the wake of a major military exercise by India in 1986.

With the demise of Zia ul Haq in 1988, there was another window of opportunity for India-Pakistan relations. However, while the ambience of the Rajiv Gandhi-Benazir Bhutto summit in July 1989 was positive, it was too late for any substantial gain. Gandhi was going in for the elections that he was to lose later that year, and Bhutto was already under pressure from the armed forces and President Ghulam Ishaq Khan.

But there was a marked shift in Indian dealings with Islamabad, perhaps because of the awareness in 1990 that Pakistan had crossed the nuclear threshold. Despite the outbreak of the Kashmir rebellion being aided and abetted by Islamabad, New Delhi maintained a policy of engaging Pakistan in an all-round dialogue. The outcome of this were agreements on not attacking each other's nuclear facilities, notification of military manoeuvres in advance, and so on. However, the growing intensity of the insurgency in Kashmir, at least till the mid-nineties, prevented any further rapprochement. But by this time, New Delhi had come to realise that while it could contain the insurgency in the state, it could not eliminate it completely as long as Pakistan kept on sustaining it. So, Prime Minister Narasimha Rao asked his Foreign Secretary J.N. Dixit to make specific proposals to Pakistan 'covering both confidence-building measures and political issues.'[37] India, now offered to talk about Kashmir, but since the militancy there was reaching its peak, Pakistan decided not to accept the Indian offer.

The next major development took place in May 1997 when Prime Minister I.K. Gujral met his Pakistani counterpart on the sidelines of the SAARC summit in Male. By this time, it was clear that the militancy was ebbing and so the two sides agreed to look at all outstanding issues. These were broken down to eight heads, the first being peace and security, the second Jammu and Kashmir, the third Siachen, the fourth Wullar Barrage/Tulbul navigation project and so on. This process of addressing all issues in an integrated fashion was termed a 'composite' dialogue.

In this period, Pakistani reluctance to open up trade with India led to a stalemate of sorts in the progression of the South Asian Association for Regional Cooperation. Periodic declaration at SAARC summits on promoting regional trade were more or less dead letters because of Pakistan's refusal to open up to India. At the Dhaka summit in 1993, the SAARC countries agreed to establish a South Asian Preferential Trade Area (SAPTA) by 1997, but there was little progress thereafter. India, in the meanwhile, moved on another track of establishing trade areas excluding Pakistan. The Indian Ocean Rim-Association for Regional Cooperation (IOR-ARC) was launched in Mauritius on 6–7 March 1997, and among its members are Australia, Bangladesh, India, Indonesia, Iran, Kenya, a number of Indian Ocean island states, and states on the littoral in East Africa and the Arabian peninsula. However, the grouping has not progressed in any significant degree. In June 1997, Bangladesh, India, Sri Lanka and Thailand Economic Cooperation (BIMST-EC) grouping was created which has subsequently been joined by Myanmar, Nepal and Bhutan and its name changed to the Bay of Bengal Initiative for Multi-Sectoral Technical and Economic Cooperation. India also moved to become a dialogue partner of the ASEAN and was invited to become a member of the ASEAN Regional Forum. Simultaneously, India began negotiating free trade agreements with several SAARC countries and signed one with Sri Lanka, and more recently with Thailand. India signed a Framework agreement with ASEAN in October 2003 to establish a Free Trade Area in ten years covering goods, services and investment. The Indian strategy has been to take Pakistan along, but not permit it to become a permanent obstacle.

With the significant detour of the nuclear tests of May 1998, the next significant India-Pakistan engagement came through the Lahore summit of February 1999. This was seen as the most significant expression of India's intention of engaging Pakistan on all outstanding issues, including Kashmir. It also represented a decision among at least some sections of the ruling class in Pakistan that there was need to normalise ties with India. The first item 'agreed to' by the Lahore Declaration was the decision of the two governments to 'intensify their efforts to resolve all issues, including the issue of Jammu and Kashmir'. Another valuable decision of the agreement, signed on 21 February, was the need to 'take immediate steps for reducing the risk of accidental or unauthorised use of nuclear weapons' and discuss other means of preventing conflict. Both sides also condemned terrorism. Equally significant was the decision by Prime Minister Vajpayee to visit the Minar-e-Pakistan, the monument to the founding of Pakistan, in Lahore, to emphasise India's commitment to the sovereign existence of Pakistan.

The Kargil war and the subsequent coup that overthrew Nawaz Sharif put this process into a limbo. Efforts to pick up the thread of negotiations with the Pakistani dictator Gen. Pervez Musharraf, at the summit at Agra, held on 14–16 July 2001, failed. The General's inexperience, as well as the lack of adequate preparation by the two sides were the reasons for this outcome.

The 2004 Thaw

Finally, towards the end of 2003, after more diplomacy and several assassination attempts on President Musharraf's life by jihadists, Pakistan expressed its willingness to take a number of steps forward. First, in November 2003, to reduce tensions, President Musharraf ordered a ceasefire along the Line of Control. For some time, Pakistan had taken the position that 'nothing was happening' on the LoC. In other words, no infiltration was taking place. But this was not India's view, and since bombardment on the LoC had been an important means of assisting infiltration across the LoC, this was an important confidence-building measure.

Of greater significance was the outcome of the summit of the South Asian Association for Regional Cooperation (SAARC) in Islamabad in January 2004. The member countries agreed to set aside the SAPTA framework and move towards creating a South Asian Free Trade Area (SAFTA) by 2015. As important as the SAARC meet and its commitment to create a free trade area, was the bilateral summit between Prime Minister Vajpayee and President Musharraf that led to a joint statement that noted:

> Prime Minister Vajpayee said that in order to take forward and sustain the dialogue process, violence, hostility and terrorism must be prevented. President Musharraf reassured Prime Minister Vajpayee that he will not permit any territory under Pakistan's control to be used to support terrorism in any manner....
>
> The two leaders are confident that the resumption of the composite dialogue will lead to peaceful settlement of all bilateral issues, including Jammu and Kashmir, to the satisfaction of both sides.[38]

Despite the change of governments in India, the two countries took up the composite dialogue and completed one set of talks by the end of the year. By this time, it also became clear that the ceasefire along the LoC was holding. The ceasefire has enabled India to build a border fence and reduce infiltration across the LoC. After initial hesitation, Pakistan also agreed to move on the other track of opening up land routes to nationals of both sides. In early 2005, the two countries agreed to reopen the Srinagar-Muzaffarabad bus route in Jammu and Kashmir, start a new Amritsar-Lahore bus service, and reopen the Khorkarpar-Munabao rail route between Rajasthan and Sind.

The one area that still remains to be worked on is on opening up trade and commerce. Pakistan has till now refused to permit India a Most Favoured Nation status, or to allow transit to Central Asia and Afghanistan. However, with India agreeing to examine a proposal to bring gas through a pipeline from Iran, this situation, too, may change.

The Indian strategy for dealing with Pakistan has now become clearer. The aim is not just to settle individual disputes, but to create an entente by a resolution of all outstanding issues, including Kashmir. The development of economic stakes and closer interaction is seen as a vital element of this policy since it could enable both sides to shift from their stated positions on contentious issues like Kashmir by making concessions less of a zero-sum outcome.

Resolving Jammu and Kashmir

In a 1990 work, Richard Haass posed the question as to why some international conflicts can be resolved, while others prove to be intractable. Looking at five of them: the Palestine-Israeli, Indian-Pakistani, the Anglo-Irish issues, South Africa and the Greek-Turkish standoff, he concluded that only if conditions were 'ripe' for solutions, could things happen. The process that is underway, is aimed at precisely that—ripening the Jammu and Kashmir issue towards a solution. Haass had identified four elements that provide a guide to the ripeness of a dispute towards a settlement—'the shared perception by the disputants that an accord is desirable, the existence of leadership on all sides that is either sufficiently strong to sustain a compromise or so weak that a compromise cannot be avoided, a formula involving some benefits for all participants, and a commonly accepted diplomatic process.'[39]

What we are witnessing in 2004 is the beginning of a movement on all these four fronts. There seems to be agreement on both sides that the dispute needs settlement, but the problems of leadership remains. Though there is consensus on the need for a settlement in India, the succession of weak coalition governments has been a hindrance. The problem is more acute in Pakistan where the leadership still remains with the Army, and it is not clear whether the entire force is behind the current leadership's efforts to normalise ties. A formula that can be hailed, or at least be acceptable in New Delhi, Islamabad and Srinagar still remains to be worked out, but a commonly accepted diplomatic process is underway. At this stage, till all the conditions ripen, it is best to work along the *process*, rather than a *formulation* since the very articulation of the outline of a compromise, could, at this stage, lead to difficulties.

One thing is clear, that any solution will require the two countries to come closer to each other politically. A Pakistan where the rights of minorities and other sects are in question is hardly the state that India can work out a condominium or joint sovereignty formula with for the Valley. Likewise, the Indian polity will also have to be more determinedly secular before Pakistan would be willing to go along with New Delhi's guarantees for anything.

Looking to the Future

Given their size and economic potential, India and Pakistan can play a significant role in Asia. But whether it is positive or negative, will only be clear from the choices they make now. Whatever be their perceptions about their disputes, both are clear that they would like to become modern, developed countries. But if India and Pakistan want to transform into developed countries by 2020 or 2025, they will not only require very high growth rates in the order of 10 per cent for India and 7 per cent for Pakistan, but also a resolution of their political issues.

If it requires the dismantling of the Great Jihad Machine in Pakistan, it also requires ensuring that the fruits of economic growth reach down to the poorest in both countries. If it requires a reaffirmation of secularism in India, it has to be based on the restoration of a liberal democratic polity in Pakistan and a move away from the sectarian and fundamentalist trends.

There can be little doubt that opening the borders to trade and commerce will prove enormously beneficial for both the countries. Indian manufacturers can exploit the existing markets in Pakistan whereas Pakistani consumers will have to pay substantially lower prices than they presently pay for the Indian goods, even as Pakistani manufacturers tap India's large market size. Joint ventures, especially infrastructure and information technology projects between India and Pakistan, would be attractive propositions for foreign investors. It is estimated, for example, that there would be a 50 per cent per unit cost reduction of steel in Pakistan, were it to be imported from India. Likewise, bicycles, pharma products and engineering goods would be cheaper by 10 to 30 per cent. Also, India could gain from reduced energy costs, if the pipelines from Iran and Central Asia ran through Pakistan.

But to achieve this, there has to be a transformation of political attitudes, particularly in Pakistan. The central problem in Indo-Pak relations is not that the two countries have a dispute over Kashmir or that one is predominantly Muslim and the other Hindu, a proposition we have shown is inaccurate anyway. The issue is Pakistan's inability to adjust to the geographical and cultural centrality of India in the subcontinent. India's centrality or 'hegemony' in southern Asia, if you will, is a function of history, size and location. The six other South Asian countries—Nepal, Bhutan, Bangladesh, Sri Lanka, Maldives and Pakistan are smaller than India, even when taken together in terms of size and population and economic potential.

Rajendra Sareen, a not unsympathetic observer surveyed Pakistani opinion two decades ago and noted that closer relations between the two countries were held up because Pakistan believed that closer cooperation with India 'would expose it to the latter's hegemony and reduce it to the level of Bhutan'. There was little, he noted, India could do about such perceptions 'since the solution lies in Pakistan's discovering for itself that its perceptions are misconceived'.

I don't know what the Pakistanis mean by 'hegemony'. India is of course a larger country with a large industrial and economic infrastructure... If good relations between India and Pakistan are contingent upon India's disintegration, the proposition is (so) absurd.... Pakistan's founding fathers were a party to the arrangement which determined India's size. They wanted to be a smaller country regardless of geopolitical considerations. Pakistan's further diminution in 1971 was unfortunate, but it cannot escape its own responsibility for that.'[40]

As of now, Pakistan's security perceptions are wholly India-centric. But the issue is not seen just as the struggle of a smaller country to guard against the hegemonic designs of a bigger neighbour, but in religio-political terms of a Muslim country determined to secure its way of life against its Hindu neighbour. This, as Ayesha Siddiqa Agha has pointed out was one of the reasons why Pakistan developed a linear approach to its security, one exclusively focusing on India. 'This linearity has kept Pakistan away from developing a strategic approach that extends beyond India and defines a more wholesome role for Pakistan in the comity of nations.'[41] Armed with nuclear weapons, Pakistan need no longer fear a physical attack by India, but it needs to overcome its psychological reservations.

Given the recent history of the subcontinent, and historical Pakistani fears about India, India needs to work at trying to alter its image in Pakistan and the rest of South Asia. This can be done through bilateral measures, which can include force reduction, re-deployment, transparency of military activity, as well as through unilateral political and economic measures through the SAARC. Given the huge asymmetry and the rest of its SAARC neighbours, there is nothing India has to fear from them on the economic front. As Shahid Javed Burki has observed that 'deep animosities among nations can be overcome by trade which produces a dynamic of inter-dependence between people and the owners of production systems'.[42]

This throws up several issues that can be fruitfully explored in the India-Pakistan context. India has shown a greater ability to adapt to the process of globalisation and absorption of technology, as well as its support infrastructure of good governance, education and market reforms. Leaving aside the important issue of parts of India being left behind in the economic surge, a major question relates to how Pakistan will adapt to this change.

India–Pakistan relations impinge on the future of Asia in two principal areas—security and economic development. As we have pointed out, India and China have managed to put their relations on a positive track by segregating their border conflict and building on their shared need for economic cooperation. In the case of Pakistan the process is at an infant stage.

Abandoning the hostile relationship towards India is essential for Pakistan's economic growth, but South Asia can prosper even if this relationship is not at an end. Unresolved problems with India will not inhibit China's economic march, neither, for that matter, continuing difficulties with Pakistan will dampen India's growth. Yet, unsettled problems do have the potential of disrupting the 'Asian century' destiny that is being talked about. The lack of normalisation of India-Pakistan relations will prevent the realisation of a SAFTA, as well as block India's direct access to Central Asia, Afghanistan and Iran. Without the resolution of the Kashmir issue, the threat of India-Pakistan military conflict remains, with its attendant possibility of a suicidal nuclear conflict. Should these issues be resolved, it is appar-ent that the gains of regional interaction and normalisation will accrue to both sides. There should be no doubt in anyone's mind that India, too, desperately needs to normalise relations with Pakistan. In percentage terms, India may be better off than Pakistan in terms of poverty reduction and growth, but in absolute numbers, India's unemployed, hungry and illiterates number in hundreds of millions.

A prosperous, stable, and liberal Pakistan can be of great help in shaping an India that will aid the overall growth and prosperity of Asia.

Given India's domestic challenges and global aspirations, it has great stakes in, first, nudging Pakistan away from its unsustainable and self-destructive path and second, in transforming the relationship from its present zero-sum approach to a cooperative win-win situation. This is a process that India cannot undertake on its own. It has, as has been seen, a limited leverage with Pakistan. In the recent past, the United States has played a significant role in moderating India–Pakistan tensions. The time has come for India to get China to play a more sustained role in moderating and transforming Pakistani behaviour. Recent developments, including a shared perception on the negative effects of Islamic radicalism and the benefits of economic cooperation, should have convinced Beijing that there are even greater gains to be had if there is a significant makeover of India–Pakistan ties.

For the first 50 years of its existence, Pakistan played a larger-than-life role in the world stage. This was more a consequence of its location than intrinsic importance. But the result was that it skewed Pakistan's attitudes towards its neighbours—India and Afghanistan. It also undermined its internal cohesion as a state and drained it economically. Ever since September 11, there is an international effort to arrange what can at best be termed a 'soft landing' for Pakistan. This involves a restructuring of its finances as well as encouraging it to set right its internal fractures. As Pakistan's only perceived adversary, and major neighbour, India has a vital role in the process.

Notes and References

1. See the executive summary, 'The 2020 Global Landscape', *Mapping the Future: Report of the National Intelligence Council's 2020 Project*, Washington DC, 2004, www.cia.gov/nic/NIC_global trend2020.html
2. Ibid.
3. 'Changing Security Dynamic in Eastern Asia', Inaugural Address by External Affairs Minister Shri K. Natwar Singh at 7th Asian Security Conference (ASC) organised by Institute for Defence Studies and Analyses at India Habitat Centre, New Delhi.
4. Ayesha Siddiqa Agha, *Pakistan's Arms Procurement and Military Buildup, 1979–99: In Search of a Policy*. New York, Palgrave, 2001, pp. 18 and 198.

5. Philip Oldenburg, 'What attitude must Pakistan change?' *The Friday Times*, Lahore, 18 January 2002, argued that India 'has slowly come to a position of accepting the permanency of Pakistan (though many Pakistanis continue to doubt this), while Pakistan has not accepted India in the same way (though this is probably the view of only the elite)'.

6. For a balanced reappraisal see Rajendra Sareen, *Pakistan, the India Factor*. New Delhi, Allied, 1984, particularly his essay on 'Partition in Retrospect'.

7. Swadesh R. Bose, 'The Pakistan Economy since Independence (1947–1950)', Dharma Kumar (ed.), *The Cambridge Economic History of India*, vol. 2, 1757–1970, Cambridge, Cambridge University Press, 1982.

8. Ibid., pp. 997–99.

9. Partha Sarthi Gupta, 'Imperial Strategy and the Transfer of Power, 1939–1951', *Power, Politics and the People: Studies in British Imperialism and Indian Nationalism*. New Delhi, Permanent Black, 2001, p. 241.

10. C. Dasgupta, *War and Diplomacy in Kashmir: 1947–1948*. New Delhi, Sage, 2002, pp. 11–12.

11. Ibid., p. 208. Also see Prem Shankar Jha, *Kashmir 1947, The Origins of a Dispute*. New Delhi, OUP, 2003.

12. Dennis Kux, *The United States and Pakistan 1947–2000: Disenchanted Allies*. Karachi, OUP, 2001.

13. Institute for Defence Studies and Analyses, *Asian Strategic Review 1998–1999*. New Delhi, IDSA, 1999, pp. 51 and 72.

14. Ayesha Siddiqa Agha, 'Pakistan's Security: Problems of Linearity,' *South Asian Journal*, vol. 3, Lahore, January–March, 2004, p. 42.

15. Ashley J. Tellis, *Stability in South Asia: Prospects of Indo-Pak Nuclear Conflict, RAND Report prepared for the United States Army*. Dehra Dun, Natraj Publishers, 1997, pp. 30–32.

16. Eric Arnett (ed.), *Military Capacity and the Risk of War: China, India, Pakistan and Iran*. SIPRI, OUP, 1997, p. 2.

17. Stephen P. Cohen, *The Pakistan Army*. The 1998 Edition with a new foreword and epilogue. Karachi OUP, 1998, p. 145. The original was published in 1984.

18. John W. Garver, *Protracted Contest: Sino-Indian Rivalry in the Twentieth Century*. New Delhi, 2001, pp. 199–204.

19. Carol Giacomo, 'US Says Pakistan Has Full Chinese Missile System', Reuters report, 13 September 1999 in www.news.lycos.com/stories/politics/19990913RTPOLITICS-MISSILES-CHINA.asp. This is only the end of the story that began when the first Bush administration became determined that this transfer was occurring and instituted mild sanctions on China.

20. Philip Oldenburg, 'What Attitude Must Pakistan Change?'

21. See Mohammed Asghar Khan, *Generals in Politics: Pakistan 1958–1982*. New Delhi, Vikas, 1983.

22. Ayesha Jalal, *The State of Martial Rule: The Origins of Pakistan's Political Economy of Defence*. Cambridge, Cambridge University Press, 1992.

23. Stephen P. Cohen, *The Pakistan Army*. The 1998 Edition with a new foreword and epilogue. Karachi, 1998, p. 105.

24. Ayesha Siddiqa Agha, *Pakistan's Arms Procurement and Military Buildup, 1979–99: In Search of a Policy*. New York, 2001, pp. 18 and 198.

25. Salman Akram Raja, 'Islamisation of Laws in Pakistan,' *South Asian Journal*, vol. 1, no. 2, October–December, 2003, pp. 94–109.
26. For the relationship between Zia and the Jamaat, see Mushahid Hussain, *Pakistan Politics, the Zia Years*. New Delhi, Konarak, 1991, pp. 178–82.
27. Khaled Ahmed, 'Islamic Extremism in Pakistan,' *South Asian Journal*, vol. 1, no. 2, October–December 2003, pp. 39–40.
28. Mohammed Amir Rana, *Gateway to Terrorism*. London, New Millenium, 2003, pp. 113–14. The book is a translation of what is perhaps the most definitive work on Jihadis, *Jihad Kashmir wa Afghanistan: Jihadi Tanzimun aur Mazhabi Jamaton ka aik Jaiza*. Lahore, Mashal Books, 2002.
29. See Abbas Rashid, 'The Politics and Dynamics of Violent Sectarianism,' in Zia Mian and Iftikhar Ahmad (eds.), *Making Enemies, Creating Conflict Pakistan's Crisis of State and Security*. Lahore, Mashal Books, 1998.
30. Strategic Foresight Group, *The Future of Pakistan*. Mumbai, International Centre for Peace Initiatives, 2002, pp. 6–7. According to another report, GDP growth declined from 6.1 per cent during the eighties to 4.2 per cent during the nineties, growth of large-scale manufacturing declined and the percentage of population living below the poverty line increased from 18 per cent in 1987 to 34 per cent in 2002. See Akmal Hussain, *Pakistan: National Development Report 2003, Poverty, Growth and Governance*. Karachi, UN Development Programme, 2003, p. 3 and Chapter I.
31. Shahid Javed Burki, 'Pakistan, India and Regional Cooperation,' *South Asian Journal*, Lahore, April–June 2004, p. 16.
32. Sharif al Mujahid, 'Jinnah's Vision of Pakistan,' in Zia Mian and Iftikhar Ahmad (eds.), *Making Enemies, Creating Conflict Pakistan's Crisis of State and Security*. Lahore, 1998. He argues that Jinnah's conversion from an unabashed modernist to an advocate of an Islamic state could not have occurred, unless the Quaid-e-Azam believed that Islamic values he was commending 'were in consonance with progress and modernity'.
33. Ayesha Siddiqa Agha, *Pakistan's Arms Procurement and Military Buildup, 1979–99: In Search of a Policy*. New York, 2001, p. 43.
34. International Crisis Group, *Kashmir: Confrontation and Miscalculation*, 11 July 2002, Brussels/Islamabad, ICG, p. 10.
35. J.N. Dixit, *Anatomy of a Flawed Inheritance: Indo-Pak Relations, 1970–1994*. New Delhi, Konarak, 1995, pp. 42–43.
36. Ibid., pp. 79–81.
37. Ibid., p. 174.
38. 'India-Pakistan Joint Press Statement, Islamabad, 6 January 2004' in http://meaindia.nic.in/speech/2004/01/06ss01.htm
39. Richard Haass, *Conflicts Unending: The United States and Regional Disputes*. New Haven, CT, Yale University Press, 1990, p. 138.
40. Rajendra Sareen, *Pakistan, the Indian Factor*. New Delhi, 1984, p. 14.
41. Ayesha Siddiqa Agha, 'Pakistan's Security: Problems of Linearity,' *South Asian Journal*, vol. 3, Lahore, January–March, 2004, p. 36.
42. Shahid Javed Burki, 'Pakistan, India and Regional Cooperation,' *South Asian Journal*, Lahore, April–June 2004, p. 57.

5

ECONOMIC REFORMS AND INTEGRATION IN SOUTH ASIA: ROLE OF INDIA IN SAARC

Mahendra P. Lama

Introduction

Unlike many other developing regions, the urge for advent and acceptance of market-led economic reforms are a somewhat recent phenomenon in South Asia. This phenomenon came to limelight only after a majority of the South Asian countries including Bangladesh, India, Nepal, Pakistan and Sri Lanka made a major departure from *dirigiste* (state-directed economic development), and vigorously adopted the 'Washington Consensus' in the form of liberalisation, privatisation, marketisation and modernisation.[1]

Despite the known political difficulty of remedial action and the likelihood of perverse short-term socio-economic effects, at least five of the seven South Asian countries including Bangladesh, India, Nepal, Pakistan and Sri Lanka, plunged into adjustment programmes in the eighties and nineties. However, adoptions and implementation of these reform measures vary across the South Asian region in terms of (*a*) time schedule, (*b*) sectoral coverage, (*c*) intensity and (*d*) sustainability. In other words, these countries are in different phases of economic reform programmes.[2]

(a) A massive dose of reforms have been injected and effected in trade, investment, technology, and the financial and capital market. Private sector, both foreign and domestic, has started playing very vital roles in areas like energy, telecommunications, banking, trade and commerce. As a result, except for a few years in-between, most of the South Asian countries have recorded higher economic growth. This is likely to massively expand both the scope and opportunities in many areas including services, infrastructure, tourism, and natural resources based economic activities which had remained unharnessed so far.[3]

(b) The effort towards integration of regional market has been further consolidated after the Agreement on South Asian Free Trade Area was signed recently under the aegis of South Asian Association for Regional Cooperation (SAARC). This will make the market more expansive with 1.3 billion people, and market access much easier both within the region, and the neighbouring Southeast and Central Asia.

(c) Vast impact on the foreign exchange reserves situations in South Asia is now witnessed. For instance, in India, it has steadily gone up from a few billion dollars in the immediate pre-reforms period to over 100 billion dollars in 2004. This has triggered a large scale foreign exchange related activities including expansion in imports, visits abroad for education, health, tourism and in many other non-traditional sectors. This could trigger off a much more integrated economic cooperation between South Asian countries and the rest of the world.

(d) The region's huge emerging market, strong institutional and legal frameworks, English-speaking professional and entrepreneurial class, and impressive scientific and technical skills are among its attractions. The most important interest of India in South Asia is continued economic reform leading to faster and well-distributed growth. Economic relations should therefore, be the focal point of India's engagement with the region. Successful economic reform and deregulation in South Asia will offer extensive commercial opportunities for India also. This is where the interdependence as a new paradigm is fast emerging.

Positive Stakeholding: India's Role

India's extensive dependence on military and political confidence-building measures (CBMs) have not really sustained the rigour of realpolitik particularly vis-à-vis Pakistan. The fate of many of these crucial CBMs were dependent upon, and determined many a times, by inept and highly unstable political regimes, pathologically insecure military generals and inward-looking bureaucrats.[4]

These CBMs were addressed to mainly those who had serious stakeholding in perpetuating the conflict and keeping the conflict alive. This meant that the stakeholders thrived on the adverse situations. Though these stakeholders have always been in microscopic minority, they have somehow been able to closely align with the power echelons and marginalise the overwhelming majority. If one draws a normal curve to show how these CBMs have worked and performed, one will find that most of these CBMs have hit the trough without reaching the peak. More interestingly, once these CBMs hit the trough, they have never been found to be worth repeating.[5]

This makes us to ponder over the vital question of designing new CBMs particularly in case of India-Pakistan conflicts. This therefore, takes us to the domain of economic CBMs where we consider the business and other economic cooperation (Track III diplomacy) as a measure of CBM and peace building in South Asia. As there are stakeholders in keeping the conflict alive, there are stakeholders for building the peace. We have never addressed ourselves to the latter.

There could be six roles of business and economic cooperation alone in peace building:[6]

(a) *Business Diplomacy*–China and Taiwan: Though there are no formal political communications, high level business contacts are often used as proxy routes.

(b) *Technology in the Service of Peace:* Role played by fax machine during the Soviet crisis in the early nineties.

(c) *Business, Development and the Environment:* The growing scarcity of natural resources has been a major source of conflict. Business can play a critical role in supporting development that sustains environmental, social and economic integrity.

(d) *Trade and Investment as Preventive Diplomacy:* Israelis' large scale participation in the joint ventures, investment and trade sector in the Palestine private sector that fostered the growth of jobs, entrepreneurship and purchasing power in Palestine.

(e) *Business as a Funding Source for Peace Building:* There are ample examples of peace institutes, and research supported by the business community. For instance, the famous Joan B. Kroc Institute for International Peace Studies located in the University of Notre Dame, USA, is wholly supported by MacDonalds chain of fast food. Business community can be a functional and a reliable impartial funding partner in organising dialogues, conferences, confidence-building projects and other events.

(f) *Business Skills and Practices for Peace Building:* Business leaders are often dealing with the same issues as peace leaders. Issues of multi-culturalism, complex systems, power, multiple stakeholders, leadership for vision, and values and partnership. These issues are as relevant to those seeking to lead their people out of conflict as to those seeking to lead large corporations. The skills, approaches and experience of the business and organisational development world in addressing these issues could be extraordinarily valuable to peace leaders and vice-versa.

In South Asia also, the CBMs built by the economic stakeholders have always sustained. In this regard, India's relations with the smaller neighbours including Nepal, Bhutan, Bangladesh and Sri Lanka have several examples to offer. There have been serious political crises these countries have faced vis-à-vis India, but they have been remarkably momentary and have showed urgent recovery mainly because of the large-scale economic stakeholding on both sides of the border.

A recent example is that of the fiercely adverse diplomatic and media exchange between India and Nepal after the hijacking of Delhi-bound Indian Airlines (IC 814) flight to Kandahar in Afghanistan. It brought the traditional–special relations between India and Nepal to the lowest possible ebb. However, as the months of March and April 2000 approached, the stakeholders in the tourism sectors on both sides of the border started making hue and cry as they were the ones who were the hardest hit by the discontinuation of Indian flights to Nepal.

These deeply entrenched stakeholders with their forward and backward linkages including travel agents, hotels, communications, trade and commerce, trekking and mountaineering, conferences and pilgrimages started pressurising their respective governments to come to the negotiating table.[7] The relationship was soon restored to the normal track. This also goes to prove that the positive stakeholdings can act as a major player in the bilateral political matrices.

Contrastingly striking has been the fact that in India-Pakistan relations, there has been no such stakeholding in the business sector. Whatever stakeholding they have, they are unfortunately all on the side of keeping the conflict alive. For example, the arms purchase lobby, smuggling syndicates and the Dubai-based traders. In other words, higher the possibility of conflict between India and Pakistan, the better and the wider are the opportunities and avenues for these, what I call negative stakeholders, to maximise their gains. One can cite several examples to conclusively show as to how some of these agencies have been playing the Kashmir card only to perpetuate narrow economic interests of the miniscule stakeholders. Even the multi-national tea companies including the Lipton-Brookbond, combined under the Lever Brothers, belong to this category of negative stakeholders.[8]

The positive players and stakeholdings are, therefore, yet to emerge. This paper seeks to highlight reform based emerging economic stakeholdings which will go a long way in building sustainable CBMs in the region. In creating, designing, building and promoting all these economic stakeholdings, India's role comes out to be of pivotal nature both in terms of a driving force and consolidating agency. India's pivotal role is however, a purely relative and positive-laden concept.[9] Its theoretical construction is based on three elements, viz., relatively advanced level of development, experience and accumulated expertise; existing or potential capacity for sharing that knowledge, and its relatively important involvement in the global economy.[10]

Importance of Trade Issues

Regionalism, besides its strategic, geopolitical and foreign policy dimensions, has been a major plank of development, cooperation and integration in many parts of the world. There are many examples of a variety of regional groupings that have transformed the conventional outlook and aspirations into more open, dynamic and wider systems and practices of peaceful coexistence, collective responsibility and regional development. There are instances where bilateral conflictual issues have been effectively dealt with by the larger concept of win–win situation generated by regionalism and multilateralism.[11] Regional cooperation has brought about significant transformations in some of the regions' strategic options, political actions, economic orientations and developmental gains.[12]

The intra-SAARC trade recorded an average annual growth rate of 31.06 per cent during the period 1990–2001 as against a very low growth rate of 3.4 per cent during the period 1980–90. On the other hand, South Asia's trade with countries outside the region grew at the rate of 11.83 and 8.15 per cent respectively during the same period. As a result, intra-SAARC trade, as percentage of South Asia's world trade has recorded an upward trend from 2.42 per cent in 1990 to 4.56 per cent in 2001. In terms of value also, the total volume of intra-SAARC trade has shown a significant 5.39-fold increase as against 3.78-fold jump recorded by their global trade during 1990–2001. (Table 5.1)

Table 5.1
SAARC: Direction of Trade

Year	Intra-SAARC Trade (a) (in billion $)	South Asia's World Trade (b) (in billion $)
1980	1.21	37.88 (3.19)
1985	1.08	43.75 (2.48)
1990	1.59	65.69 (2.42)
1995	4.25	104.16 (4.08)
2000	5.8	144.06 (4.08)
2001	6.53	143.44 (4.56)

Source: IMF, *Direction of Trade Statistics Yearbook, 2001* and other old issues.
Note: Figures in parentheses indicate (a) as per cent of (b).

Though the exact impact of SAARC Preferential Trading Arrangement (SAPTA) alone on the intra-regional trade in South Asia, has not been carried out or not known as yet, the spurt in the volume of trade in South Asia in the last couple of years has been mostly attributed to rapid liberalisation under bilateral trade and WTO regimes rather than SAPTA. Sri Lanka, Nepal, Bangladesh and Pakistan have liberalised their trade regime in a much more extensive and intensive manner than India under WTO regime.

Balance of Trade Deficit

The huge deficit in the intra-regional balance of trade, particularly vis-à-vis India, has been the most pervasive phenomenon of the South Asian countries. This has been reflected in the negligible intra-regional import figures of India of 0.40 per cent of its total world import in 1990, and 0.77 per cent in 2000. Though a genuine concern of the smaller neighbours, this has been politically often overplayed.

There is a constant fear that it is/will be India who is/will be the only partner country to gain maximum out of any trade liberalisation efforts in the region. This is substantiated by the fact that during the period 1995–2000, India alone constituted over 70 per cent of the exports made within the region and 13 per cent of the imports made from within the region. Bangladesh, Nepal and Sri Lanka remained the three major countries that figured prominently in the intra-regional imports. (Table 5.2).

Table 5.2
Percentage Share of Member Countries in their Total Intra-regional Exports and Imports

Country	Exports		Imports	
	1995	2000	1995	2000
Bangladesh	4.1	3.2	51.34	34.2
India	76.4	72.33	8.8	12.34
Maldives	0.54	1.07	2.0	4.79
Nepal	1.48	6.5	5.9	17.46
Pakistan	12.58	10.2	7.53	8.31
Sri Lanka	4.9	6.7	24.4	22.9
Total (Million $)	2021	2797	2242	3057

Source: IMF, Direction of Trade Statistics Yearbook, 2001 and other old issues.

India's Restrictive Trade Practices

The traders in South Asia, however, still find that there are a host of barriers in India, which prevent the free flow of goods and other economic ties. These are as follows:

(a) Indian importers are finding it much cheaper to import goods like vegetable ghee, acrylic yarn and copper scraps via Nepal and Sri Lanka as their tariff barriers are much lower than in India. Though the unweighted average tariff in India has steadily gone down from 128 per cent in 1990–91 to 35 per cent in 2002–03[13] (as against Pakistan's all products simple average rates of 18.2 per cent in 2002–03), there are a large number of tariff lines which are still relatively on the higher side.[14]

Nepal's and Bangladesh's ongoing tussle with India on certain export items and the subsequent imposition of counter-vailing duties and quantitative restrictions are also considered to be anti-dumping measures. The exercise of these measures is vehemently protested by both Nepal and Bangladesh. The Government of India has thus imposed quota ceilings on vegetable ghee, acrylic yarn, copper products and zinc oxide from Nepal as per the Trade Treaty of 2002. Further, the certificate of origin has also been made more complex.

(b) India also assesses high surcharges and taxes on a variety of imports. Major non-tariff barriers include sanitary and phyto-sanitary restrictions, import licenses, regulations that mandate certain products only to public sector entities, discriminatory government procurement practices, and the use of export subsidies.[15] India continues to maintain a number of inefficient structural policies which affect its trade, including price controls for many 'essential' commodities, extensive government regulation over many sectors of the economy, and extensive public ownership of businesses, many of which are poorly run.

Trade Liberalisation in SAARC: India's Pivotal Role

The SAARC Preferential Trading Arrangement (SAPTA), which has been operational since December 1995, is considered to be one of

the boldest steps taken by the SAARC, particularly against the vitiated
background of bilateral political chicanery, the historico-cultural-
topographic roots of mistrust and suspicion in this subcontinent, and
dismal level of economic interactions among some of these countries.

Detailed studies are now being carried out to examine the impact
of SAPTA in the last eight years of its operationalisation. A study[16]
reveals that Bangladesh most extensively used the import liberalisation
extended by India under SAPTA. Its exports of the items on which
preferential treatment was extended by India rose from a mere
Rs 925.7 million in 1996–97 to Rs 2,434.2 million in 2000–01. In case
of Pakistan, the same increased from Rs 933.7 million to Rs 1,533.8
million during the same period. On the other hand, expectedly, India
made extensive use of the preferential treatment facility extended by
the contracting member countries. India's export of preferential
products extended by Bangladesh doubled from Rs 1,010.6 million
in 1996–97 to 2000.5 million in 2000–01 (Table 5.3).

Table 5.3
**India's Exports of Products Offered Concession by Other
Contracting States under SAPTA (in Million Rs)**

Exports to	1996–97	1998–99	2000–2001	Remarks
Bangladesh	1,010.6	994.1	2,000.5	as non-LDC*
Bhutan	13.3	12.9	1.5	as non-LDC
Maldives	2.9	2.4	6.8	as non-LDC
Nepal	1,186.2	1,521.5	1,732.3	as non-LDC
Pakistan	1,427.5	2,091.1	2,347.7	as non-LDC
Sri Lanka	13.4	130.0	1.5	as non-LDC

Source: Indra Nath Mukherji, 'Towards a Free Trade Area in South Asia: Charting
a Feasible Course for Trade Liberalisation with Reference to India's Role', Jawaharlal
Nehru University, New Delhi in collaboration with the Research and Information
System, New Delhi, October 2002.
* LDC: Least Developed Countries.

However, the SAPTA could hardly be termed as any effective means
to enhance the level of intra-regional trade as it has a serious limitation both in terms of weight of the scheduled products in the
tradeables and the depth of tariff cut. The non-deployment of other
agreed arrangements like para-tariffs, non-tariff measures and direct
trade measures has made it more ineffective.[17]

All the three rounds of SAPTA negotiated and operationalised so
far have been too tedious, tardy and ineffective. Member countries

have given tariff concessions on non-tradeable products.[18] The tariff cuts have not been deeper enough to de-attract their imports from other countries. The country bias in the product identification is distinct.[19]

Could only the tariff concessions raise the level of trade interaction and exchanges among the South Asian countries? This is a very fundamental question that needs to be addressed particularly against the backdrop that the low level of trade within the region could broadly be attributed to (a) politico-strategic-hegemonic impression and fear emanating from India's sheer size and economic might based on diverse industrial base, (b) extremely limited export basket and relatively inefficient and uncompetitive production structure in the neighbouring countries, (c) destination diversification triggered by both domestic compulsions and foreign aid-investment binding arrangement, and (d) trade barriers and unmanned border-led expansive practices of informal-illegal border.[20]

Since the provisions of SAPTA partially addressed only to the fourth inhibiting factor, its outreach and efficacy has been expectedly dismal. The trade ailments are, in fact, much complex and intriguing both in terms of varieties and depth. The 'frequently addressed' tariff and non-tariff barriers are simply the tip of icebergs.

The 12th SAARC Summit held in Islamabad in January 2004 signed a framework agreement on South Asian Free Trade Area (SAFTA) which will be ratified by and implemented with effect from 2006. Till the agreement is ratified, the SAARC member countries have to thrash out and decide upon the four crucial issues, namely, (a) formulation of rules of origin, (b) the preparation of the 'sensitive' or the negative list, (c) the creation of a fund for compensating the Least Developed Countries (LDCs) for loss of revenue from the elimination of customs duties, and (d) the identification of areas for providing technical assistance to these countries.[21]

Four least developed countries including Bangladesh, Bhutan, Maldives and Nepal are worried about the revenue loss arising out of free trade regime, particularly when customs revenue constitute a large portion of their total revenue generation. Their concern is also based on the fact that they have been massive importers from India. The experience with regard to the rules of origin criteria under the bilateral trade arrangement has been controversial and worrisome.

The size of negative list in the free trade agreement is a very vital question. The bigger it is, the more farcical and restrictive is free

trade. A noted Sri Lankan economist writes that 'the free trade agreement (between India and Sri Lanka) does not guarantee free access to all Sri Lankan exports as it excludes about 400 items from preferential trade'.[22]
India has to play a very pivotal role in all these four areas.

(a) It has to evolve mechanisms and institute committees to monitor progress of implementation in the elimination of NTBs and TBs.
(b) The level of development in the manufacturing sector varies considerably among the individual countries in SAARC. In few cases, the manufacturing sector is large in size, complex in structure, and important in terms of its contribution to total GDP. In many cases, the sector it is at an early stage of development and its contribution is very low. This brings in a range of reservations and inhibitions among the contracting nations. This is where India has to play a critical role in investing in manufacturing sector in these countries with arrangements like buy back. There should be a clear integration of trade and investment activities. This implies an in-built mechanism that allows free access to the products of these investor companies in any of the member country's markets.
(c) India's private sector is fairly strong and could make a solid economic instrument along with the private foreign investors. From the experiences of other regional bloc, one could convincingly argue that wherever the private sector tended to decide the agenda and also heavily influence the direction and contents of trade liberalisation measures, the groupings have seen quite a few breakthrough in the process towards a free trade regime.
(d) A free trade regime requires not only a total reorientation of the existing systems and legal regimes but also a massive intervention in terms of infrastructural and institutional reforms. India has to initiate this process immediately and also help the member countries in coping with the needs and other specifics required in the new trade regime. It also requires a considerable degree of harmonisation and coordination in some of the macroeconomic policies, particularly trade.
India has to adopt very comprehensive trade facilitating measures simultaneously with the process of liberalisation in

the area of customs cooperation including simplification and harmonisation of trade documents and procedures so as to reduce the cumbersome, time-consuming and costly proced- ures that were currently faced by the business community in the conduct of international trade.

(e) India has to be pro-active in the promotional measures to enhance the volume of intra-regional trade manifold. These include:

- Broadening assistance to business community to help it take advantage of existing intra-regional opportunities.
- Organising buyer–seller meetings, marketing missions, general trade fairs, specialised trade fairs, investment pro- motion.
- Extending support to chambers of commerce and industry across South Asia.
- Providing specialised services in export financing, export quality management and export packaging trade at the regional level.
- Training trade related human resource development and import operation and techniques at the regional level.
- Campaigns for regional products.[23]

Investment: Challenges and Options

Despite massive reforms and widely liberal foreign direct investment policies in most of the SAARC member countries, this region has received very insignificant foreign direct investment inflows (Table 5.1). The FDI flow to South Asia started picking up only in the mid-nineties. As compared to the 1986 inflow, the 2001 inflow of FDI increased more than 15-fold from $255 million to $4,069 million as against a little over nine-fold increase in the global total foreign investment flows. As a result, the share of South Asia in the global FDI flows gradually reached 0.55 per cent in 2001 from a mere 0.23 per cent in 1990. Similarly, its share in the total FDI inflows to developing countries and Asian countries also recorded a marginal increase from 1.8 to 1.99 per cent and from 3.6 to 3.99 per cent respectively during the 16-year-period of 1986–2001 (Table 5.4).

Table 5.4
Foreign Direct Investment: Inflows and Outflows
Percentage Share of World Total (in Million US$)

	Inflows (% of World)			Outflows (% of World)		
	1990	1995	2001	1990	1995	2001
World	203,812	331,844	735,146	240,253	357,537	620,713
Bangladesh	0.00	0.00	0.01	0.00	−0.02	0.00
Bhutan	0.00	0.00	0.00	0.00	0.00	0.00
India	0.08	0.65	0.46	0.00	0.03	0.12
Maldives	0.00	0.00	0.00	0.00	0.00	0.00
Nepal	0.00	0.00	0.00	0.00	0.00	0.00
Pakistan	0.12	0.22	0.05	0.00	0.00	0.00
Sri Lanka	0.02	0.02	0.02	0.00	0.00	0.00
SAARC-7	0.22	0.89	0.54	0.00	0.01	0.12

Source: UNCTAD, *World Investment Report*, various issues.

Why has there been a halting pace in the FDI inflows to South Asia, is a question asked many a times. Besides the usual explanations of poor infrastructure, bureaucratic hurdles and politically unstable situations, one argument that may provide a theoretical underpinning to this is the basic development strategy based on import substitutions followed by the South Asian countries.[24]

India has been consistently taking an overwhelming part of the FDI flows into South Asia which has gone up from 34 per cent in 1980–85 to 83.6 per cent in 2001. On the other hand, the shares of Pakistan and Sri Lanka have drastically gone down (Table 5.5).

Table 5.5
Percentage Share of SAARC Member Countries in the Total Foreign Direct Investment Inflows in South Asia: 1986–2001

Year	SAARC Countries	Bangla-desh	India	Maldives	Nepal	Pakistan	Sri Lanka
1980–85	178.8	−0.06	34.68	−0.17	0.11	41.95	23.49
1990–95	1,184.8	0.51	59.33	0.59	0.51	32.83	9.28
1990	458	0.66	35.37	0.00	1.31	53.28	9.39
1995	2,753	0.07	71.34	0.25	0.18	26.12	2.03
2000	3,095	9.05	74.93	0.42	0.00	9.85	5.75
2001	4,069	1.92	83.63	0.29	0.47	9.46	4.23

Source: UNCTAD, *World Investment Report*, various issues.

This is despite the fact that Sri Lanka started economic reform measures in 1977 and together with Pakistan has one of the most liberalised foreign investment regimes, whereas India is yet to open the services sector and other sectors like agriculture. This relatively better inflow to India can broadly be attributed to better infrastructural facilities, long spell of political stability, availability of technical manpower and professionals of a huge variety, long established traditions of corporate bodies and private sector, and international exposure in terms of trade, professional and technology transfer.

State of Intra-regional Investments

The continuous absence of any cross-border investments from within the region has been a major issue in strengthening the process of regional cooperation and integration in South Asia. Except a number of Indian joint ventures in Nepal, Sri Lanka, Bangladesh and Bhutan, there are no intra-regional reciprocal investments worth the name.

The bias against the regional partners are inborn in the governmental machineries which so far monopolised the decision-making process, and literally kept the private sector alienated from the mainstream economic participation. Otherwise, how can we explain the flourishing of a large garment sector in many parts of South Asia with clandestine association of the private sector from across the region?

The issues related to FDI from within the region stand to be very critical in today's context, particularly when the focus is increasingly turning towards the regionalisation of economic benefits. This needs to be looked into, as extensively as possible, keeping natural resource management, technology, domestic participation, labour market and internal resources in mind.

The SAARC should more vocally address itself to these issues of regional investments so that the cream of business and industrial activities remain in the region. The SAARC Fund for Regional Projects, established in 1991, mainly to make funds available for identification and development of regional projects, has completed 13 feasibility studies in different areas.

In spite of distinct proximity, market advantage and socio-cultural similarities, South Asia has never been a destination for the Indian investors. The share of South Asia in the total Indian joint ventures have hardly been 6 per cent (total 65 units) in 1976, 8 per cent (total 140 units) in 1983 and 14 per cent (total 185 units) in 1995. Southeast Asia constituted over 30 per cent, Africa over 15 per cent and Middle East over 10 per cent. In Bangladesh, registered foreign investment up to June 1999 stood at 1,005 units in which the regional partners have very insignificant presence, i.e., India (7 per cent), Pakistan (5 per cent) and Sri Lanka (1 per cent). Origin of investors and sectors of India investment are also varied in Bangladesh (Table 5.6).

Table 5.6
Characteristic Features of Indian Investment in Bangladesh

Investor's Origin	No. of Units	Sectors	Present Status
Bangalore	2	Readymade garments accessories; vegetable seeds.	11 units in production,
Mumbai	7	Automobile; basic pharmaceuticals; fertiliser; industrial chemical; LPG storage, bottling, distribution and marketing; cement clinker.	2 units in operation, 9 units implemented,
Kolkata	31	Textiles; air-conditioning; building industry; cement concrete poles, railway slippers; software development; jute; hospital and clinics; lamination for packaging materials; audio, video, satellite cable television equipments; dyes, chemicals and pigments and colours; bead wire ring; cold storage; woollen textiles, power transmission distribution and telecommunication instrument; steel MS and GI; amusement parks; plywood; copper wire; hotels; khair catechu; flaps used in tyres; jam, jelly squash, fruit piece; wood veneer.	6 units under implemen- tation, 42 units not yet implemented.
Delhi	9	Building industry; textile spinning; hatcheries and poultry; readymade garments; media paper; cutting polishing and finishing of natural stones, IE granites, marble slate; adhesive and chemicals; hotel and motel; cold rolling steel mill.	
Chennai	4	Bakery and confectionery; drugs and pharmaceuticals; cosmetics, non-metallic mineral processing.	
Others	17	Motorcycles; toiletries and cosmetics; ball point pen; electric meter; tea processing packaging and bagging; printing lamination, multi-layer film; integrated agro-based project; transformers; fertiliser and chemicals; hospital.	

Source: Board of Investment, Dhaka.

India is a major player in Nepal constituting almost 33 per cent of the total number of industries under joint ventures with foreign companies. Over 49 per cent Indian joint ventures in Nepal are in the manufacturing sector followed by 24 per cent in tourism sector and 21 per cent in services sector (Table 5.7). Again, despite so much of talk about the hydel potentials of Nepal and the known captive market in India, there is not a single major Indian joint venture in this particular sector as yet. This clearly shows that there continues to remain a whole array of hitches that make the hydel sector unattractive.

Table 5.7
Joint Ventures in Nepal, 1988/89—2002/03

Country	No.	Total Project Cost (in Million Rs)	Total Fixed Cost (in Million Rs)	Foreign Investment (in Million Rs)	Employ- ment
Bangladesh	10	330.67	175.74	99.22	3,401
Bhutan	3	27.26	20.58	3.61	98
China	77	8,051.06	6,635.74	2,498.13	7,571
France	21	441.17	375.63	110.94	1,043
Germany	38	1,691.88	1,548.05	560.79	2,657
Hong Kong	12	1,221.79	1,067.60	437.62	2,064
India	279	29,322.77	22,473.00	7,861.42	36,346
Italy	13	1,234.90	1,121.40	188.81	295
Japan	88	2,809.20	2,421.26	925.23	5,247
Pakistan	10	307.34	222.17	129.47	2,331
South Korea	37	1,701.94	1,424.52	876.76	2,942
Sri Lanka	3	79.15	55.90	37.41	83
Switzerland	18	513.90	441.86	135.88	324
UK	27	1,888.40	1,625.09	166.61	5,240
USA	84	12,629.68	11,496.67	4,018.18	7,810
Others*	115	21,484.00	17,492.01	4,538.88	14,873
Total	835	83,735.11	68,597.22	22,588.96	92,325

Source: Department of Industry, HMG/Nepal, July 2003.
* Others include Australia, Austria, Belgium, Bermuda, Brazil, Canada, Denmark, Finland, France, Germany, Guatemala, Iran, Ireland, Israel, Italy, Malaysia, North Korea, New Zealand, Norway, Panama, Philippines, Taiwan, Thailand, Turkey and Ukraine.

India is the third largest foreign investor in Sri Lanka. The total number of Indian companies approved by the Board of Investment (BOI) in Sri Lanka, as on August 2003, is 108 with the amount of investment of Rs 32,685.22 million. Out of these projects, 60 companies are in commercial operation in various sectors. The preferred sector by Indians has been textiles, cement, steel mills,

light engineering, pharmaceuticals, agriculture, dairy, food process-
ing, hotels, restaurants, computer software, chemical, petroleum,
rubber and plastic (Table 5.8).

Table 5.8
Indian Investment in Sri Lanka under BOI (as on August 2003)

Project Status	Number of Companies	Estimated Investment (in Million Rs)	Manpower
Approved/Awaiting agreement	15	8,907.71	1,629
Awaiting implementation	18	7,057.31	2,294
Awaiting commercial operation	15	2,994.88	1,656
In commercial operation	60	13,725.32	10,330
Total	108	32,685.22	15,909

Source: Board of Investment of Sri Lanka, 2003.

At present, the leading sectors attracting investment to Sri Lanka are
steel, cement, rubber products, tourism, computer software, IT training and other professional services. The major Indian companies that
are participating in the investment activities in Sri Lanka include:
Gujarat Ambuja, Asian Paints, Larsen & Toubro, Tata Infotech,
Aptech Ltd, NIIT, Apollo Hospital, Ansal Housing Construction Ltd,
Mahindra British Telecom, Life Insurance Corporation of India and
Indian Oil Company. In the meantime, CEAT and Taj Hotel are
expanding their operations in Sri Lanka. The entire profile of investors has undergone visible changes. Other big players have emerged.
It is mostly private parties rather than the government-aided JVs.
Sectoral participations have also recorded drastic changes. Previously, the emphasis was mainly on agriculture-based activities, and
now it is essentially manufacturing and the services sector. Merger
and acquisition (M&A) operations across the border have started
taking place. Berger India has acquired Jenson and Nicholson Nepal
which was a 100 per cent subsidiary of Jenson and Nicholson in India.

Regional Allocations

The direction of Indian investment within a country, in terms of both
location and sectors chosen, also needs to be readdressed if these
investments are to make some social contributions for the long-term
interest of the host countries. This is more so as regional disparity
has been prominently figuring in many of these countries as one of

the major factors behind the internal discontentments and squabbles. Lack of productive activities and sustainable income sources in some specific region have been the major cause for regional disparity and income inequality. If adequate income generating activities are initiated in these regions, the situation could drastically improve. In other words, development has to take place in the conflict zones then only can one grapple with the conflictual dynamics. It is seen that most of the Indian investment ventures in Nepal are concentrated in the Central Development Region, i.e., in and around Kathmandu,[25] whereas there is virtually no venture in the most neglected areas, including western regions, where Maoists have now established themselves firmly (Table 5.9).

Table 5.9
Nepal: Development Region-wise Location of Operational Joint Ventures

	Eastern	Central	Western	Mid-West	Far-West	Total
India	2	48	2	1		53
Bhutan	1	1				2
Pakistan		1	1			2

Source: Computed from *Nepal and the World: A Statistical Profile* (various issues), Federation of Nepalese Chambers of Commerce and Industry, Kathmandu, Nepal.

Similarly in Sri Lanka, the factories are concentrated in the Western Province, especially in the Colombo and Gampaha districts. This is because of proximity to harbour and airport, close access to product and labour markets, and infrastructure facilities. This has created problems related to scarcity of labour and poor infrastructure, environmental pollution, escalation of real estate prices and congestion in the city. Board of Investment (BOI) now actively encourages the setting up of export-oriented factories in other parts of the country including in the newly developed industrial zones at Koggala zone where it finds easy to provide infrastructure facilities and security and to monitor these enterprises.[26]

The proposed India-Sri Lanka land bridge between Dhanushkodi (Southeast of Tamil Nadu state) and Talaimannar (North-West Sri Lanka) will have a relatively high impact on the northern part of Sri Lanka.[27] Being a multi-purpose project, this land bridge initiative will enhance trade in both manufacturing and a number of service sectors, which are strategically important for both countries. Apart from quick movement of goods and passenger traffic, it can facilitate transmission of electricity and natural gas, and integrate the telecommunication links. The proposed bridge can also establish a link between northern Sri Lanka and southern India, and generate multifaceted benefits to the people of both countries.

While bringing about drastic changes in its traditional mode of economic diplomacy, based more on specific geopolitical considerations, India has to play a pivotal role in the following areas:

(a) The idea of establishing a Business Council on Investment Flows with the private sectors of each country, basically to analyse the role of MNCs, to develop South Asia-based MNCs, to explore possibilities of trade creating joint ventures, to maintain inventory of investment laws, accounting and legal regimes, and to harmonise them across the region, should be given the top priority.

(b) A comprehensive regional convention encompassing the details, potentials and implications of investment both from within and outside the region needs to be put in place. The SAARC Secretariat has already initiated this process which needs to be debated and deliberated by the entire spectrum of stakeholders. This could finally lead to a Common Investment Area.[28]

(c) To encourage investment within the region, a green channel for investments, technology transfer, joint ventures, etc., should be set up thereby according the investor from the region the same status as the domestic investor.[29] A mechanism should be evolved which allows these investing companies to enjoy the benefits of free trade environment immediately, without having to wait until SAFTA is realised.

(d) The Group of Eminent Persons (GEP) recommended that the relatively more developed countries of South Asia should permit partial convertibility of their respective currencies on capital account, for the limited purpose of investment in the least developed and small economies of the region.[30]

India and South Asia in WTO

There are several issues that the SAARC member countries can work together for in the international forum. In fact, this will be one of the most crucial ways in which the member countries can build confidence among themselves, and to a large extent, dilute conflicts emanating from outstanding bilateral and regional politico-strategic chicaneries. Though SAARC clearly lays down 'strengthening co-operation with other developing countries; strengthening cooper-ation among themselves in international forums on matters of common interests and cooperating with international and regional organisations with similar aims and purposes'[31] as its major objectives, the process of making a common stand in the international forum and collective bargaining started only in the last few years.

The Seattle Meeting of World Trade Organisation held in Decem-ber 1999 triggered off an array of activities by South Asian Govern-ments and other bodies. This was for the third time[32] that the SAARC countries showed some kind of collective will to address their com-mon concerns and problems. The WTO-related issues are now taken seriously by the SAARC member states as a collective voice and effort. A Joint Statement was released by the SAARC Commerce Ministers from Male in August 1999. This was issued with a view to adopting a common position in advance of the Third WTO Ministerial Meeting at Seattle in 1999.[33]

Movement of Natural Persons

For a region like South Asia, remittances from abroad are very crucial in its balance of payment and foreign exchange management. More than this, the real integration with the world economy of this region will only be possible if there are free flow of goods, services, capital, and the people to other countries. There are 1,678,765 Indians in the US,[34] which is the single largest destination of Indian migrant labour. Beneficiaries from India dominate the H–1B programme—accounting for nearly half of the total in 2000 and 2001. Not only in IT, India born beneficiaries lead in other occupations as well.

International Monetary Fund published a list of 20 developing countries with the volume of remittances and its percentage share of GDP (Table 5.10). A majority of the South Asian countries figured in this wherein India ranked as number one in terms of the volume of remittances with US $11 billion, and that contributed 2.6 per cent of the GDP. For all these countries, the US is a vital source. For Pakistan, the highest of its remittances come from the US, which is over 30 per cent.

Table 5.10
South Asian Countries: Remittances from Abroad

Rank	Country	Remittances (US $ Million)	% of GDP
1	India	11,097	2.6
7	Bangladesh	1,803	4.1
8	Pakistan	1,707	2.7
18	Sri Lanka	1,056*	6.9

Source: International Monetary Fund, *Balance of Payment Statistics*, Washington, 2000.
* 61.7 per cent from Middle East countries, and 7.3 per cent is from North America, 13.6 per cent from European Union.

Therefore, at least the demand in general by the developing countries about Temporary Movement of Natural Persons (TMNP–Mode 4) is vital in the ongoing trade negotiation process.[35] As of today, the TMNP accounts for less than 2 per cent of global services trade. A study done by Walmsley and Alan Winters in 2002 indicate that through increasing developed countries' quotas on inward labour movements by 3 per cent of their labour, world welfare would rise by $156 billion.[36]

In the past, responses of most of the developed countries, including the US, to this demand of the developing countries have been marred by a large number of questions and resistance.[37] This included extreme political sensitivity to the very question of TMNP as reflected in various laws and other legal regimes, including the immigration provisions, and conscious equating of temporary mobility with the larger issue of migration, both legal and illegal, and forced and voluntary.

This is in sharp contrast to the market demand situation in the developed countries where demand for skilled work forces has increased as against the backdrop of fast ageing population. The existing skilled workers in the developed countries cater mostly to the upper echelons of the job market, thereby leaving a major supply gap in the lower echelons.

The South Asian countries are at fault too. There are scores of examples ranging from illegal emigration to misuse of even H–1B and L–1 visas by the South Asian people and the companies.[38] The domestic pressure on United States regarding the rights of and job opportunities for locals have brought visible frictions. Potential friction results from a combination of social, economic and political factors. So the problem has to be tackled on all fronts in a coherent manner.

However, for the South Asian countries Mode–4 is very important from the bilateral, regional and multilateral perspectives to promote and exploit linkages between supply of services, and trade in goods. These countries have specifically asked for commitments of the US on:

(a) a visa system to ensure fulfillment of sectoral and horizontal commitments undertaken, as well as grant of multi-entry visa for professionals;

(b) on independent professional, de-linked from commercial presence;

(c) allowing inter-firm mobility to professionals;

(d) expansion in the scope and coverage of other persons and specialists to include middle level professionals;

(e) sector specific movement in architecture, health, computer related services, audio-visual services, tourism, etc.;

(f) issue of recognition of qualification which needs establishment of multilateral principles and monitoring mechanism;

(g) quota limits that should be raised to meet higher demand in USA.

India has to play a major role in putting forward these demands of SAARC member states in collaboration with other partners in the WTO forum.

Conclusion

South Asia's huge natural resources endowment, emerging market, strong institutional and legal frameworks, English-speaking professional and entrepreneurial class, and impressive scientific and technical skills have attracted many nations towards itself, and have ushered in the phenomenon of market-led economic reforms and tremendous growth. The most important interest of India in South Asia lies in encouraging and supporting continued economic reforms in the region leading to faster and well-distributed growth. This would provide both expanded market and political stability—the two key elements in India's foreign policy dynamics. Economic relations in non-traditional ways and sectors should, therefore, be the focal point of India's engagement with the region. The interdependence that is emerging as a new paradigm in the region should be India's pet project rather than the present scattered approach to multi-regionalism.

Notes and References

1. Fiscal austerity, privatisation and market liberalisation are the three pillars of Washington Consensus extended throughout eighties and nineties. Rehman Sobhan, *Experiences with Economic Reform: A Review of Bangladesh's Development, 1995*. University Press Limited, Dhaka, 1996; S.P. Gupta (ed.), *Liberalisation: Its Impact on the Indian Economy*. Macmillan, Delhi, 1993; Bibek Debroy (ed.), *Challenges of Globalisation*. Konark, Delhi, 1998; B.M. Jauhari, *Economic Liberalisation and Globalisation*. Commonwealth Publishers, Delhi, *1996*, Syed Nawab Haider Naqvi and Khwaja Sarmad, *External Shocks and Domestic Adjustments: Pakistan's Case 1970–1990*. Oxford, Karachi, 1997, S.A. Mirza, *Privatisation in Pakistan*. Ferozsons (Pvt) Ltd, Lahore, 1995; W.D. Lakshman (ed.), *Dilemmas of Development: Fifty Years of Economic Change in Sri Lanka*. Sri Lanka Association of Economists, Colombo, 1997.
2. Mahendra P. Lama, 'Globalisation and South Asia: Primary Concerns and Vulnerabilities', *International Studies*. Sage, April–June, New Delhi, 2001.
3. Mahendra P. Lama, 'South Asia—US Trade and Economic Relations: Opportunities and Challenges in the Changing Dynamics of Interdependence', in the workshop on 'America's Role in Asia: South Asia Workshop' organised by Asia Foundation, Dhaka, February, 2004.
4. E. Voutira and Shaun A.W. Brown, *Conflict Resolution: A Review of Some Non-Governmental Practices*. Refugees Studies Programme, 1995, and Raimo Vayrynen (ed.), *New Directions in Conflict Theory: Conflict Resolutions and Conflict Transformations*. Sage, London, 1991.
5. For further theoretical and case study discussions, see Hugh Miall and others, *Contemporary Conflict Resolution*. Polity Press, Cambridge, 2001 and M Cranna, (ed.), *The True Cost of Conflict*. Earthscan, London, 1994.
6. *Business and Conflict Resolution*. Institute for Multi-Track Diplomacy, Washington DC, 2000; Maurice Schiff and L. Alan Winters, *Regional Integration and Development*. World Bank and Oxford, Washington, 2003; Miroslav N. Jovanovic, *International Economic Integration: Limits and Prospects*. Routledge, London, 1998.
7. Mahendra P. Lama, 'Designing Economic Confidence Building Measures: Role of India in South Asia', in *India's Pivotal Role in South Asia, CASAC*. New Delhi, 2000.
8. This author has done an empirical study of how MNCs act as negative stakeholders essentially thriving on adverse relationship between India and Pakistan.

Mahendra P. Lama, Monograph on *Regional Economic Cooperation in South Asia: A Commodity Approach* published by the Society for Peace, Security and Development Studies, Dept of Defence and Strategic Studies, University of Allahabad, Allahabad, 1997, and also 'Integrating the Tea Sector in South Asia: New Opportunities in the Global Market', *South Asian Survey*, Delhi, January–June, 2001.

9. Mahendra P. Lama, 'Changing Facets of Conflict and CBMs in South Asia,' paper presented in the Faculty Workshop on 'Peace and Conflict Studies: South Asian and Western Perspectives', organised by JNU and Kroc Institute, University of Notre Dame, USA, New Delhi, March 2000.

10. Sakbani, Michael, 'Pivotal Countries in a Two-Track World: Regionalization and Globalization', *Cooperation South*, no. 1, New York, 1998.

11. Mansfield, Edward D. and Helen V. Miner, *The Political Economy of Regionalism*. Columbia University Press, New York, 1997. Also see Maurice Schiff and L. Alan Winters, *Regional Integration and Development*. World Bank and Oxford, Washington, 2003; Miroslav N. Jovanovic, *International Economic Integration: Limits and Prospects*. Routledge, London, 1998.

12. El-Agraa, Ali M., *Regional Integration: Experience, Theory and Measurement*. Macmillan, London, 1999.

13. World Bank, 'Trade Policies in South Asia: An Overview', Poverty Reduction and Economic Management, South Asia Region, May 2003 (unpublished draft).

14. The major item falling in this category are vegetable ghee, acrylic and other synthetic yarn, plastic and articles in case of Nepal's exports to India and copper-related products including scraps from Sri Lanka. See Mahendra P. Lama, 'Nepal' in 'Trade Cooperation and Economic Policy Reform in South Asia (TRACE): The Cases of Bangladesh, India, Nepal, Pakistan and Sri Lanka', organised by Bangladesh Institute of Development Studies, Dhaka and European Union Dhaka (to be published in 2004), and in Mukherji, Tilani Jayawardhana and Saman Kelegama, 'Indo-Sri Lanka Free Trade Agreement: An Assessment of Potential and Impact', Research paper prepared for South Asia Network of Research Institutes (SANEI), New Delhi, 2003.

15. Historically, India maintained extensive non-tariff barriers on many imports, bases on balance of payments reason. However, in 1999, a WTO dispute panel ruled that these restrictions were no longer justifiable, which prompted India (in 2001) to remove many of its quantitative import restrictions (although many of these barriers were replaced with high tariffs). Congressional Research Service (CRS) Report for Congress received through the CRS web; Wayne Morrison and Alan Kronstadt, 'US-Indian Economic Relations', Foreign Affairs, Defense, and Trade Division.

16. Indra Nath Mukherji, 'Towards a Free Trade Area in South Asia: Charting a Feasible Course for Trade Liberalisation with Reference to India's Role', Jawaharlal Nehru University, New Delhi in collaboration with the Research and Information System, New Delhi, October 2002.

17. 'Para tariffs' mean border charges and fees, other than tariffs, on foreign trade transactions of a tariff-like effect which are levied solely on imports, but not indirect taxes and charges, which are levied in the same manner on like domestic products. Import charges corresponding to specific services rendered are not considered as para-tariff measures. The 'non-tariffs' mean any measure,

regulation or practice other than tariffs and para-tariffs, the effect of which is
to restrict imports, or to significantly distort trade. 'Direct trade measures' mean
measures conducive to promoting mutual trade of contracting states, such as
long and medium-term contracts containing import and supply commitments
in respect of specific products, buy back arrangement, state trading operations
and government and public procurement. *Agreement on SAARC Preferential
Trading Arrangement (SAPTA)*, SAARC Secretariat, Kathmandu, 1993.

18. SCCI, Consolidated National Schedules of Concessions Granted by each Member Country under 1st, 2nd & 3rd Rounds of Trade Negotiations under SAPTA, 1999.
19. Poonam Barua, *Towards a Free Trade Arrangement in South Asia*. IIFT, New Delhi, 1995; 'Making SAFTA a Reality: India's Critical Role', a three page note circulated in Public Affairs Management, August, Delhi; B. Bhattacharya and Vijaya Katti, *Regional Trade Enhancement: SAPTA and Beyond*. IIFT, New Delhi, 1996; Mukherji, *South Asian Preferential Trading Arrangement: Assessing Trade Flows in the First Round of Trade Negotiations*. Friedrich-Naumann-Stiftung, New Delhi, 1995; Mahendra P. Lama, 'SAARC: Shallow Regionalism, Political Abstinence and Economic Imperatives', *BIISS Journal*, vol. 21, no. 1, Dhaka, 2000.
20. Mahendra P. Lama, 'Trade will Bring us Together: Lets Trade', *Himal South Asian*, Kathmandu, 2000.
21. SAARC Secretariat, *Framework Agreement on South Asian Free Trade Area*, Kathmandu, 2004.
22. J.B. Kelegama, 'Indo-Sri Lanka Free Trade Agreement', *South Asian Survey*, vol. 6, no. 2, July–December, New Delhi, 1999.
23. UNCTAD, *Handbook of Economic Integration and Cooperation Groupings of Developing Countries*, vol. 1, Geneva, 1996, p. 62.
24. Mahendra P. Lama, 'Investment in South Asia: Trends and Issues', *South Asian Economic Journal*, Colombo, March 2000.
25. Most of the Indian joint ventures in Nepal are located in Kathmandu. HMG, Department of Industries, Kathmandu.
26. *Sri Lanka Investment Policy and Incentives*, Board of Investment of Sri Lanka, 2003; *Annual Reports* (various issues), Central Bank of Sri Lanka, Colombo; *Socio-Economic and Consumer Finance Survey* (various issues), and Muthukrishna Sarvananthan, 'Needs Assessment for Employment Generation through Local Economic Development in the North and East Province of Sri Lanka', ILO, March 2003.
27. The Government of India and the Government of Sri Lanka signed a Memorandum of Understanding to build a bridge across the Palk Strait in July 2002. This is aimed at connecting the island nation with the mainland of South Asia by road and rail through India.
28. UNCTAD, *Handbook of Economic Integration and Cooperation Groupings of Developing Countries*, vol. 1, Geneva, 1996. Augusto de la Torre and Margaret R. Kelly, *Regional Trading Arrangements*. IMF, Washington DC, 1992.
29. Recommended by the PHD Chamber of Commerce and Industry, New Delhi, September 1999.
30. Group of Eminent Persons (GEP), *Executive Summary and Recommendations of the Report of the Group of Eminent Persons*. New Delhi, 1999.

31. *South Asian Association for Regional Cooperation: A Profile*. SAARC Secretariat, Kathmandu, 1998; *Declaration of the Tenth SAARC Summit, Colombo*, Kathmandu, 1998.

32. The first time a common position was adopted by the member states of SAARC which was prior to the United Nations Conference on Environment and Development (UNCED) held in Rio de Janeiro also known as Rio Summit in 1992.

33. *Newsletter*, March–April and September–October 1999, SAARC Secretariat, Kathmandu.

34. *Dynamics of International Migration from India: Its Economic and Social Implications, August 2003*, Ministry of External Affairs 2001, as quoted by ESCAP.

35. The General Agreement on Trade in Services (GATS) covers four different modes of supply:
    Mode 1: cross-border supply of services
    Mode 2: consumption abroad
    Mode 3: establishment of a commercial presence
    Mode 4: movement of persons providing the service.

36. Presentation by Manab Majumdar, WTO Division, FICCI, New Delhi, 2003.

37. *Making Global Trade Work for People*. UNDP, New York, 2003.

38. Some law makers while making presentation to the International Relations Committee of the House of Representatives alleged that made corporations including premier Indian information technology companies outrageous and fraudulent abuse of L visas programme. *The Hindu*, New Delhi, 6 February 2004.

6

THE UNITED STATES AND
THE ASIAN POWERS

Chintamani Mahapatra

When World War II came to an end, there was not a single country in Asia worthy of the name—Asian Power. But its global reach and a robust military presence in Asia eminently qualified the United States to be an Asian power. Today, there are three countries, which are generally considered as Asian powers—Japan, China and India. Soon after the end of World War II, Japan was a war-devastated country with thousands of American troops present in that country as an occupation force. China was undergoing a civil war between the nationalist forces and the communist forces. India was fighting the last leg of its struggle against the British colonial rule. During a large part of the Cold War era, Japan was a strategic ally of the United States, China was for some time in the hostile camp led by the USSR, and for some time made a common cause with the US to contain the spread of Soviet influence in Asia; and India remained a non-aligned country. However, the United States had viewed these three countries in more or less black and white terms in view of its strong Cold War relations with the USSR. The end of the Cold War more or less coincided with the Chinese economic boom, the Indian initiative to institute far-reaching economic reforms, and lacklustre performance of the Japanese economy. The US, having acquired the status of the sole superpower, accordingly, began to readjust its equations with the three Asian heavyweights on the basis of uncertain political ties and economic realities of the post-Cold War era.

Japan

Japan was regarded as one of the Big Five international powers since World War I. Japan had worked closely with the US since the late nineteenth century until 1931.[1] But it did not work as a junior partner of the US. It was a great power by its own merits. When Japan attacked Russia in 1904, President Theodore Roosevelt welcomed it thinking 'Japan is playing our game'. However, he 'soon feared that an overwhelming Japanese victory could threaten American interests as much as Russian expansionism did, so he skillfully mediated an end to the war'.[2] Japanese people perceived that Washington did not allow their country to consolidate the gains in the war and this led to anti-American riots in Tokyo.[3] Anti-Japanese sentiments in the US, in the wake of the Pearl Harbour, were equally strong, which led to the internment of 110,000 Japanese people (two-thirds of them US citizens) in western United States.

The Second World War ended in the Asia-Pacific with a big bang. Destruction of two Japanese cities by the American nuclear bombs not only culminated in Japanese surrender but also heralded the dawn of the nuclear age. More significantly, the war ended with the loss of major power status for Japan. Thus the US began its interaction with Japan in the post-war period by destroying its status as a major power. But Japan's defeat in the war not only altered its status and role but also turned it into an American occupation zone for about seven years until it regained its full sovereignty in 1952. The emergence of China as a communist country, the end of the Korean War without a clear victory for the US, and the simmering crisis in Indochina threatening the rise of another communist power in Asia led to a strategic reassessment of Japan's role in Washington's Asian strategy. If Chiang Kai-shek would not have been defeated in the Chinese civil war, he would have offered his service to turn China into a key American strategic partner in the Asia-Pacific region. The outcome of the Chinese civil war made it clear that Japan needed to be rehabilitated and befriended to act as a close American strategic ally in the region. It was certainly considered strategically unwise to leave Japan to its own fate, because Japan, left to itself, could reemerge as a military power with revengeful attitudes. The US policy makers considered it essential to rehabilitate Japan, turn the erstwhile adversary into an ally and use it as stepping stone to combat the emerging primary threat of the post-war era—spread of Soviet influence and communist ideology. How would the US befriend Japan, a country it nuclear bombed, in waging a Cold War against a war-time ally—the Soviet Union? The US policy makers decided to turn Japan into an anti-communist ally through a careful process of shaping its polity, encouraging and assisting its economic growth and prosperity, and simultaneously keeping it away from developing an independent military capability. With a new constitution almost dictated by the US occupation force and with in-built constitutional restrictions against militarisation, Japan's political and economic evolution unfolded during the Cold War era.

Japan found itself an American strategic ally by signing an agreement on bilateral security alliance in 1961. Japan provided military base facilities to the US and financial and material support to US forward-deployed forces. Under the US–Japan Treaty of Mutual Cooperation and Security, Japan continues till date to host a carrier battle group, the Third Marine Expeditionary Force, the Fifth Air Force, and the Army's Ninth Theater Support Command. The United States, moreover, continues to station thousands of US troops in Japan, and currently maintains more than 50,000 troops in Japan, about half of whom are stationed in Okinawa.[4] Throughout the Cold War period, Washington viewed its alliance with Japan as 'the cornerstone' of its security interests in Asia, and 'fundamental to regional stability and prosperity'.[5]

While Tokyo's role as a key ally of the US in the Cold War conflicts was largely confined to the Asia-Pacific region, rapid growth of the Japanese economy in the seventies and the eighties altered the image of Japan in the US. Japan came to be perceived as a threat to the US interests, particularly because of a coinciding decline of American influence in the world, and uninspiring national economic performance at home. Japanophobia gripped the United States, and books and articles proliferated explaining the rising power of Japan. There was a rising demand in the US to 'contain' an economically galloping Japan. The Japanese were accused of making use of their wealth to buy strategic land assets in the United States. As Japan came out as the largest creditor and number one banker in the world and evinced interest in playing a larger political and security role in the region, it appeared to Americans as if Tokyo was on the road towards playing a more independent role in Asian affairs. American apprehensions about Japan's promising proactive role in the Asia-Pacific were compounded by the outbreak of the second Cold War in the Southwest Asian region. In less than five years after the American military withdrawal from Indochina, and the rise of an independent and unified communist Vietnam, the Soviet Union militarily intervened in Afghanistan, put a puppet regime in Kabul, and threatened to expand its influence in the oil-rich Persian Gulf region.

Japan's role as a very crucial Cold War ally was less visible in America's anti-Soviet programmes and operations in Afghanistan in the eighties. The American focus had shifted from the Asia-Pacific in the post-Vietnam era to Southwest Asia, where Washington made use of Pakistan to drive the Soviet troops out of Afghanistan. It was China which played a larger role in containing Soviet influence in Indochina rather than Japan. Consequently, when the Cold War ended, US–Japan security relations began to drift rapidly. A bipartisan report by the Institute for National Strategic Studies of America's National Defence University correctly captured the mood in Washington and Tokyo in early nineties. It said:

> Once freed from the strategic constraints of containing the Soviet Union, both Washington and Tokyo ignored the real, practical, and pressing needs of the bilateral alliance. Well-intentioned efforts to find substitutes for concrete collaboration and clear goal-setting have produced a diffuse dialogue but no clear definition of a common purpose. Efforts to experiment with new concepts of international security have proceeded fitfully, but without discernable results in redefining and reinvigorating bilateral security ties.
>
> This lack of focus and follow-through has been evident in both countries. Some in Japan have been drawn to the notion of 'Asianization', and the hope that economic interdependence and multilateral institutions would put the region on a path similar to that of Europe. Many in the United States regarded the end of the Cold War as an opportunity to return to economic priorities.[6]

The drift in alliance stopped when North Korean nuclear ambitions came to the surface and a rape incident in Okinawa fuelled anti-American sentiments in Japan. The China-Taiwan political conflict in the wake of missile tests by China, during an election in Taiwan, and Washington's dispatch of a carrier battle group to South China Sea, further renewed American and Japanese attention to the need for redefining the bilateral security alliance in the new context of the post-Cold War era. The result was the 1996 US-Japan Joint Security Declaration and the revised Guidelines for US-Japan Defence Co-operation. The Okinawa incident was also tactfully handled and the two countries vowed to cooperate in expediting the development and deployment of missile defence systems.

However, the US came to lose interest in sustaining a high level attention on Japan by the late nineties. The prolonged Japanese recession made Japan appear 'incapable of renewing itself'. Some Japanese came to look at the US as 'arrogant' and 'unable to understand that its prescriptions are not universally applicable to other's economic, political and social needs'.[7] The US, at the same time, came to focus more on the growing Chinese economy, and the Washington's engagement of China, discouraged and dispirited Tokyo a great deal.

It appeared as if successful Japanese economy makes America nervous and lackluster performance of Japanese economy make Washington less caring of Japan. It was nonetheless obvious that the US policy makers did not plan to develop a strategic partnership with China at the cost of Japan. The US goal was only to take advantage of the growing Chinese economy. Beijing, in fact, did not keep its views secret that US-Japan alliance aimed at containing China's role in the region.[8]

Nuclear crisis in the Korean Peninsula, terrorist strike against the US, and the consequent US-led war against international terrorism, and the US military intervention in Iraq once again brought the US and Japan together. The American analysts now justify the importance of US–Japan security alliance on the following grounds:

> Major war in Europe is inconceivable for at least a generation, but the prospects for conflict in Asia are far from remote. The region features some of the world's largest and most modern armies, nuclear-armed major powers, and several nuclear-capable states. Hostilities that could directly involve the United States in a major conflict could occur at a moment's notice on the Korean peninsula and in the Taiwan Strait. The Indian subcontinent is a major flashpoint. In each area, war has the potential of nuclear escalation. In addition, lingering turmoil in Indonesia, the world's fourth-largest nation, threatens stability in Southeast Asia.[9]

All these make it important that the US and Japan stay together. Japan's strategic value to the US may have declined relative to China in recent years, but as the second largest economy in the world, with long-standing alliance relations with the US, Japan continues to cooperate with the US on strategic issues, and on issues of peace and conflict in Asia. Over the past several years, Washington has encouraged Japan to assume non-combat role in regional contingency. There are no fundamental differences between Japan and the US on vital questions of Asian security. The US successfully encouraged Japan recently to deploy naval ships in the Indian Ocean to support US military operations in Afghanistan, launch intelligence satellites, fund research on missile defence, buy Patriot missiles, and contribute troops to Iraq for facilitating reconstruction there—the first Japanese troops deployment to a combat zone since World War II. The passage of historic legislation allowing Japanese forces to participate in reconstruction and humanitarian mission in Iraq had US encouragement and backing. Japan, moreover, has been the most ardent supporter of the Bush administration's North Korea policy. It is with the US in latter's multilateral approach to North Korean nuclear issue in contrast to the bilateral one demanded by North Korea. While not supportive of the preemptive doctrine, it advocates, unlike China, Russia and South Korea, use of coercive diplomatic measures against North Korea.[10] Under US influence, Japan also made substantial contribution to reconstruction efforts in Afghanistan, and the political and economic rehabilitation of Iraq. The US currently supports the idea of raising the military capabilities of Japan. The US Department of Defence has prepared plans for giving necessary training to the Japanese military forces in appropriate US bases. This is viewed by some as the necessary first step towards reducing the US military troop deployment in Japan.[11] Washington is very well aware of a rising trend of nationalist sentiments in Japan. North Korean stand on nuclear issues and missile developments have further fuelled such sentiments in Japan. Some analysts in the US have raised indirect concern over open demand in Japan for acquiring nuclear weapons as a deterrent, but the US Administration does not seem perturbed. In fact, US officials in early 2003 obliquely told their Chinese counterparts that Japan might go nuclear unless the Chinese government succeed in persuading North Korea to abandon the nuclear path.[12]

Whatever may be the public posture of Washington on Japanese nationalism, no US government will allow Japan to develop a nuclear weapon capability. A nuclear Japan will find the American troops

deployment on its territory irrelevant, and demand immediate withdrawal of US soldiers. A nuclear Japan will reduce the American
predominant influence in Southeast Asia and the Pacific region.
Japanophobia may rise in the region in response to Japanese nuclear
tests, but it will be short-lived and the regional countries will soon
come to grips with the new situation by readjusting their policies to
the new ground realities. The US perhaps would be more concerned
about a nuclear Japan than even China and is generally expected to
reign in Japan's probable nuclearisation.

China

The US never had best of relations with China during the early Cold
War years. In fact, the tone was set by the very civil war in China,
in which the US sided with Mao's arch rival and nationalist Chiang
Kai-shek. The US had connived with Soviet leader Joseph Stalin
against Mao's communist forces. Stalin himself was apprehensive of
the emergence of a strong communist state to the east. In return for
several territorial and other benefits, he was ready to side with
Chiang. When Mao approached the US for friendship after knowing
Stalin's move, the Truman administration was not in a position to
accept Mao's offer of friendship.

The US policy makers, however, were visibly pleased with the
expanding Sino-Soviet rift since the mid-fifties and which continued
until the rise of the Gorbachev phenomenon in the former Soviet
Union. The reverses during the Korean War, specially after the
Chinese entry into the war, gradual US involvement in the Indochina
crisis and the growth of the Chinese military power, particularly
acquisition of nuclear capability, had made Americans increasingly
uncomfortable. When China conducted nuclear tests in 1964,
denuclearising China or helping India in developing a nuclear weapon
capability were very much in the air during official deliberations.[13]
By the late sixties, the US discovered that the Soviet Union was
getting more powerful, and the relative strength and influence of the
US around the world was diminishing. With intensification of the war
and rising US casualties in Vietnam, the Nixon–Kissinger team
adopted a new strategy and took a major step to use one communist
power to contain the spread of influence of the other in a new balance

of power game. The alternative in Washington's perception was emergence of a Chinese-dominated Southeast Asia, particularly if the US would abandon its involvement in Indochina crisis. President Richard Nixon and his national security advisor Henry Kissinger decided to open a line of communication with China with the ultimate goal of playing Beijing against Moscow. Later, President Jimmy Carter and his national security advisor Brzezinski cleared the ground to play the China card. China, of course, equally played the 'American card' vis-à-vis the Soviet Union. The US opened diplomatic relations with China, recognised Chinese claim over Taiwan on the basis of a 'one China and two systems' policy, enhanced its trade relations with that country, and began a process that would subsequently terminate the enemy image of the Chinese.

At the same time, the US sought to ensure that China's efforts to modernise its military remained within limits. A booming Chinese economy would materialise American dream of enjoying access to one of the largest markets of the world, but a militarily powerful China could pose a threat to American national security threats. President Bill Clinton, the first post-Cold War President of the US, criticised his predecessor during the 1992 presidential election for 'cuddling China'. But once in power, he ensured that his country developed a robust economic relations with China. Trade, Tibet, Taiwan and Human rights issues continued to hunt the US relations with China, and caused considerable political tension. But it was President Clinton who successfully initiated steps to de-link the human rights concern from bilateral trade issues and in the process, removed one of the strong irritants in the relationship. It was also President Clinton who fought for a permanent normal trade relationship with China and made the US Congress oblige him with the passage of a law in that regard. Washington, moreover, encouraged and supported the Chinese membership in the World Trade Organisation.

US-China trade relations reached a new peak during Clinton's presidency, and in fact, more than a hundred billion dollars of China's trade surplus created new irritants in the relationship. But more than economic friction, it was strategic issues that kept the trade partners divided. China was accused of spying in the US for missile technology and other high technology secrets. Clinton took a tough stand during the Chinese missile tests across the Taiwan Strait to influence the election outcome in Taiwan. The accidental bombing of the Chinese embassy during the NATO operations in Kosovo generated tremendous heat in US-China relations. During the 2000 Presidential elections, George Bush characterised China as a 'strategic competitor' and not a 'strategic partner' of the US raising Chinese suspicion of US motivations to new heights. The collision of a US spy plane with a Chinese aircraft over China's air space in early 2001 raised new political confrontation between the two countries.

The Americans remain divided over the country's China policy. There are anti-China lobbies and pro-China lobbies in the US. China's human rights record, continuation of communist rule, Chinese perennial mistrust of the US, Beijing's characterisation of the US as a hegemonic power, and China's enthusiasm to create a multi-polar world and alleged spying activities of the Chinese to acquire high-tech military technology in the US are cited by the anti-China groups to oppose the Government's cooperative policy towards China. But the trade and investment linkages with China have created a very robust pro-China lobby in the US. The American traders and business houses lobby against any strong US response to perceived Chinese misdeeds even in foreign policy and security areas. The oft-repeated argument is sometimes based on concocted figures about the number of American jobs linked to economic relations with China, which would be adversely affected if hostility between the two governments erupted.

The US Government realises the potential role of China in conflict resolution and conflict prevention in Asia. Although President George Bush initially branded China as a 'strategic competitor', the September 11 incident induced him to abandon that notion and quickly mend fences with the Chinese leaders. China offered strong public support to US war on terrorism, cooperated with the US in counter-terrorism efforts, publicly supported the US bombing operations in Afghanistan and is holding regular counter-terrorism dialogues with the US.[14] The US also managed to bring China on its side to deal with the nuclear dilemma of the Korean Peninsula. While China has its own stakes in a nuclear-free Korean Peninsula, it is believed that it was Beijing that assisted North Korea's WMD programmes, and often sided with North Korea against perceived excess Western pressure on the North Korean regime.

The US policy makers are very well aware of the benefits of Chinese cooperation in international arms control and proliferation efforts. They have also knowledge about the negative fallout of Chinese intransigence. By building robust economic linkages with China, the US has been able to develop a positive stake in China's growth and simultaneously erected leverages in that country. More than 100 US-owned multinational companies do business in China. Thousands of American-Chinese joint ventures have been worked out. The US investment in mainland China is more than $35 billion and in Hong Kong it is more than $40 billion. Thousands of American citizens live in Hong Kong to carry out their business activities. The two-way trade between the two countries is about to touch a hefty $200 billion. The bond between the two countries has been cemented to an extent where overt hostility and armed conflict can be safely ruled out.

India

The American political thinkers and policy makers never had the image of India as a huge market for American traders and business-men. When the US industrial progress led to a search for markets abroad in the late nineteenth century, it was Chinese market—not the Indian one—which looked attractive to the Americans. It was for China that the US had an open door policy. The reason is not difficult to find. India was under the tight control of the British Raj. And the British would clearly not entertain any 'open door' policy in the 'jewel' of their Crown. Even when India became independent a couple years after the end of World War II, the Americans did not look at India as an economic prize. There were several other places in the world, which were considered attractive for American business and investment. However, there was a big hope that India as a democratic country would join the US in its Cold War with the Soviet Union. When the Indian foreign policy under Prime Minister Jawaharlal Nehru's stewardship adopted a non-aligned strategy, it appeared to be a big blow to America's embryonic Asian strategy. Not many American analysts may subscribe to this view. But it was possible that a cooperative India at a time when China went communist and Soviet influence was spreading rapidly could have brought big bonanza for the US containment strategy. When US Secretary of State John Foster Dulles depicted non-alignment as immoral, his uneasiness with the Indian policy was amply mirrored on it.

However, a non-aligned India was never considered a potential threat to the US security interests. Had it been so, a United States which turned a hostile Japan into an ally and made common cause with communist China against its main communist adversary could have exerted additional efforts to keep India on its side. India could neither become an economic prize nor a strategic partner· of the United States in the post-war era. As India remained non-aligned and Pakistan surfaced as an intimately aligned country to the US, Indo-US political confrontations became frequent during the entire Cold War period. Supply of American weapons to Pakistan posed serious challenge to Indian security in view of Pakistan's persistently aggressive designs against India. When it appeared that India was being contained by advancing Pakistani military capabilities, some analysts believed that the United States was opposed to the expansion of Indian power, and considered Indian military augmentation as antithetical to American national security interests.

In any case, Washington had little anxiety, as Indian military capabilities, like its economy, had a 'Hindu rate' of growth. The Indian political leadership under the towering influence of Nehru never contemplated to make India a major military power. When the first commander-in-chief of the Indian armed forces, General Robert Lockhart, presented a paper to Prime Minister Nehru outlining the defence plan for expansion of independent India's Army, he said: 'We don't need a defence plan. Our policy is non-violence. We foresee no military threats. You can scrap the army. The police are good enough to meet our security needs'.[15] In fact, he directed on 16 September 1947 that the army's strength of 280,000 be brought down to 150, 000.[16] The Pakistani invasion of Kashmir in 1948 was a big bolt from the blue for India. But Nehru still did not have any grand desire to make India a military power of the region. He did foresee India as an Asian power and wanted India to play a significant role in Asian affairs, but not in the military and defence arenas. He followed a non-aligned foreign policy, which was against the very idea of formation of military alliances and which opposed foreign military presence—bases and/or troops. India did not have well-trained and well-equipped mountain divisions when China invaded Indian territory in 1962. A couple of years after invading India, China detonated a nuclear device and heralded the entry of China to the exclusive club of nuclear powers. Prime Minister Nehru was disappointed at the Chinese aggression, but stuck to his opposition to making India a nuclear power even after the dreadful experience with the Chinese. It is difficult to speculate how Nehru, if alive, would have reacted to the detonation of a nuclear device by China.

The United States had little to worry about India's idealistic foreign policy, and nothing to be apprehensive about a militarily weak India that was apparently pleased with its moral position and leadership in the non-aligned world. Some officials in the US government toyed with the idea of encouraging India to develop a nuclear weapon capability in the wake of imminent Chinese nuclear weapon tests, but soon abandoned the idea.[17] Indians themselves did not appear to be ready for taking a bold decision on going nuclear even in the post-Nehru era. With growing anticipation of a Chinese nuclear test, Indian nuclear physicist Homi Bhabha had, more than once, clearly articulated the need for developing a deterrence capability, but judging the mood of the political establishment, had expressed the view that if other nuclear powers would provide a nuclear umbrella there was no need to develop a weapon capability. Less than a year before the Chinese nuclear test, Homi Bhabha said during a Pugwash Conference in early 1964,

> nuclear weapons coupled with an adequate delivery system can enable a State to acquire the capacity to destroy more or less totally the cities, industry and all important targets in another State.... With the help of nuclear weapons, therefore, a State can acquire what we may call a position of absolute deterrence even against another having a many times greater destructive power under its control.[18]

Then he went on to argue,

> if any State is to be asked to renounce a possible dependence on nuclear weapons to redress the balance of power against a larger and more powerful State not having nuclear weapons, such as China, its security must be guaranteed by both the major nuclear powers.[19]

In other words, he hinted that India would need the guarantee from the US and the USSR against a possible nuclear strike before it would abandon a possible recourse to going nuclear.

The US would have disliked the emergence of a non-aligned nuclear weapon power as much as it did when communist China developed nuclear capability. But simultaneously, neither the Western Powers led by the US, nor the former Soviet leadership desired to extend a nuclear guarantee to non-aligned India. History is witness how Prime Minister Lal Bahadur Shastri sought in vain nuclear guarantee from other major powers, including the US after the Chinese nuclear tests. As if to add insult to India's injury, the US, along with other major powers, initiated steps that would seek to perpetuate the existing nuclear club, and simultaneously close the membership to any other country in the world. The outcome was a well-crafted discriminatory document known as the Nuclear Non-Proliferation Treaty (NPT) that would hunt US-Indian relations for decades to come.

While the non-aligned India was no threat to the American security, closer Indo-Soviet relations since the early seventies became a thorn in US-Indian relations. The relative decline of the American power and influence in the 1970s, the expansion of the Soviet influence around the world, and simultaneous growth of Indian conventional military power coupled with a nuclear test in 1974 hardly generated a propitious atmosphere for any positive upgrading in US-Indian relations. The American attempts to contain the Soviet influence by improving ties with China and equipping Pakistan with sophisticated military hardware especially since the Soviet invasion of Afghanistan in late seventies, in a way, got thwarted by rising Soviet influence in India and Indochina—on two sides bordering China. Washington appeared agitated, but could do little to forcefully address the issue.

This was precisely the time when the strategic planners in the US would not have liked to see the emergence of a militarily powerful India. The challenge of military supplies from the Soviet Union to India was met by promoting Pakistan's conventional military competence. The US kept making noises on nuclear proliferation at a time when India continued to refrain from developing nuclear weapons, and adopted a policy of keeping the options open. On the other hand, around this time, Pakistan relentlessly followed an aggressive and clandestine policy to acquire a nuclear weapon capability. What was clandestine for the large parts of the world were almost transparent for the US policy makers! Pakistan developed a nuclear weapon capability right under the American nose, even as the Regan and the senior Bush administrations maintained studied silence. They did not want to risk the policy to keep Pakistan on the American side in the war against the Soviet military presence in Afghanistan. India—the perceived Soviet friend—keeping options open for developing nuclear weapons, and Pakistan—a close American ally— developing a nuclear weapon capability—suited the larger American national security interests at the time.

However, as the Cold War relaxed and a new period of détente emerged in the late eighties and the early nineties, US-Indian relations turned increasingly positive and cooperative. The disintegration of the Soviet Union, irrelevance of non-alignment as a foreign policy strategy, institution of wide-ranging economic reforms in India, and the steady decline of Pakistan's strategic relevance in the post-Cold War world led to a re-examination of India policy in the US. There was a growing understanding in the US that India was emerging as an important international player in view of its long diplomatic experience, military capabilities, and prospective economic role in the world of trade and business. American analysts were not sure yet about India's place in the emerging world order, but began to perceive India as a probable new major player in global politics.

The American think tanks and analysts urged the new President Bill Clinton to take a fresh look at India. A report—*India and America after the Cold War*—prepared by the Carnegie endowment for International Peace urged the Clinton administration to give increased priority to India as a 'potential partner' in efforts to resolve disputes in and around the world.[20] Another study by Asia Society Study Mission—*South Asia and the United States after the Cold War*—recommended that economic issues should be the focal point of US engagement in South Asia.[21] The earlier US engagement in the region was largely focused on political and security issues. Indian economic reforms and the potentially huge market opportunities apparently caused such new thinking.

The US began to make friendly overtures towards India since the waning days of the Cold War, but more vigorously in the aftermath of the Soviet collapse. India optimistically responded. While economic engagement between the two countries intensified, enhanced level of military-to-military interactions too was contemplated. The Kickleighter proposal for improving military ties was presented to the US government around the time the Narashimha Rao government announced its economic reforms package. There was an emerging convergence of views in India and the US to forge stronger bilateral ties between the two countries in economic, as well as in military fields. While the rationales were different in New Delhi and Washington, the goal was similar. Ashley J. Tellis captures the mood in the US and India at this time when he writes:

> In the waning years of the Cold War, India responded eagerly to American overtures to cement a new relationship between the two countries...it was hoped that a deepening association with the United States across multiple dimensions—growing economic interaction, enhanced political understanding, increasing intelligence exchanges, and greater military-to-military ties—would provide India with a high level of strategic reassurance that would minimise the need for 'go it alone' strategies, including the necessity for dramatic changes in India's nuclear posture.[22]

The United States, on the other hand,

> viewed its evolving relationship with India from the perspective of a global power; it sought to acquaint itself with India as a regionally influential state that might some day become more powerful, and to the degree possible, sought to incorporate India into its vision of furthering regional stability in Asia.[23]

India did emerge as a more powerful country when it conducted a series of nuclear tests and declared itself as a nuclear weapon power. Such a development was never expected in the US. It, for a while, shocked and angered the US policy makers. India came under sanctions and a dark cloud appeared over the sky of US-Indian relations. But India soon proved itself to be a responsible new nuclear power. The dependability and credibility of nuclear India was best reflected in the way it handled the Kargil misadventure by Pakistan. Months after it tested nuclear devices and called itself a nuclear weapon power, Pakistan initiated the fourth round of armed hostility against India in Kargil. New Delhi saw to it that Pakistan was unable to raise the nuclear scare. In the mean time, the Indian economy, unlike that of Pakistan, prospered despite US sanctions, Asian financial crisis, and international recession. With a booming economy and new nuclear capabilities, India came to be viewed as a new Asian power on the rise. The roaring growth of information technology sector further altered the traditional image of India in the international community.

By making a path-breaking trip to India in 2000, President Bill Clinton laid the foundation of a new kind of relationship between a new nuclear India and the United States. He issued a vision statement with Prime Minister Atal Bihari Vajpayee to elevate the bilateral relations to new heights. How did the American analysts look at India in the post-Pokharan II era? Stephen Cohen, a seasoned analyst of South Asian affairs, came out with a new book—*India: Emerging Power.* He wrote:

> In the past four centuries India's influence in Asia has reached two high tides: under the Mughuls, India was one of Asia's two dominant cultural powers; under the British, it became the center of a pan-Asia empire. During the cold war, its power dwindled because of competition from the United States, Britain, and France in regions where (during the Raj) it had once held considerable influence.... Since the end of the cold war, the prospect of a resurgent India-in-Asia has become more realistic....[24]

But Cohen still had doubts about India's future. He wrote: 'In brief, India has the interests and ambitions of a great Asian power, although it still lacks some critical resources....'[25] One of the steps that India would have to take, according to Cohen, is

> to determine its relationship with the one non-Asia power that remains a power in Asia, the United States. In the past, New Delhi considered American interventions in Asia largely detrimental to its interests. Yet as long as American power remains in the region, India must come to grips with it.[26]

Joseph Nye Jr., a former chairman of the US National Intelligence Council and assistant secretary of defence in the Clinton administration, wrote:

> India too is sometimes mentioned as a future great power, and its population of a billion people is four times that of the United States. For decades, India suffered from what some called the 'Hindu rate of economic growth'...but in the last decade that has changed...India has an emerging middle class of several hundred million, and English is an official language spoken by

some 50 million to 100 million people. Building on that base, Indian information industries are beginning to play a transnational role. In addition, India is a military power, with several dozen nuclear weapons, intermediate range missiles, 1.2 million military personnel, and an annual military expenditure of nearly $11 billion. In terms of soft power, India has an established democracy and was long regarded as a leader of nonaligned countries during the Cold War. India has an influential diaspora, and its motion picture industry is largest in the world in terms of the number of films produced yearly, competing with Hollywood in parts of Asia and the Middle East.[27]

While recognising India's achievements, Nye did not ignore the limitations of India. He nonetheless stressed that Indian power was unlikely to work against the US interests. He has argued that India alone could pose no threat to the US interests, and that India, along with China and Russia, could challenge the US, but such a triangular strategic alliance was implausible and improbable in view of inherent contradictions.[28] Henry Kissinger's observation earlier was not much different from that of Joseph Nye and Stephen Cohen. According to Kissinger,

> The international system of the twenty-first century will be marked by a seeming contradiction: on the one hand, fragmentation; on the other growing globalisation. *On the level of relations among states, the new order will be more like the European state system of eighteen and nineteenth centuries than the rigid patterns of the Cold War. It will contain at least six major powers—the United States, Europe, China, Japan, Russia, and probably India....*[29] (emphasis added).

Kissinger was not yet sure about India's role and went on to observe that

> As for India, which is now emerging as the major power in South Asia, its foreign policy is in many ways the last vestige of the heyday of European imperialism, leavened by the traditions of an ancient culture.... Absorbed by the struggle to feed its vast population, India dabbled in the Non-aligned movement during the Cold War. But it has yet to assume a role commensurate with its size on the international political stage.[30]

Whatever may be the observations of the American analysts, Indo-US relations picked up momentum at an unprecedented level when George Bush became the US President in 2001. It has been remarkable that relationship between India and the US have moved a long way from decades of estrangement to years of engagement to a new era of strategic partnership. Both Indian and American political leaders and foreign policy pundits now increasingly use the phrase 'natural partner' while describing the Indo-US relations. The change in the US administration's views of India was reflected in the *US National Security Strategy Report* of 2002, which said:

> The United States has undertaken a transformation in its bilateral relationship with India based on a conviction that US interests require a strong relationship with India. We are the two largest democracies, committed to political freedom protected by representative government. India is moving toward greater economic freedom as well. We have a common interest in the free flow of commerce, including through the vital sea lanes of the Indian Ocean. Finally, we share an interest in fighting terrorism and in creating a strategically stable Asia. Differences remain, including over the development of India's nuclear and missile programs, and the pace of India's economic reforms. But while in the past these concerns may have dominated our thinking about India, *today we start with a view of India as a growing world power with which we have common strategic interests. Through a strong partnership with India, we can best address any differences and shape a dynamic future*[31] (emphasis added).

The Bush administration and the NDA government in India actually took several measures in the defence and security field that culminated in a series of military-to-military exercises in heat of Agra, heights of Alaska, jungles of Mizoram and waters of the Indian Ocean. The defence cooperation involved all sections of the armed forces of the two countries, which included counterterrorism cooperation involving the special forces. The military cooperation, which was limited to holding seminars, extended to the field of exchanging notes on military doctrines and even arms purchase. Indo-US defence cooperation, which unfolded during the Bush administration, was unthinkable during the Cold War years.

One of the most significant developments in the emerging context of a strategic partnership between the two countries is the recent announcement by President George Bush to forge closer ties in the 'trinity' areas of civilian nuclear cooperation, civilian space programmes and high technology trade with an ultimate goal of establishing 'strategic partnership with India'. Before the announcement came, the officials from the two countries had worked over these issues for about two years through painstaking and detailed negotiations. In a way, Bush's announcement sought to give a shape to Vajpayee–Bush vision of a strategic partnership made public, way back in 2001. The statement by Indian prime minister and American president in 2001 said that India and the US were partners in controlling the proliferation of mass destruction, and the means to deliver them.

If viewed in the broader context of the budding Indo-US security cooperation in recent years, the announcement appears more significant. Months after the announcement, Indian and American officials agreed to implement the understanding on 'trinity' areas of high technology cooperation. More significantly, this agreement was made after there was a change of government in India. The UPA government had replaced the NDA government after the national parliamentary elections of summer 2004. It reflected an Indian consensus in building cooperative ties with the US. While anti-terrorism cooperation between the two nations has intensified since September 11, deeper defence ties in the areas of military-to-military exercises have emerged as one of the most promising areas of the relationship. Since 2002, numerous military exercises, involving all branches of the two militaries have taken place, including the joint Special Forces exercise in Ladakh near the India–China border. As US Under-secretary of Commerce noted recently in a speech at Mumbai:

> From our perspective, a strategic partnership between our countries serves both of our interests. A strong and vibrant India will be most effective in advancing our shared objectives of promoting peace and stability in Asia, combating global terrorism and stemming the proliferation of weapons of mass destruction. As this audience well knows, *the level of cooperation for the last two years between our two countries across a broad range of issues has been nothing short of extraordinary*[32] (emphasis added).

Such developments have prompted some US analysts to laud increased US-India security ties as providing potential counterbalance to the growing Chinese influence in the region. But the goal of Indo-US military cooperation is far from being an anti-China one. Neither the Bush administration nor the Vajpayee government have contemplated a policy of containing China. As a matter of fact, both the US and India have positively engaged China in a number of areas, including trade and investment.

The emerging strategic partnership between India and the US is unlikely to contain a Cold War type alliance system. Since the two natural partners have not forged normal relations in the security field for decades, recent improvements of relations and new frontiers of collaboration make the initiative appear grand and unprecedented. According to a recently released report by the US-based Council on Foreign Relations, 'US-India military-to-military cooperation is evolving along lines that the Pentagon has established with many non-allied but "friendly" countries' and 'the policy challenge is to continue this enhanced cooperation and, where possible, to enlarge its parameters'.[33]

In fact, Indian software, back-office facilities, outsourcing activities of US companies, etc., are increasingly becoming dominant issues in Indo–US relations. India now seems less concerned about the Bush administration's efforts to hug, praise and cooperate with Pakistani President Pervez Musharraf in various areas, including arms sales and military assistance. Nor is Washington bothered about Russia's continuing security ties with India. China has ceased to become a major negative factor in Indo-US relations, as both the countries are seeking an improved state of relations with that country. India does more trade with China than with Germany. The US sells five times more goods to China than to India.

However, this emerging US-Indian relationship is not completely problem-free. First, some old issues have persisted and new issues are coming to the surface. For instance, India currently figures in a 'brewing' political storm in the US with some politicians linking up offshore outsourcing as one of the main causes of job losses in the country. As the telecom workers union made noises, the state of Indiana recently cancelled a contract with Tata Consultancy Services. Outsourcing has also become an election issue in the US. Second, some sections in the US have begun to express fear about the possible erosion of American dominance over information technology. Unless tackled tactfully, Indo-US private sector cooperation in the knowledge industry could run into serious trouble.

As far as the government level high technology cooperation in defence-related areas is concerned, the Pakistan factor appears to be still at work to keep it at a lower level. So long as Pakistan remains relevant to US war on terrorism, Washington would be careful in its defence-related cooperative ventures with India to ward off an impression that it is contributing to increasing military strength of India. Second, the Cold War mindset in the State Department, the non-proliferation fundamentalists in Washington, and Pakistan supporters in the policy making circles will continue to demarcate the boundary of Indo-US cooperation in high technology area.

The government of India is no doubt seeking to establish cooperation with the US in civilian nuclear technology, space programmes, and missile defence research. The US government still appears reluctant to open the gate in these areas. As US Undersecretary of Commerce Kennneth Juster said recently, in the past fiscal year, the US approved 90 per cent of export license applications filed for India, and that US licenses only apply to sensitive dual-use goods and technologies, representing approximately 1 per cent of US exports to India. The government of India, nonetheless, views US willingness to cooperate in these 'sensitive areas' as a test case for improved Indo-US cooperation. Continuation of restriction on duel-use technology would mean sustained US suspicion of India. The future of the bilateral relations will thus hinge on tackling hurdles in high technology cooperation.

Conclusions

The US strategic thinkers and analysts viewed Japan, China and India with a little amount of suspicion at various times. The anxiety over an Asian power hurting American interests periodically surfaces in the American foreign policy debate.

In the eighties, as American strategic focus was in Afghanistan, speedy growth rate of Japanese economy raised considerable threat perceptions in the US. A *Newsweek* report in 1989, for instance, said: 'In boardrooms and government bureaus around the world, the uneasy question is whether Japan is about to become a superpower, supplanting America as the colossus of the Pacific and perhaps even the world's No. 1 nation.'[34] Others predicted a new Pacific bloc emerging and Japan emerging as a nuclear superpower.[35] Nothing of the sort happened. As the world entered the nineties and the Japanese economy faced a persistent economic downturn, concern about the rising Japan vanished. It was Chinese economic miracle that drew attention.

In the nineties, a large number of American analysts and foreign policy pundits came to view China as a rising superpower. Henry Kissinger, for instance, wrote:

> China is on the road to superpower status. At a growth rate of 8 per cent, which is less than it has maintained over the eighties, China's Gross National Product will approach that of the United States by the end of the second decade of the twenty-first century. Long before that, China's political and military shadow will fall over Asia and will affect the calculations of other powers....[36]

The US administration under the leadership of Bill Clinton devised a policy of 'constructive engagement' of China. President George Bush, Clinton's successor, initially viewed China as a strategic competitor and failed to continue the same momentum of bilateral relations. But cooperative ties with China soon came to be viewed as of utmost importance in the wake of terrorist attacks on the US. US-Japan alliance was officially strengthened, but Japanese recession and China's galloping economic performance pushed Japan to the background in the list of US foreign policy priorities. The rise of Chinese influence commensurate with its economic growth, and decline of Japan's regional influence due to its jaded economic performance led to lessening of its 'strategic value' to the United States.[37]

Now in the twenty-first century no one talks much about China taking over the United States. The talk has somewhat shifted to India. No one predicted the emergence of a nuclear India, but it happened. No one was very optimistic about India's economic performance, but Indian economy grew in the midst of Asian financial crisis and international recession. The rise of the Indian power and influence, however, has not been as spectacular as that of Japan and China in the eighties and the nineties respectively. Consequently, the explanations about the rising power of India have not accompanied panic portrayal of yet another emerging threat to the US interests in Asia. US Undersecretary of Commerce Kenneth Juster said in November 2003: 'India has the potential of becoming one of the great democratic powers of the 21st century' and observed that 'a recent Goldman Sachs study projects India to be the world's third largest economy

by the year 2050 if a number of structural barriers to trade and
investment are removed'.[38] Juster also praised India's human resources saying, 'We recognise and greatly admire India's technical
competence in information technology, life sciences, and other disciplines of high technology'.[39] It is this area that has caused a
controversy in the US and has created a modest level of scare in the
US about India's emergence as an information technology superpower, which has affected the US jobs due to rising 'outsourcing'
of such jobs by the American companies.

But India—a new nuclear power and new economic power—has
emerged as a new security partner of the United States. India's
decision to go nuclear, failure of the US sanctions policy, and rapid
growth of the Indian economy altered the traditional image of India
as a country of nothing but potentials. Indo-US multidimensional
military cooperation has led many to observe that the two countries
are inching towards forming an alliance relationship. Several Indians
and Americans also described the bilateral relationship as the one
between two 'natural partners'.

It is a notable fact that the US has successfully developed and
employed a policy of constructive engagement of all three major
powers in Asia. First, it has led to the prevention of rise of an anti-
American regional power in Asia. Second, while Washington's relations with these three Asian powers are not without their respective
bilateral problems, it is improbable that in the foreseeable future,
there is going to be any major clash of interests between the US and
the Asian powers. Third, the US would remain the most powerful
military entity in Asia, but Japan, China and India would act as
powerful centres in the emerging balance of power in Asia. Fourth,
the US desires that China does not grow militarily, Japan does not
go nuclear, and India does not deploy its new nuclear weapons and
missiles. Last but not the least, Washington would seek to maintain
the Asian balance by nurturing cordial ties with Japan, China and
India, and simultaneously work towards preventing a situation where
these three Asian powers could unite against the US interests.

Notes and References

1. Walter Lafeber, *America, Russia, and the Cold War, 1945–2000*. New York,
   McGraw-Hill, 2002, p. 71.

2. David Gold Field, Carl Abbott, Virginia DeJohn Anderson, Jo Ann E. Argersinger, Peter H. Argersinger, William J. Barney and Robert M. Weir, *The American Journer: A History of the United States*. New Jersey, Prentice-Hall, 1998, p. 450.

3. Ibid.

4. http://www.state.gov/r/pa/ei/bgn/4142.html

5. Ibid.

6. 'US and Japan: Toward a Mature Partnership', Report by the members of a bipartisan study group under the auspices of the Institute for National Strategic Studies, National Defense University of the US, 19 October 2000. http://www.atimes.com/japan-econ/BJ19Dh01.html

7. Ibid.

8. Ibid.

9. Ibid.

10. Mark E. Manyin, 'Japan–North Korea Relations: Selected Issues', CRS Report for Congress, 26 November 2003.

11. Eugene A. Matthews, 'Japan's New Nationalism', *Foreign Affairs*, vol. 82, no. 6, November–December 2003, p. 88.

12. Ibid., p. 83.

13. Suggestions about helping India in developing a nuclear weapon capability were revealed in the newly released declassified documents in 2001. See Walter Lafeber, *America, Russia, and the Cold War, 1945–2000*. New York, 2002, p. 263.

14. 'Background Note: China', Bureau of East Asian and Pacific Affairs, US Department of State, March 2003. http://www.state.gov/r/pa/ei/bgn/18902.htm#relations

15. According to a retired Indian Air Force Officer, Nehru hated the men in the uniform. For details, see rediff.com special Series: 40 years after the Sino-Indian 1962 War. www.rediff.com/../../news/2002/dec/18chin.htm

16. Ibid.

17. J.N. Dixit argues that India had nuclear ambitions since the Chinese nuclear tests, although it abjured the 'acquisition of nuclear weapons, despite suggestions to the contrary by the US in 1963....' See J.N. Dixit, *Across Borders: Fifty Years of India's Foreign Policy*. New Delhi, Picus Books, 1998, p. 421.

18. Quoted in George Perkovich, *India's Nuclear Bomb*. Oxford, Oxford University Press, 2002, pp. 60–61.

19. Ibid.

20. For details, see Chintamani Mahapatra, *Indo–US Relations into the 21st Century*. New Delhi, Knowledge and IDSA, 1999, p. 15.

21. Ibid.

22. Ashley J. Tellis, *India's Emerging Nuclear Posture: Between Recessed Deterrent and Ready Arsenal*. Santamonica, Rand, 2001, p. 80.

23. Ibid., p. 81.

24. Stephen P. Cohen, *India: Emerging Power*. Washington DC, Brookings Institution, 2001, pp. 264–65.

25. Ibid.

26. Ibid.

27. Joseph S. Nye Jr., *The Paradox of American Power*. Oxford, New York, Oxford University Press, 2002, p. 28.

28. Ibid., p. 29.
29. Henry Kissinger, *Diplomacy*. New York, London, Simon and Schuster, 1994, p. 23.
30. Ibid., p. 26.
31. The National Security Strategy of the United States of America, The White House, September 2002. http://usinfo.state.gov/topical/pol/terror/secstrat.htm#nssintro
32. 'Under Secretary of Commerce Juster Praises India's Economic Potential', Press Briefings and Release, US Consulate, Mumbai, 20 November 2003. http://mumbai.usconsulate.gov/wwwhwashnews1021.html
33. 'New Priorities in South Asia: US Policy Toward India, Pakistan, and Afghanistan,' Chairman's Report of an Independent Task Force Cosponsored by the Council on Foreign Relations and the Asia Society, October 2003.
34. Quoted in Joseph S. Nye Jr., *The Paradox of American Power*. Oxford, New York, 2002, p. 23.
35. Ibid.
36. Henry Kissinger, *Diplomacy*. New York, London, 1994, p. 26.
37. Morton Abramowitz and Stephen Bosworth, 'Adjusting to the New Asia', *Foreign Affairs*, vol. 82, no. 4, July–August, 2003, p. 119.
38. Press Releases and briefings, United States Consulate, Mumbai. http://mumbai.usconsulate.gov/wwwhwashnews1021.html
39. Ibid.

7

REFORM AND RESURGENCE: THE TRAJECTORY OF CHANGE IN WEST ASIA

Girijesh Pant

The trajectory of change in a region in the present phase of global-isation is increasingly defined by the global flows.[1] The exclusive and inclusive nature of these flows is fragmenting regions vertically but integrating horizontally. The vertical divide, obviously is between those included—the successful, and those excluded—the unsuccess-ful. On horizontal plane, both the gainers and the losers are getting engaged in integrative processes. While the former are collaborating across the national territories on globalising market mode, the latter are forging linkages and bonds of solidarity of discontents across the region. In West Asia, the twin processes are manifesting in the form of reform and resurgence. The participants in the inclusive processes of globalisation are making structural changes by integrating markets at global and regional level under various forms like proposed Cus-tom Union by GCC, the Middle East Free Trade Area (MEFTA), or even bilateral Free Trade Agreements (FTAs). At a broader level it is being conceived as the New Middle East project facilitating the linkages between the region with the globalising world. Resurgence, on the other hand, is the manifestation of protest from the marginalised community further excluded by the globalisation processes across the region, interacting and communicating to resist the attempts of reforms. The contention of this paper is that the trajectory of change in West Asia is going to be determined by the dialectics of reform and resurgence.

The Region on Margin

West Asia has been the region in slow motion though its history since the second war is full of events both of implosive and explosive nature. It also has been the region with high external intervention. The paradox of being a volatile region yet moving at slow pace is reflected in the make-up of structures, institutions, and the culture giving distinct profile to the region often described as exceptional attributes of West Asia. These include the prevalence of authoritarian polity, the archaic institution of governance, and the highly restricted freedom in socio-cultural space, distancing the region from the mainstream. In retrospect, it appears that West Asia found a kind of comfort on being on the margin. It did not make serious attempt to overcome the barriers or possibly did not see them as barriers in its evolution. It can even be argued that West Asian region has been purposely made to sustain on the strength of it being on the margin. By virtue of being at distant location, it could possibly protect its 'pristine' character. It may be clarified here that being on margin does not mean disengagement. It is an engagement from distance not inducing change but endorsing status quo. This engagement was perpetuated, if not, promoted by the Western powers. Thus the stakeholders both from within and outside found in it a win-win situation.

The interface between West Asia and the world during the last 50 years has been critically influenced by the Palestinian–Israeli conflict, and the Western stakes in its oil. While the former has been used effectively to construct a regional threat–security regime to rationalise the arm build-up including nuclear power, to transfer billions of aid, for political mobilisation at convenient occasions, both by palace and street, the latter has contributed in crippling the pace by pushing the region into rentier mode. It can be a safe hypothesis that establishment of Democratic Secular Palestine alone could have contributed in strengthening the processes retrieving the region from margin. The attempts to ensure the security of Israel aborted the nationalist ferment in the region at very embryonic stage. The June 1967 war was the final blow to Arab nationalist movement. The defeat also created grounds for the rise of regressive forces, which eventually occupied the civil society and thinking space in the region. This was encouraged by the ruling classes and supported by the Western powers as ideological contest against the nationalist, Bathist and communist dispensations. It eventually reinforced the societal worldview and stake in favour of 'Umma'. To further perpetuate and consolidate the ideological orientation of the society, the ruling classes promoted religion-based, highly centralised education system freezing the frame of reference to the glorious past. The intellectuals too contributed to it. 'Arab intellectuals who ought to encourage change have failed in that role. For the most they did not detach themselves from the tribal traditions of defending "ours" causes in the face of "enemy"—they help stereotype themselves before being stereotyped by any enemy'.[2] This stereotyping further restricted interaction with outsiders, keeping the region on the margin. No wonder that it has created a psyche, resisting to come to terms with developmental challenges of contemporary times. It also helped the ruling classes including the religious establishment having share in the power structure to rationalise all their deficiencies in terms of corrupting influences of the outsiders. The point made here is that by closing the communication, the region space was protected from possibility of any kind of accountability. Importantly to legitimise the mode of governance a new set of names were given to old institutions like the Islamic banking, Islamic science, etc. In short, the stakeholder did see a distinct advantage in distancing the region in the name of identity.

Oil contributed in freezing the evolution of the economy by providing the life support of massive revenue to the prevailing structure and institutions. It empowered the ruling political class with the strength to devise its own format of governance under the rubric of Islam on patron–client mode. This suited well for Western stakeholders to negotiate for an international oil regime compatible to their interests. In case of countries where oil revenue have not been sufficient like Jordan and Egypt, the strategic rent was available in the form of aid to sustain the format of governance. The peace dividend earned by Egypt while the conflict remains in perpetuity is a brilliant example of locational rent. President Mubarak of Egypt traded the support for US coalition against Iraq for $250 billion in debt relief. The oil-based development undermined those economic processes, which compel the region to build linkages with the external world on a wider scale. The nature of engagement encouraged by the rent seeking transactions provided the local oligopolies and monopolies power to restrict the competition.

The sustenance of West Asia on margin was based on the assumption that the rent will continue to be available in increasing proportion to meet the expanding demands of the region. Ironically, the end of the Cold War and the decline in oil revenue led to the shrinking of rent. This was further reinforced by the shift in the global premise from geopolitics to geo-economics, necessitating renegotiation of contract among the stakeholders. Though Western stakes on West Asian energy continue to remain, but the rise of non-OPEC oil, emergence of natural gas and new sources of hydrocarbon in central Asia and Africa have remapped the global energy configuration eroding the leverage enjoyed by the West Asian oil exporters in the seventies. Moreover, the investment needs of the region's oil regime to upgrade its aging wells and export capacity have moderated their managerial capacity and clout. In other words, West Asia for the last decade has been under pressure to relocate its position from the margin. The relocation demands a new road map. Apparently, reforms are the pointer of the new direction towards which the region intends to move.

Dialectics of Reforms:
Re-negotiating the Contract

The terms and reference of the new contract among the stakeholders are defined by the new geography of globalisation. Like other regions, West Asia too has to come to terms with the deconstruction of its space into strategic sites—the 'trans-locals'. Translocality refers to 'linkages and connection between places (media, travel, import/ export, etc.).[3] This spatial interface undermines the sovereignty of the nation space thereby the power quotient. 'The loss of power at the national level produces the possibility for new forms of power and politics at the sub national level. The national as container of social process and power is cracked. This cracked casing opens up possibilities for a geography of politics that links sub national spaces.'[4] It also changes the character of the stakeholders. It is argued that this will see the birth of 'first generation of aspirants'[5] linking these strategic sites to the global flows and processes. Simultaneously, it will also create a 'second generation of moralisers' opposing the linkages at vertical level, and forging the ties horizontally across the region or even beyond. The former are seeking patronage in 'democracy and market' construct and the latter looking for refuse in resurgence of discontent. This inevitably changes the power equation among the stakeholders.

The ruling class faced with depletion of solvency caused by declining rent, reluctantly accepted the market mode on the suggestions of IMF and World Bank, the structural adjustment programme. However, it resorted to all kinds of tactics to delay its implementations.

Regional governments and elites have so far shown a marked preference for a gradual, even dilatory pace of reform. The reasons for this vary from case to case, but are typically combination of two factors: (1) regimes fear—with some reason—that the social dislocations which full-scale economic reform would entail run a high risk of being politically destabilizing. (2) Powerful vested interests either block reforms or ensure that the specific kind of reform yields disproportionate benefits to them, at the expense of other social groups. The result has been a very mixed picture, in which regimes have embraced some, often many, economic reforms (especially in macroeconomic policy) yet have postponed or evaded more complex reforms, such as privatization, reform of regulatory rules, and development of the rule of law. Whether as a result of the inherent difficulties facing any economic policy, or thanks to the unevenness of reform, the results have been relatively disappointing.[6]

Despite the slow process of adjustment, the social consequences are visibly felt due to downsizing of the state affecting the employment and cut in subsidies and expenditure in social sector. The sharpening of exclusionary tendencies enhanced the constituency of discontent spilling the protests beyond the region. It is the changing profile of protest that made the external stakeholders to impress upon the regional governments to enhance the scope of SAP by adding on democratic underpinning to it. It is illustrated by the Bush–Mubarak meeting of 12 April 2004, where the US President recalling the role Egypt played in Camp David, asked categorically, the President of Egypt, to set 'the standard in the region for democracy by strengthening democratic institutions and political participation'.[7]

Though the ruling classes have been feeling uneasy with the stagnant region in midst of fast changes triggered by the information revolution, the democracy-market format of reform has come from external stakeholders. The Greater Middle East Initiative of President Bush is in US description a 'forward strategy of freedom in the Middle East'.[8] The proposal has triggered a fierce debate in West Asia. The potential beneficiaries—'first generation of aspirants'—though do see their stakes in the reforms, yet are finding difficult to sell it as a proposal coming from USA, as the superpower is notoriously seen as pursuing its agenda unilaterally. From Cairo to Riyadh it received hostile response. The sentiment across the region has been that America has no business to impose its version of democracy. The suspicion is so deep that those fighting for democracy felt that it could even setback their hard work. Saudi Arabia and Egypt in a joint statement rejected outside imposition of reforms in the Arab world, the two countries 'affirmed that Arab states proceed on the path of development, modernization and reform in keeping with their peoples' interests and values'.[9] It is even observed that the ulterior objectives behind the reforms is to divide the countries of the region geologically. In the words of *Sarah Al-Ansary*, 'In their recent history, Arabs faced all forms of colonialism, but mostly economic and military. The Greater Middle East Initiative is colonialism under another title.'[10]

However, faced with serious crisis of legitimacy and governance, the ruling class could ill afford to reject the proposal. In fact, their response was not against the reforms. It was primarily against the American posture and apprehension about the message that it could send to the people. This becomes clear from the observations of the Secretary General of the Arab League: 'the Americans should listen to us so as we will listen to them and considered that there is "no opportunity" for any initiatives that is not discussed with those concerned'.[11] So much was the concern of its American origin that Syria even insisted that the word reform should be replaced with 'development and modernization'.[12] Thus, to make it an authentic regional initiative, the Arab League called a summit with the agenda to define the content and processes of its implementation. On May 2004 in the summit held in Tunis, it passed a resolution:

> to pursue reform and modernization in our countries, and to keep pace with the rapid world changes, by consolidating the democratic practice, by enlarging participation in political and public

life, by fostering the role of all components of the civil society, including NGOs, in conceiving of the guidelines of the society of tomorrow, by widening women's participation in the political, economic, social, cultural and educational fields and reinforcing their rights and status in society, and by pursuing the promotion of the family and the protection of Arab youth.[13]

The moderating impact of the summit was carried forward by Egypt by soliciting support from the civil society. On state initiatives, a conference was organised in collaboration with Arab Academy for Science and Technology, Arab Business Council, Arab Women's Organisation, Economic Research Forum, Arab Organisation for Human Rights, on 12–14 March 2004, at the Bibliotheca Alexandrina (Alexandria Library) on 'Arab Reform Issues: Vision and Implementation.' The Alexandria Statement endorsed and even advocated the necessity of reforms in the field of polity, economy, society and culture. Its main emphasis was that the roadmap would have to come from within, and it may not be identical as every society has its own values, culture and milieu.[14]

Since reforms aim at the reconstruction of the space by shrinking the state and expanding the market space, it was needed that the stakeholders of market—the private sector—be energised and mobilised to undertake the task of building linkages with globalisation. The World Economic Forum at the Extraordinary Annual Meeting 2003 in Jordan established, the Arab Business Council (ABC)—the voice of Arab business community. Drawing membership from the private sector of the region, the Council is to function as forum to facilitate the integration of the region with the global economy. It resolved that the region, 'today stands at a very critical juncture. Sustaining the status quo will only widen the development gap between this region and the developed world.' It also adopted a blueprint of economic reforms across the region 'to concentrate on economic liberalisation and reforms, governance and human resource development. The blueprint is one of the first steps taken along the road to an Arab Renaissance'.[15] The Council visualises that together the three pronged process would 'help the region its rightful place in the fast evolving global economy'.[16]

It is important to note that on economic dimensions of reforms, there were neither noticeable resistance, reservation nor assertion for regional roots and identity as against on issues of political. The

disjuncture between the economic and political could be explained
in terms of paralysing impact of the rentier mode of regional economy.
The economy is more susceptible to external pressures. Thus the
globalisation has direct impact on reforms. While the region is still
engaged in defining the politics of reforms, it has already moved
a distance on its economics. Most of the countries are members of
the WTO. Consequently, under its obligation, are reorganising their
rules and institutions. Some of them have moved a bit faster by
signing bilateral Free Trade Agreements. It is significant to note that
Jordan, Israel, and Bahrain have signed the FTA with the USA.
Apparently, the trajectory of reforms in West Asia is going to be
defined by the economy.

The reform discourse in the region acquired new perspective with
the publication of Arab Human Development Reports 2002 and
2003. Dr Rima Khalaf Huanidi, director of the Arab Regional Bureau
of the UNDP, under whose leadership these reports were prepared,
pointed out that the Report 'was written by Arabs for Arabs'.[17] The
AHDR has redefined the rationale of reform by juxtaposing the
regional deficiency in human resources against the imperatives of
building a knowledge society. By linking development with freedom
it has put the ruling class on the defensive. Its emphasis that knowledge requires an unrestricted flow of information is challenging the
survival of those who have been thriving on close-rentier society. Its
thrust on linking social malaise like corruption and moral decline to
the skewed distribution of power, is going to threaten the stakes of
the class who, so far, enjoyed the central power. These reports are
impressing upon corrective action at the foundation level beyond the
traditional prescriptions. Importantly, these reports have identified
the three deficits impeding the progress of the region as:

   (a) the freedom deficit,
   (b) the women's empowerment deficit,
   (c) the human capabilities/knowledge deficit relative to income.

The reports are not taken kindly because of the obvious implications of its far-reaching consequences. The responses therefore have
not been very encouraging from the perspective of change. The
contention of the report that the freedom, knowledge and gender
deficits are causes of underdevelopment is questioned.[18] In support
of the argument, it is pointed out that countries like the East Asian

Tigers and China have achieved remarkable development under authoritarian regimes. Further, the empowerment of women in the West came as a consequence of the Industrial Revolution (development) and was not a cause of it. Interestingly, the linkage between development and democracy was also contested: 'That, the issue of individual freedom, while important in itself, should be separated from that of development...that an equitable distribution of income should take precedence over granting economic freedoms'.[19] Some critiques went to the extent that the report portrays a gloomy picture and could even be used by the Western media to further tarnish the image of the Muslim societies or could be used for opposing change from outside. The debate summed up by Dr Baroudi clearly shows that the thinking community in the region is wary and apprehensive of loosing its stakes, 'This preference for strong (but not necessarily tyrannical) states remains rampant among Arab intellectuals. Many of them have experienced a certain upward mobility thanks to greater state intervention in the economy and society (e.g., through free education at state universities)'.[20] Though the opinions are divided yet there is recognition across the region and among all the segment of stakeholders that the region cannot be sustained on the present format of governance and development paradigm. The greater awareness, despite close skies, is drifting the dynamics of change in the form of backlash. The gap between the state and people has widened to the magnitude that informal systems are surfacing at local level beyond the reach of state governance. While the region is still engaged in the reform debate, some significant developments towards the reforms are already on the anvil indicating the trajectory of change. The two important issues referred in the AHDR are being addressed, namely, the education reforms and women empowerment education and curricula has received wide attention to prepare the society towards knowledge building. Saudi Arabia known for relatively more restricted freedom has recently initiated a national dialogue. The first two constituencies being addressed are the women and youth. While the recently established National Dialogue Forum on the rights of Saudi women has been carrying the debate on women freedom issues, the Saudi state has taken a landmark decision 'allowing women to obtain commercial licenses. Previously women could only open a business in the name of a male relative, and religious and social restrictions excluded them from all but a few professions such as teaching and nursing'.[21]

Though the reform debate in West Asia has yet to resolve whether polity or economy will set the ball rolling, there is agreement among all stakeholders that the region has to enhance its engagement with the globalising mainstream. In the words of prominent scholar from the region Mr Ismail Sirageldin, 'There was unanimous recognition that there can be no survival for an immobile society in a world that is fast moving forward and changing rapidly. Those who do not participate in the development of global knowledge and science— and reject the new—only choose slow suicide'.[22] This is clear departure from earlier proposition that to be on margin served the interest of the stakeholders. The external stakeholders are pushing for political reforms by underlining the need of good governance. The World Bank report 'Better Governance for Development in the Middle East and North Africa' argues that the development in the region 'is being handicapped by the weakness in the quality of public governance in which the region lags behind the rest of the world'.[23] Political reform is also required to meet the criteria of development defined as efficient and effective delivery of services. It further argues that a climate of confidence needs to be created by ensuring transparency and accountability to accelerate the pace of the economy by attracting investment and create job opportunities for a fast growing, volatile and young working population.

Apparently, though the political class is gradually accepting to share power under pressure, yet it has eloquently expressed its reservation for the transfer of power to the people in the name of distinct cultural and civilisational milieu of the region. The reluctance for liberal political processes is also justified by expressing the prospects of 'Algerian syndrome'. The pressure for accelerating political reforms is coming because of the failure of the political class to contain the resurgence of discontent within its own territorial space. What is known as terrorism today, has its roots in West Asian polity not religion. It was the state which used religion to gain legitimacy, and it is its failure that has led to it becoming a voice of protest. Political Islam might have failed at state level, but certainly it has gained strength at popular level. The political Islam is not confined to militancy. It is evolving and growing, and even acquiring a transnational dimension. It is deriving its resources from globalisation processes in its own way. Ironically, the resolution of the essentially political problem is sought by military means. While it might be argued that disengaging religion from polity in the region is a very arduous process, but certainly, military way is no solution. Moreover, it cannot be ignored that in attempting the processes of disengagement, care has to be taken of the belief that in Muslim society religion is not totally a private affair. Removing and imposing of regime is no way to develop the democratic political culture. In the region where political culture is highly fragmented on sectarian and tribal lines, a composite political culture would require institutions and policies to arrest the processes of alienation of the people and creating their stakes. Equally important is to recognise that there is a strong feeling across the social strata that the region is suffering from loss of sovereignty, and is exposed to cultural invasion and erosion of identity. At the more extreme level there is even fear of being targeted by the Christian world. The confidence-building therefore, has to begin at the popular level with the constituency of discontent.

Resurgence of Discontent:
The Eleventh of September

Resurgence of discontent in West Asia, spilling over beyond its boundaries, reaching Washington in its most violent form on 11 September 2001 has underlined the scale of drift that it has undergone, and the need to contain it by engagement. From the perspective of trans-localisation of subaltern polity of West Asia, 11 September marks the beginning of a new phase. Ironically, the way the Twin Tower tragedy is diagnosed and responded to, is further pushing the region into the periphery. West Asia is given a new identity—the region of terror, and to make the matter worse, a prefix is also added to it—the Islamic, thereby expanding the expanse of the so-called community of terrorists. By using vocabulary like 'crusade' and 'civilizational war', a divide has been created having a wider connotation. It also projects a flawed image of the region as a monolithic entity. What is not appreciated is that the mere fact that all the participants in the ghastly act of September 11 were from the region does not make West Asia a community of terrorists. West Asia, like any other region, has multiple spatial dimensions with local variations. The way the West Asians were treated in the aftermath of 11 September, the embarrassing situation the American allies in the region were put in, have sent impulses making the region more introvert. In fact the 'demoralization' of political leadership of the region encouraged many violent attacks targeted at them. Consequently, despite the condemnation of the violent act of terrorism, West Asians are pushed to rethink their position. An unprecedented distance has been created leading to searching queries in binary frame like 'Why do they hate us' and 'the Challenge of Islam'. What is more alarming is that the state in the region has become more incapacitated, and the society is getting further polarised and alienated. This is happening when the popular sympathy for extremist forces, i.e., violence, is on the decline. That does not mean that the popular political Islam is on retreat. On the contrary, as argued earlier, 11 September has further contributed to its consolidation. They perceive a causal relationship between their despair and the USA. Even though the American contribution to the making of discontent could be a matter of debate, the impact of the overwhelming presence of the superpower on regional sensitivities is not disputable. The policy to retaliate the expression of regional anger by military might has further reinforced its growth. Iraq illustrates it.

The constituency of discontent is not only growing but communicating and forging linkages across the region. According to one study,

> The poll revealed ubiquitous feelings of solidarity with coreligionists in the *umma* (Muslim community) and widespread support among Muslims surveyed for the notion that Islam was under threat, though the perceived sources of threat were multiple and predominately reflected local concerns.[24]

Apparently, spatial dimension is transforming its character. In the era of ICT such linkages are inevitable. Efforts to contain them by censoring are going to be self-defeating. Therefore, the strategy to negotiate with the constituency of discontent requires a three-level approach—global, regional and national.

The task for the ruling class, particularly the American allies, to engage the society in reform process, has become much more difficult. However, the redeeming feature of increasing violence has been the public debate that it has triggered, and the changed nature of discourse at least among the intelligentsia. According to Sateh Noureddine, managing editor of the Lebanese newspaper *As-Safir*, the debate 'could pose the larger and more important question of how qualified are the Muslim religious establishment and clergy to lead a political platform?' 'Right now, Muslim youths can choose only between Osama bin Laden and semiliterate clerics,' Noureddine added. 'What is required is an Arab religious establishment that's civilized, educated and vigilant'.[25] 'Rearranging the Arab house has always been a pressing matter, but now it is an inescapable one', wrote Mustafa al-Fiqi, an Egyptian diplomat and member of parliament, in the pan-Arab daily *Al-Hayat*.[26] Abd al-Hamid al-Ansari, dean of the College of Sharia and Law at the University of Qatar, wrote in *Al-Hayat*: 'We should be responsible for confronting the idea of terrorism in our midst. There is paralysis in our society that is forcing young people to become involved with terrorist groups.' Prof. Abd al Khaliq, from the United Arab Emirates, observed unless the Arabs blended the 'innovations of the modern world with the best influences and beliefs from our own Arab and Islamic legacy', they will 'remain in a state of permanent fracture, division, extremism, and confrontation one with another', and become the producer and exporter of terrorism.[27]

The debate has still to gain wider acceptability at the popular level. It is quite revealing, as pointed by one opinion survey in Saudi Arabia in the wake of the Municipal election, 'fifty-five percent of those polled thought society was not going to accept the new electoral experience; only seven percent believed that society would appreciate it. Ninety-two percent of the respondents did not discuss the elections with their families or friends'.[28] However, the fact that issues of fundamental nature are being discussed in public domain underlines a qualitative shift in the regional ambiance. It is illustrative to refer the way the Saudi women are reacting to this political opening. Arab News from Saudi Arabia published a feature article, 'Am I Not Saudi?' where the writer raised some basic questions very candidly, 'Silently I kept asking myself, if I am a Saudi national, why am I treated as a second-class citizen? Why can't I get an ID card, without anyone's permission, proving that I am a national? Why do I need a male mediator between my government and me?'[29] The National Dialogue Forum on the rights of Saudi women is the emerging face of civil society in the region. The debate in these forums are going to put the ruling governments under pressure by raising uncomfortable questions specially on issues like the Palestinian homeland. No wonder, as observed by the AHDR 2003, that some regional countries are using terrorism as an excuse to restrict the civil and political freedom. Such moves to suppress the public opinion are bound to further rejuvenate the discontent.

The strategy to retrieve the ground requires efforts at three levels—global, regional and national, not as exclusive space. From the global perspective, the region needs to regain its sovereignty and autonomy even in the limited sense available to other regions in the present phase of globalisation. In specific terms, region needs to be free from military presence of external powers, particularly USA. In situations like Iraq, international coalition under the UN could take the responsibility of resolving the issues. This could be a difficult decision for the superpower as it amounts to retreat. But the expansionist mode of the present kind too cannot serve its objectives. American foreign policy has still to come out of the Cold War mindset. American engagement in West Asia needs to be changed.

At the regional and national levels, the constituency of discontent needs to be contained by addressing to the issues that contributed to its resurgence. The ailing economy has been the prime factor behind the source of discontent. Faced with the situation of depleting rent, the political class attempted to resuscitate the economy, by initiating structural adjustment programme under the guidance of IMF-World Bank. SAP however failed to deliver. The economy did not generate the needed momentum. With the state cutting the social expenditure and pruning its size, the society witnessed sharpening of income disparities and rise of unemployment. What is more alarming is the growth of informal sector in society gaining sustenance from informal economy. The informal economy, 'includes unreported income from the production of legal goods and services, either from monetary or barter transactions—hence all economic activities which would generally be taxable were they reported to the state (tax) authorities'.[30] Thus rise of informal economy implies growth of economy beyond the control of the state. All the activities supported by this economy become out of the reach of governance. The second feature of the informal economy is the link with poverty.

There a link between working in the informal economy and being poor. Average incomes are lower in the informal economy than in the formal sector. As a result, a higher percentage of people working in the informal economy, relative to the formal sector, are poor.[31]

Estimates show that the informal economy is on rise in West Asia, ranging from 20 to 35 per cent of the economy. The rise of informal sector is the reflection of the rising pressure of the labour market and limited capacity of the organised sector to generate employment. In terms of inter regional comparison, unemployment in the region is highest in the world even more than sub Sahara Africa. According to ILO, it is around 19 per cent in this region, while 14 per cent in the case of sub-Saharan Africa.[32] The problem has acquired more serious dimension with organised jobs becoming high tech and highly skilled, posing the question of employability. The Economic Commission on West Asia in its study points out:

> The extensive investment in physical and human capital of the past three decades has had poor results. This may be because of the poor quality of investment in the education sector and the lack of incentives for private sector participation. Moreover, the institutional structure of the labour market has been such that, for many, 'rent seeking' has yielded a higher return than more productive and growth-enhancing activities. Developments have tended to encourage jobs for semi-skilled or unskilled labour that produced inferior products in a highly protective environment. Educated persons have preferred jobs in the public sector and education has been geared towards administrative and managerial jobs. As a result, workers have had few incentives to improve their skill levels and educational attainment has remained low. Furthermore, labour market rigidities and distortions did not reward appropriate human capital accumulation. Such distortions reduced the social returns of investment in education and reduced the incentive to accumulate skills.[33]

The poor economic performance of the region could be seen by the fact that the 'Per capita GDP decreased by an average 1.0 percent per year in the 1980s, a rate worse than that of any other developing region, except Sub-Saharan Africa. Although per capita income stopped contracting in the 1990s, it still grew by a mere 1.0 percent per year'.[34] Average financial flow from International Financial market to West Asia was $38 billion in the seventies, and $45 billion in the eighties, but dipped sharply in the nineties to $12 billion. The flow for the same period in Asia-Pacific has been $350 billion, $480 billion and $625 billion, for Latin America $255, $280, $210 billion.[35]

The increasing demographic burden on the society can be appreciated from Table 7.1. It may be noticed that in countries like Egypt,
Jordan, Saudi Arabia, Iraq, and Yemen, the economy has to move
at a very rapid pace of 5 to 6 per cent to generate space for new
entrants to engage them as stakeholders in the society.

Table 7.1
Population in Select West Asian Countries in millions

Country	2000	2010	2020
Bahrain	0.64	0.74	0.83
Egypt	67.89	83.53	102.46
Iraq	22.95	30.59	41.07
Jordan	4.91	6.60	8.73
Kuwait	1.91	2.27	2.63
Oman	2.54	3.66	4.87
Qatar	0.56	0.66	0.77
Saudi Arabia	20.35	29.44	39.36
UAE	2.61	3.01	3.36
Yemen	18.35	28.66	43.43

Source: Arab Human Development Report 2002.

The shrinking formal economy has driven the unemployed youth
to find place in the informal sector. The informal sector has its own
dynamics, code of conduct, norms and ethics.

The vast majority of the labouring classes remains dispersed in the
informal urban economy. In general, trade unions have failed to
link community concerns to those of the workplace. For this
reason, urban grassroots movements may find a space for collective action in the community or neighbourhood, rather than the
workplace. People are, for the most part, facing the same challenges of day-to-day living: finding secure housing, being able to
pay rent, acquiring urban amenities, and having adequate schools,
clinics, cultural centres and the like. Community-based struggles
for such collective consumption, through institutional settings
characterise, in some sense, urban social movements. However,
community activism in the form of urban social movements is rare
in the Middle East. Local soup kitchens, neighbourhood associations, church groups, or street trade-unionism are hardly common features in the region. The prevalence of authoritarian and
inefficient states, the legacy of populism, and the strength of family

and kinship ties render primary solidarities more pertinent than secondary associations and social movements.

There is, however, an argument that considers the Islamist movements in the region as the Middle Eastern version of urban social movements. No doubt Islamist movements notably that of social Islam represent a significant means through which some disadvantaged groups survive hardship and better their lives. These movements contribute to social welfare not only by direct provision of services and assistance to the needy; they also tend to compel rival social groups and institutions, such as state agencies and secular NGOs, to do the same.[36]

The most disturbing trend in the region is the perceived uncertainties with respect to future and sense of helplessness. Alarmingly this has been found at much higher level in the most affluent society of the region. 'The degree of insecurity in both its economic and cultural dimensions presumably relates to actual economic performance, embodying possibilities of both virtuous and vicious circles. In this regard, the recent experiences of Saudi Arabia could be read as a cautionary tale: weak economic performance leading to pessimism about the future, possibly counterproductive policy interventions, and bouts of political extremism.'[37]

Renewing the Social Contract: Ensuring Human Security

West Asia is evolving into spatial mould, where at one level, there is little transaction reflected in low turnover of intra regional flow of goods and commodities and trans-border collaborations, but at another level, trans-localisation of space is taking place, where the growing marginal segment of society is interacting on issues impinging on their sensitivities, which include besides the continuing struggle of Palestine, all kinds of protest movements across the Muslim societies. The reactions on the street and the slogans are not only expression of their solidarity, but more importantly, participation in the larger cause. In fact, it is perceived as their duty and obligation—the part of morality. Unlike other peripheral societies, West Asia is witnessing along with the resurgence of protest, formation of transnational polity from below. The ICT has further contributed in consolidation of the resistance. It is interesting that while the state has been restricting the free flow of information, the society is not beyond the reach of cyber communication. The restricted, yet accessible information regime is transmitting images and understanding of the worldview creating paranoid mindset at street level.

> Nothing in history has threatened the Muslim like the Western media; neither gunpowder in the Middle Ages...nor trains and the telephone, which helped colonize them... The Western mass media are ever present and ubiquitous; never resting and never allowing respite. They probe and attack ceaselessly showing no mercy for weakness or frailty.[38]

The ramifications are obvious. The new politics of West Asia thus is going to be determined by emerging translocalisation of regional space. The state will have to devise a new social contract embedded into new realities.

The new social contract has to be premised not as much on devolution of power, as on arresting the exclusionary processes. In the fractured polity of West Asia partially, power already resides beyond the formal polity.[39] The informal polity thrives on failure of the state to create institutions where the stakes of the people could be protected. The question thus arises whether moving into unknown will promote the required political culture to expand the formal polity. Brumberg rightly observes,[40]

> Consider the basic political requirements of a genuine democratization strategy. To be effective, it would require at its most elemental level a substantive shift—away from a demand-side, civil society—focused approach to a supply-side, state-focused approach. By the latter I do not mean narrowly conceived technical programs that are geared toward showing legislators how to pass bills or would-be candidates for office how to draft an election manifesto. Those are indeed state-focused, supply-side initiatives, but their narrow scope does little to address the core of the problem, which is the excessive and mostly unchecked power of unelected executives, or of executives who are 'elected' in state-managed polls that usually give them 90 percent or more of the vote.

To build on supply side initiatives, the burden of change has to be on rejuvenating the social sector, which has been neglected, as can be seen from the declining allocation for resources for the sector. A political commitment needs to be renewed, 'to widely valued social policies—a new social contract that links reform to the principles of poverty reduction, income equality, and income security that have guided political economies of the region for almost 50 years'.[41] The key thus lies in ensuring social security. The World Bank admits that the

region now faces economic and social risks that threaten investments in human capital and compromise the welfare of the population. Particularly vulnerable population groups include the poor, who are unable to engage in high-risk, high-return activities; children, who face the risk of entering informal labour markets prematurely; small landowners, who remain exposed to unanticipated changes in weather and fluctuations in prices; first-time job seekers and low-skilled workers, who face the risk of unemployment; and the elderly, who may lack access to sustainable health insurance and pension systems.[42]

The state has to reinvent its role as guaranteer of social security. A conscious choice has to be made that the space of social sector is not to be handed over to the market. The so-called neo liberal economic regime premises politics on the centrality of market as the efficient allocater of resources. It rationalises a trade-off between efficiency and equity, relegating the social sector on development agenda. The market institution in West Asia are neither ready nor do they enjoy the popular trust. What is needed is to build participatory polity by developing a participatory economy. Thus, without compromising on the efficient utilisation of resources, stakes have to be created for marginal segments in the economy but not by re-distributive mechanism alone.

All countries in the region have put in place comprehensive social protection systems that combine labour market programs, social insurance programs, and social assistance programs. The goal of these programs is to assist individuals in managing social risks, man-made (unemployment, inflation) and natural (adverse weather, disease). The social protection system becomes a mechanism to insure investments in human capital and to promote the accumulation of human capital among the poor and vulnerable. Most social protection systems, however, are facing problems.[43]

The capacity building at societal level could be the pathway to engage the millions from the informal sector. What is being argued here is that a synergy needs to be created between the state and civil society to strengthen the social sector, thereby bringing stakes of the informal society into the mainstream.

Summing up, the trajectory of change in West Asia is unfolding on the contradictions of weak reforms and strong discontent (resurgence). Democratic deficit as the main agenda of the reform could be a desirable condition, but as argued earlier, it is not sufficient to contain the sources of discontent. The twin factors, the birth of Palestinian nation and the dependence on regional hydrocarbon, continue to have bearing on the regional psyche. The unipolar globalising world has yet to demonstrate its sensitivities in adequate measure towards the discontent it is creating in West Asia. In other words, the strength of reforms in West Asia critically hinges on the position of the external stakeholders on the two issues mentioned earlier. It can be hypothesised that a satisfactory resolution of Palestinian-Israeli conflict alone can change the popular political preferences. It will weaken the polarised polity and widen the political choices, and thereby the prospects of electoral results. At the regional level, the strengthening of reform has to be predicated on retrieving the space from the informal formations by addressing the concerns of marginalising segments of society by empowering the social sector on the strength of economy. Hence, the disjuncture promoted by the market, by relegating social issues to be taken care by the trickledown effect, has to be contested in the context of societies with skewed asset distribution. The state cannot absolve and retreat its social responsibility. This certainly does not make a case for authoritarian state. The state in West Asia has been on authoritarian mode because the economy has not been democratic. It is only a participatory economy that could contain the alienation of the society, the distance between government and society, and create political temper for democracy to go beyond becoming merely an electoral exercise.

India and the Emerging West Asia

Resurgence and reform in the emerging West Asia has implications for India. The region is seen by India as its extended neighbourhood. History of Indian interaction with the region tells the intensive and extensive nature of mutual influences in all aspects of life. In contemporary times too, India is a major buyer of energy from the region, earns rich remittances from Indians working there. Its presence is quite visible in the developmental activities of the region. Besides, the largest minority in India shares religion with the majority of the region. Thus India cannot remain isolated from the developments in the region. The drift and despair of discontent from the region has been spilling over to India. Its energy security is susceptible to the region's energy flows. The stakes are huge both material, as well as ideological. From West Asian perspective, India might not have been a substantive actor in their external engagement during the Cold War years, but it has gained new significance as an emerging energy market and software power. Besides, 11 September has forced the political class in the region to review their excessive engagement with the West and look for energising ties with the eastern neighbours.

The issues that acquire significance from the Indian perspective could be classified as global and the regional. The globalising-unipolar world, working on the doctrine of preemption is not in conformity with Indian worldview. It doesn't serve the interest of West Asia either. It restricts the space for autonomy for both. This is a matter of mutual concern. While a benign presence of USA in the region, in the short run, could be of some relevance, prospects of Pax Americana is detrimental to the Indian interest. Therefore, India needs to extend its support to the region to undermine the American hegemony. It may be recalled that India, along with Egypt and other Afro-Asian countries, did articulate common concern by conceptualis-ing the doctrine of non-alignment. It provided India an ideological clout. Particularly in West Asia, the Nehru–Nasser for-mulation even if not accepted by many regimes of the region, created the image of India resisting the dominant paradigm. India, despite its poverty and backwardness, contributed in the nation-building process in West Asia by providing undefined and invisible inputs. India needs to take initiative of similar nature against the negative stereotyping of the region as Islamic world and terrorism, as justi-fication for intervention. From Palestinian issue to Iraq, from pro-motion of religious militancy in the Cold War days to the war on terror, and recently, the WMD, the region has been paying for the flawed diagnosis, many times based on wrong informations and even fiction. The consequences of these policies impinge seriously on Indian interest. Indian diplomacy ought to hedge against such fall-outs by widening the terms and reference of debate on the strength of its own historical interface with Islam to provide a more realistic and holistic understanding. Indian intervention in the debate could be both authentic and effective. Many countries in the region do expect a proactive role from India on correcting distorted hegemonic nature of the debate. What is not well recognised by the Indian establishment is that spillover of such flawed policy could create a context, forcing them to be the party in promoting unilateralism, defeating the basic premise of the Indian foreign policy. Indian approach towards the so-called fight against terror illustrates the point. This is not the place to elaborate; it will suffice to mention the two self-explanatory developments brought to light by non-West Asian sources—one, that Saddam Hussein had no linkages with Al Qaeda and that post-Saddam Iraq has groups having ties with various transnational outfits including the Al Qaeda, and second, the number of people killed by US-led multinational forces are much larger than the Iraqi insurgents. It is imperative that in the light of emerging facts a reappraisal is made of the fight against terror by looking into the totality of the context. It requires appreciation of regional concerns without undermining the global sensitivities, and forge a regional coalition to contain all that which goes in its making. A regional approach would be a more realistic policy. It may be mentioned that terrorism even though spreading across the globe is not a monolithic entity. It is neither religious nor limited to West Asia. It needs to be disaggregated than forced to forge collective identity. India's West Asia policy thus has to engage on a range of issues on structured and sustained basis. One such issue disturbing the West Asian psyche where India could play a role would be against the cultural homogenisation threatening the cultural identity.

'Culture is the heart of a nation. As countries become more economically integrated, nations need strong domestic cultures and cultural expression to maintain their sovereignty and sense of iden-tity.' This does not mean cultural protectionism but underline the need to recognise 'that cultural diversity, like biodiversity, must be preserved and nurtured. As the world becomes more economically integrated, countries need strong local cultures and cultural expression to maintain their sovereignty and sense of belonging'.[44] As pointed out earlier, West Asia is suffering from acute sense of loss of sovereignty and threat to the identity. India too is witnessing, though in lesser proportion, the anxiety of cultural hegemony. It may be emphasised that the perceived loss of cultural space at popular level is a factor in encouraging the so-called fundamentalism in all societies not in West Asia alone. It can be contested only by preservation of cultural space, cultural autonomy. Making of West Asia Regional Coalition on Cultural Diversity reinforcing the global cultural diversity could be the Indian initiative in this direction. The Indian civilisation based and survived on cultural diversity provides the natural advantage and vision to articulate towards a worldview on global cultural diversity. To achieve these objectives Indian diplomacy has to work at two levels—one, to create a regional debate and dialogue on cultural diversity in the era of globalisation; second, to mobilise regional resources for the development and implementation of a new instrument equivalent to the World Trade Organisation's trade agreements which set out rules appropriate for cultural expression.

Another area where India can contribute could be in upgrading their social infrastructure and institutions to meet the demands of globalisation and sustain it. The region suffers from technologically inadequately developed infrastructure in the areas which are going to set the pace in the coming decade, i.e., the information technology and the knowledge economy. The human resource base of the region is poor not only in quantitative terms, but also qualitatively to meet the demands of the high-tech and high skilled production processes and entrepreneurship. The R&D strength of the region is very weak so are the institutions not compatible with market economy. Economic institutions are not geared to face the demands of the global market. In these areas, India, despite its own share of poverty, has made significant progress and has experience, which could be complementary to the demands of the West Asian economies. India needs to reinvent its West Asia policy breaking the prevailing inertia, with the changed mindset to play a meaningful role in the world affairs.

Notes and References

1. 'The nation state has become a dysfunctional unit for understanding and managing the flows of economic activity that dominate today's borderless world. Policy makers, politicians and corporate managers would benefit from looking at "region states"—the globe's natural economic zones—whether they happen to fall within or across traditional political boundaries. With their efficient scales of consumption, infrastructure and professional services, region states make ideal entryways into the global economy. If allowed to pursue their own economic interests without jealous government interference, the prosperity of these areas will eventually spill over.' Kenichi Ohamae, 'The Rise of the Region State', *Foreign Affairs*, Spring, 1993.

2. Hazim Saghie, 'It's not all America's Fault', *Time*, 15 October 2001 quoted in Trevor Mostyn, *Censorship in Islamic Societies*. London, Saqi Books, 2002.

3. Peter Mandaville, *Transnational Muslim Politics*. London, 2001, p. 50.

4. Saskia Sassen, 'A New Geography of Power?' http://www.debalie.nl/artikel.jsp? articleid=16225

5. C.M. Henry and R. Springborg, *Globalisation and the Politics of Development in the Middle East*. London, Cambridge University Press, 2001.

6. Alan Richards, 'The Political Economy of Economic Reform in the Middle East: The Challenge to Governance Prepared for RAND', http://sccie.ucsc.edu/ documents/working_papers/2001/challenge_econreform.pdf

7. Michele Dunne, 'The United States and Political Reform in Egypt: A New Era', *Arab Reform Bulletin*, vol. 2, no. 5, May 2004, Carnegie Endowment for International Peace.

8. Remarks by President George W. Bush at the 20th Anniversary of the National Endowment for Democracy, Washington DC, 6 November 2003. Quoted from http://www.meib.org/articles/0407_me2.htm

9. Arab News, 29 May 2004.

10. Aljazeera_Net - Arab reform alternative.htm

11. http://www.arabicnews.com/ansub/Daily/Day/040221/2004022113.html

12. Ron Synovitz, World: Arab League Adopts First Joint Reform Plan Radio Free Europe/Radio Liberty © 2004 RFE/RL, 23 May 2004.

13. http://www.arabsummit.tn/en/tunis-declaration.html

14. Alexandria Statement March 2004. Final Statement of 'Arab Reform Issues: Vision and Implementation', 12–14 March 2004, Bibliotheca Alexandria.

15. 'Arab Business Council Announces New Blueprint for Economic Reform in the Middle East', *World Economic Forum*. http://www.weforum.org/

16. Ibid.

17. Press Review: Special issue on UNDP Arab Human Development Report, 5 July 2002, United Nations Information Centre (UNIC), Beirut.

18. *Al-Hayat*, 4 October 2002, p. 10.

19. *Al-Nahar*, Beirut, 16 August 2002, p. 13.

20. Sami E. Baroudi, 'The 2002 Arab Human Development Report: Implications for Democracy UNDP 2002'.

21. http://english.aljazeera.net

22. Ismail Sirageldin, 'What Next after the Alexandria Declaration?' News Letter, Of The Economic Research Forum for the Arab Countires, Iran and Turkey, vol. 11, no. 2, Summer, 2004.
23. World Bank Better Governance for Development in the Middle East and North Africa. http://lnweb18.worldbank.org/
24. Marcus Noland and Howard Pack Islam, 'Globalisation and Economic Performance in the Middle East', *International Economics Policy Briefs*, no. PB04-4, June 2004.
25. Donna Abu-Nasr. Arab intellectuals soul-searching over terrorism in the name of Islam. http://ap.tbo.com/ap/breaking/MGBW8UMYCZD.html
26. Michael Theodoulou, Arab Press Finds Roots of Terrorism Closer to Home. Public Debate is Emerging Over the Link between Political Oppression and Militancy. www.http/csmonitor_com.html
27. Ibid.
28. Arab News, 8 October 2004.
29. Ibid.
30. Friedrich Schneider, 'Size and Measurement of the Informal Economy in 110 Countries Around the World', July 2002. rru.worldbank.org/Documents/PapersLinks/informal_economy.pdf
31. Marilyn Carr and Martha Alter Chen, 'Globalization and the Informal Economy: How Global Trade and Investment Impact on the Working Poor'. www.wiego.org/papers/carrchenglobalization.pdf
32. ILO Global Employment Report.
33. Globalisation and Labour Market in ESCWA Region, Economic and Social Commission on Western Asia, 2001.
34. Macro Economic Trends in the Middle East and North Africa', Economic Research Forum Cairo, Egypt.
35. 'Globalization of Financial Markets: Implications for the ESCWA Region, Economic and Social Commission for Western Asia, Beirut, 2002.
36. Asef Bayat, 'Social Movements, Activism and Social Development in the Middle East Civil Society and Social Movements Programme', Paper Number 3, November 2000. United Nations Research Institute for Social Development.
37. Marcus Noland and Howard Pack Islam, 'Globalization, and Economic Performance in the Middle East', *International Economics Policy Briefs*, no. PB04-4, June 2004.
38. A.S. Ahmed, *Post Modernism and Islam, Predicament and Promise*. London, Routledge, 1992.
39. Lisa Anderson, 'Political Decay in the Arab World', www.dayan.org/mel/anderson.pdf
40. Daniel Brumberg, 'Beyond Liberalisation?' *The Wilson Quarterly*, Spring, 2004.
41. 'Creating 100 million jobs for fat growing work force'. http://lnweb18.worldbank.org/mna/mena.nsf/Attachments/EmploymentOverview/$File/Employment-overview.pdf
42. http://lnweb18.worldbank.org/mna/mena.nsf
43. http://lnweb18.worldbank.org/mna/mena.nsf/Sectors
44. http://www.cdc-ccd.org/Anglais/welcome.html

8

CENTRAL ASIA'S SECURITY: THE ASIAN DIMENSION

Ajay Patnaik

Introduction

The disintegration of the former Soviet Union resulted in the independence of five former Soviet Central Asian republics—Kazakhstan, Kyrgyzstan, Uzbekistan, Tajikistan and Turkmenistan. Kazakhstan is the largest in terms of area, while Uzbekistan has the largest number of population. Titular nationality constitutes majority in each republic and, except in Tajikistan, is of Turkic ethnicity. Tajiks belong to the Persian-speaking group. At the time of independence, there were a substantial number of Russians and other Slavic population in Central Asia. In Kazakhstan, they formed more than a third of the population, and in Kyrgyzstan about a quarter. Central Asia experienced some violent inter-ethnic clashes just prior to independence. Rising ethno-nationalism combined with religious revivalism resulted in large-scale migration of Slavs. The challenges to independent statehood came not just from forces that threatened internal instability, but also from heightened insecurity from external threats. Along with the euphoria of independence, there was a certain degree of vulnerability on account of economic and military weakness. Disputed borders and complex ethno-territorial legacy added to the security worries of Central Asia.

Soviet disintegration changed the geopolitics of Central Asia, and so also the security scenario in the region. Central Asia acquired not only immense geopolitical significance but also experienced a power vacuum. As a result, this region became key to the security of many neighbouring countries, big and small. The fear of some adversary filling the vacuum prompted neighbouring states to seek influence in the region. Russia and China were worried about the possible threats to their internal stability emanating from Central Asia. Others such as Turkey, Saudi Arabia, Iran and Pakistan were eager to gain maximum influence at the cost of their regional rivals. Regional rivalries were getting mixed up with various forms of religious radicalism. This resulted in making the region very volatile.

With the coming of Taliban to power in Afghanistan in 1996, the threat to security of the Central Asian states grew manifold. Mounting cross-border terrorism, supported by the Taliban government, backed by international terrorist groups and sustained by drug money, became the biggest challenge to their external security and internal stability. Central Asia's threat perception heightened and the relationship with most of its Islamic neighbours cooled. The role of Russia and the United States increased in the region to ensure regional stability. The engagement of two mighty global powers is presumed to take care of Central Asia's security needs so comprehensively that there may not be any role left for Asian powers in the region.

This paper underlines the significance of Central Asia for the security and stability of some Asian countries, and vice versa. Despite the threat emanating from its Asian neighbourhood, there is a common threat perception that the Central Asian states share with some of their Asian counterparts. The role of three Asian countries is highlighted in this paper. The three countries chosen—China, Iran and India—are Asian powers, affected by the developments in Central Asia, and have made positive contribution to strengthen peace and regional stability. India and Iran have strong links with Tajikistan, as well as with important elements in the post-Taliban Afghanistan. China has taken major steps to meet some of the security worries of Kazakhstan, Kyrgyzstan and Tajikistan. As countries that are likely to be adversely affected by threats to peace and stability in Central Asia, these Asian powers cannot ignore the region, and should aim at policies that would strengthen their engagement in Central Asia.

Security Scenario in Central Asia

Independence was so sudden that the new states in Central Asia did not know what kind of relations would evolve among themselves and with their regional neighbours. Given the territorial disputes, presence of large ethnic minorities, and the recent incidents of inter-ethnic conflicts in 1989–90, the spectre of war and civil war between neighbours was not ruled out. Lack of a strong regular armed force heightened their fears vis-à-vis more powerful neighbours. The vulnerability of the new states could start a competition for influence in Central Asia. Some scholars even talked of a 'new great game', especially with the region's oil and gas resources coming to international limelight.

Central Asia's security scenario until now has evolved through three phases. The first phase was till the mid-nineties before the coming of the Taliban to power. During this period, though Central Asian states were part of the Commonwealth of Independent States and its security complex, they sought to intensify their relations with Islamic states. The second phase includes the Taliban years in Afghanistan. During this period Russia became the main security guarantor, and sustained the anti-Taliban front with support from states like Tajikistan, India and Iran. The third stage set in since the 11 September 2001 terrorist attack in the United States. USA and Russia increased their presence in the region and Central Asia is insulated from external threats by the strong security cover provided by these two military superpowers.

During the first phase (1991–96), Central Asian countries sought closer collaboration with the Islamic states, though they remained linked with Russia by joining the Commonwealth of Independent States (CIS), which was formed in December 1991. The CIS framework guaranteed the territorial integrity of the Central Asian states. Not only were Soviet-created borders recognised by their CIS neighbours, the Central Asian states were also protected from outside threats by the CIS security structure. All of them barring Turkmenistan entered into a CIS Collective Security Treaty signed in May 1992 that also included Russia and Armenia.

However, during the early days of independence, the euphoria of nationalism and religious revivalism propelled these new states towards their Islamic neighbours. An open-door policy was followed with the hope that an extended cultural neighbourhood would stabilise their independence and lessen their dependence on Russia. Funds started pouring in from Saudi Arabia, Iran, Pakistan and Turkey to augment religious and cultural institutions. Groups propounding political Islam were finding ideological and material support from these states. A struggle for cultural influence in the region began. It was expected that due to historical, cultural and religious affinities, and because of their own military and economic weakness, Central Asian states could be brought under their influence.[1]

Central Asian states joined the Organisation of Islamic Conference (OIC) and other regional groupings such as Economic Cooperation Organisation (ECO) to strengthen their ties with Islamic countries.[2] Economic limitations of the member states and tension between them made these organisations ineffective. Early hopes of strengthening economic integration with Islamic neighbours have not materialised. These powers were interested in spreading their own brand of ideology to obtain hegemony that hardly helped in ensuring security or development in Central Asia. Competing perspectives and limited objectives of Central Asia's southern neighbours (in West Asia as well as in South Asia) were bound to impinge on their capacity to have a strong influence in the region.[3]

For example, in the early years of Central Asia's independence (late 1991 to early 1993), Iran took the lead in encouraging and shaping religious revival in Central Asia. This included sponsored missionary activity, distribution of religious books, broadcasting of Iranian television and radio in Central Asia, training of mullahs in Iranian *madrasahs*, and opening of religious schools and mosques. Iran was reportedly supporting the Islamic Revival Party (IRP) of Tajikistan. The initial fervour, however, calmed down as Saudi Arabia and Pakistan entered in a big way in this fray and Iran subsequently, became less aggressive in religious proselytising, and concentrated more on good diplomatic and economic relations.[4]

The involvement of Islamic neighbours, especially in Tajikistan, brought Russia right back to Central Asia after initial hesitation. The fear of religious extremism and instability from Central Asia could affect Russia's Caucasus and Volga region, where bulk of its Muslim nationalities reside. The beginning of the Tajik civil war in 1992 and cross-border support to Islamic opposition in Tajikistan led to the stationing of Russian troops on Tajik-Afghan border, which ensured Tajikistan's territorial integrity during and after the civil war.

The rise of the Taliban and its coming to power in Kabul, dramatically changed the security scenario in Central Asia. The region was in the danger of being sucked into a world of radical Islam, the foundations of which had been laid in Afghanistan. However, the victory of the Taliban also ended the illusion that secular and moderate Central Asia can integrate with its Islamic neighbours in a larger cultural space for mutual advantage. Some states, like Iran, changed course feeling the heat from the Taliban, and others like, Saudi Arabia and Pakistan, sided with the Taliban.

During this phase (1996–2001), Russia became the major security guarantor of Central Asia, and China looked beyond economic opportunities in the region to issues of regional stability and religious extremism. India, faced with the escalation of cross-border terrorism emanating from Pakistan and Afghanistan, looked at Central Asia as a region with which its security interests converged. Symptomatic of these changes were the settlement of the Sino-Central Asian border problems and the creation of the Shanghai Five. Iran's role in conflict resolution in Tajikisan, and India and Iran's role in coordinating their efforts with Russia to help the Northern Alliance in Afghanistan were symbolic of the positive role these Asian powers played in preserving peace and stability in Central Asia.

The terrorist bombings in the United States on 11 September 2001 radically metamorphosed the geopolitics of the Central Asian region, which became vital to US security interests. Both energy and international terrorism drew US physical presence to the region. Though earlier it operated through NATO's peace programmes, it now became the main security alternative for the Central Asian states. The US presence in the region has alarmed Russia, and its presence in the region has equally grown. Both have troops and military bases in Central Asia. There is a danger that US-Russia cooperation could marginalise the Asian powers in the region and jeopardise their interests. However, in a variety of ways, China, Iran and India have contributed to the stability in the region and met some of its security needs. Given their economic and military potential, the political goodwill they enjoy in Central Asia, and friendly relationship with Russia, these three Asian powers are expected to remain involved in the Central Asian security scenario.

China-Central Asia Relations

Bordering on three Central Asian countries—Kazakhstan, Kyrgyzstan and Tajikistan—China's significant size, fast growing economy, and powerful military make it a potential major player in Central Asia. From the Chinese perspective, according to Guangchang Xing, the strategic importance of Central Asia will increase. China considers Central Asia in the context of Eurasia, and these states have a linking role not just in the geographical sense but also in a political and cultural sense—a bridge between East and West. However, if there were to be turbulence around the 'bridge', the future political and economic cooperation in the whole Eurasia would be seriously affected. That is why Chinese political and economic cooperation is viewed as vital to the stability and prosperity in the region, adds Xing.[5]

At the time of Soviet disintegration, ideological and political problems apart, China's major apprehensions included security challenges along China's northern frontier provinces, especially the Xinjiang-Uighur region. Issues of ethnicity and religious revivalism, in addition to the lingering problem of border disputes, were key problems that defined the security parameters of China's relations with Central Asia, according to Gerald Segal.[6] China was also concerned about the nuclear threat emanating from Central Asia, especially when Kazakhstan's President Nazarbaev declared in early 1992 that his country has a right to remain nuclear. Subsequently, under US persuasion, it signed the NPT as a non-nuclear weapon country in May 1992, and in the same month, signed the Lisbon Protocol of START treaty maintaining its non-nuclear status. By mid-1995 all nuclear warheads in Kazakhstan were either transferred to Russia, or destroyed. Before that in February 1995, the Chinese government had already issued its security assurance to Kazakhstan, and urged all nuclear-weapon states to undertake the same commitment.[7]

Central Asia's concerns included territorial disputes and presence of Chinese forces on the border in huge strength. There were also apprehensions over China's nuclear testing and Chinese economic projects on Central Asia's border that might cause environmental problems. China's rising military and economic power is both a matter of advantage and concern. China looks towards Central Asia's rich deposits of oil and gas and other minerals and metals, access to which will fuel China's rapid industrial development. The Central Asian states look to China for its huge market, capital investment potentiality and access to the sea.[8]

China and Central Asian states have several common concerns in the region and they have made positive moves to meet those, and in the process have been able to create a regional organisation for security and cooperation, known as the Shanghai Cooperation Organisation (SCO).

Settlement of the Border Issues

For China as well as bordering Central Asian states, there was a common imperative to stabilise the frontier and create a favourable external environment for improvement in bilateral relations. China shares nearly 3,500 km border with Kazakhstan, Kyrgyzstan and Tajikistan. Border talks were carried out on the basis of: (*a*) respect for agreements already entered into in the Sino-Soviet border talks; (*b*) recognition of existing treaties as basis for future negotiations; (*c*) willingness to settle all disputes in accordance with established rules of international law; and (*d*) mutual consultation on equal footing or mutual accommodation. The Sino-Kyrgyz and the Sino-Tajik Joint Communiques in 1992 and 1993 confirmed these principles. Sino-Kazakh border agreement signed on 27 April 1994 finalised in principle the delineation of the 1,700 km long border. Both countries signed an agreement on 4 July 1998 that finally brought an end to their long-standing border disputes. Subsequently, understanding was also reached on the China-Kyrgyzstan and China-Tajikistan border.[9]

Talks to resolve the border issue culminated in a Summit of the five countries in Shanghai in April 1996, the focus of which was to settle the border question and secure tension-free relationship among them. The five states included China and the four former Soviet republics (Russia and three Central Asian states) that share border with China. At the time of its formation in 1996, the Shanghai Five members formed a regional border security forum, and agreed to cut their armed forces along their common border, and refrain from using force against each other.

The April 1996 Shanghai Five Agreement on Mutual Military Confidence-building Measures was the first collective agreement between Russia, China and three Central Asian republics. Besides an accord on mutual troop reduction on the borders to a level that would make offensive action impossible, the parties agreed not to use force or threaten to use force in case of disputes nor would seek unilateral military superiority. In the next Summit at Moscow in 1997, Russia proposed a zone of peace along the borders. The Moscow Agreement on Mutual Reduction of Military Forces in the Border Region, signed in April 1997, committed the five countries to reduce military forces in the border, and maintain only defensive troops. They also agreed not to use weapons or threaten to use them to seek to maintain military superiority, and to reduce number of ground forces, air forces, air defence forces and border defence forces, and the number of major weapons deployed within 100 km on either side of the border. The members further committed to define the size of the forces remaining after the reduction, and the manner and timetable of this reduction, to exchange relevant information on their forces deployed in the border region, and to conduct regular verification of the implementation of the agreement. The agreement is valid till 2020, but can be extended. The information exchanged on the military forces in the border area will be kept secret from third parties.[10]

The whole process of border negotiations was based on such a spirit of cordiality and mutual accommodation that the delimitation of the borders has been more or less smooth. The formation of the regional grouping, Shanghai Five, symbolised the significance the five countries attached to harmonious relations between them. A joint declaration signed by the Shanghai Five leaders in Tajikistan's capital Dushanbe on 5 July 2000 further emphasised the highest priority given to state sovereignty by the members, thus signalling that border issues are unlikely to pose any military crisis among them.

Border agreement has helped Central Asian states in demobilising to a large extent their limited armed forces from the Chinese border. They are now able to focus and concentrate their troops against threats from other sources. Military confidence-building has also been extended to cooperation in the defence field. While Russia remains the main external supplier of military and defence hardware to all the rest, China has taken a few, though limited, steps to augment the defence capabilities of Central Asian states. Military delegations have been exchanged between China and Central Asia states on a regular basis since 1995. China provided an aid of 11 million yuan to Kazakhstan's armed forces during the visit of the Kazakh defence minister in April 2000, and is seeking closer military ties with other Central Asian states as well. The Turkmen defence minister who visited China in September 1999 expressed interest in cooperation in the field of military training and use of equipment. A Chinese military delegation visited Tajikistan on 13 July 2000. China has also enhanced its military ties with Uzbekistan, which is under great pressure from Islamic militancy and extremism. Before 11 September 2001, apart from Russia, China was the only other power to supply lethal weapons to Central Asia. China provided Uzbekistan with sniper rifles as well as flak jackets. China has provided Kyrgyzstan assistance worth $600,000, to include tents and army gears, and in June 2001, the Kyrgyz and the Chinese defence ministers agreed to the training of Kyrgyz soldiers at a training centre in Guangzhou in China.[11]

Religious Extremism and International Terrorism

There is a mutual concern regarding religious extremism and cross-border terrorism. China fears that such movements could emerge from Central Asia to threaten China's north-west region, home to Turkic-Muslim ethnic groups that are culturally similar, and can be influenced by the independence of neighbouring former Soviet republics and the revival of Islam there. Central Asian states (some have substantial Uighur population), in turn, are concerned that separatism and religious radicalism among Uighurs in China's Xinjiang could create problems in their own states.[12]

All the member states of Shanghai Five have faced threats to internal stability from radical forces backed by external terrorist groups. After the victory of the Taliban in Afghanistan the terrorist activities increased substantially. Common threat perception and need to cooperate resulted in an agreement at the Almaty Summit (Kazakhstan) in 1998. Members pledged to reject 'all manifestations of national separatism and religious extremism' and to ban on their territories 'activities harmful to state sovereignty, security and public order' of any of the member states. At the fourth summit of the Shanghai Five in Kyrgyz capital Bishkek (August 1999), the member states agreed to make joint effort to fight 'ethnic separatism, religious extremism and international terrorism'.[13]

The threat of religious extremism in Central Asia fuelled by Taliban regime in Afghanistan triggered stronger coordination among the five states. In fact, going beyond the border issue made the organisation open for membership to other neighbouring states that faced challenges of cross-border terrorism. Uzbekistan joined the organisation in January 2002, and since then, it is named as Shanghai Cooper-ation Organisation (SCO). For all the six states, terrorist camps in Chechnya, Xinjiang, in the Ferghana Valley region, and the southern belt bordering on Afghanistan have been a major source of worry. The SCO decided to specifically focus on these regions and on terrorist organisations like the Islamic Movement of Uzbekistan (IMU).

However, there was a greater imperative for making SCO a larger security organisation that can effectively deal with international ter-rorism and regional security. As a result, at the same summit in January 2002, the presidents of all the member states signed a charter transforming the SCO security bloc into a full-fledged international organisation with a permanent secretariat based in Beijing. They also agreed to set up a regional anti-terrorist structure, and signed a political declaration underlining the SCO's joint goals. The charter makes the regional anti-terrorist structure as a permanent organisation within the SCO. The political declaration stated that the aim of the Shanghai group is to fight terrorism, prevent conflicts, and ensure security in Central Asia.[14]

In 2004, the Shanghai Cooperation Organisation formally operationalised two permanent bodies—a secretariat and an anti-terrorist set-up. The secretariat will handle organisational and paper-work for the SCO's apex bodies that include four councils consisting of heads of states, heads of government, foreign ministers and national coordinators. The anti-terrorist centre is charged with com-bating terrorism, extremism, separatism, and the illegal narcotics trade. With these two working bodies in place, SCO began operating 'as a full-fledged international organisation complete with its work-ing mechanism and budget'.[15]

Expanding Economic and Energy Cooperation

A major strategic objective for China is related to economic aspects of China's relations with Central Asia. The former has emphasised a gradual regional economic cooperation between the latter and Xinjiang. Immediately after the emergence of new states, China established rail and road links with bordering Central Asian republics. Cheap Chinese consumer goods flooded the region.[16]

One of the biggest oil-bearing basins in Asia, the Tarim basin lies in the Xinjiang Uighur Autonomous Province of China. The long-

term economic aim of China is to develop its north-western region.
Central Asia is important not only for China's territorial integrity
but also for its future energy and economic development. China
equally needs to find new markets for its consumer goods in nearby
markets such as Central Asia. The implications of Western interests
in exploiting the oil and gas resources are but an added factor in this
overall Central Eurasian matrix for China, according to Svante
Cornell and Maria Sultan. Attempts are being made by Beijing to
develop a broader conceptual framework for regional cooperation on
the basis of cooperative security, and the shared principles of interaction in the bilateral and regional power-framework in Central Asia,
they add.[17]

The Chinese business has also moved in a big way into Central
Asia. Official sources in China reported that Chinese investment in
Central Asia was to the tune of $1 billion in 2004. Beijing has trade
missions in all the countries there. China's trade with Central Asia
registered a ten-fold increase in a decade since 1994.[18] China can
extend access to sea for the landlocked states through its ports on
the Pacific, which helps the latter in their search for alternative routes,
and reduces their dependence on Moscow. In view of Western
projects to take Caspian oil and gas westward through a new network
of pipelines, China is keen to ensure that the Caspian oil and gas are
not delivered only to the West.[19]

In the field of energy, the economies of Central Asian Republics
and China are mutually complimentary. While the Central Asia has
natural resources, China has market, capital and technology.
Turkmenistan and Kazakhstan are the main focus of China, which
is particularly interested in gaining access to their resources and
ensure its own future energy security. A joint statement issued during
President Jiang Zemin's visit to Turkmenistan's capital Ashgabat on
6 July 2000 attached special importance to strengthening mutually
beneficial cooperation in the energy sector. Central Asian republics
also realise that increased cooperation with China will link their
economies with the Asia-Pacific economic boom.[20]

Similar views were expressed by Sebastian Bersick, a research
fellow at the European Institute for Asian Studies in Brussels, which
is preparing a major study for the European Commission on Europe's
interests in East Asia. According to Bersick, Central Asia could
benefit from China's move to forge strong regional bonds in East
Asia. The likely development of a free trade area between China and

some ASEAN countries would offer trade opportunities for Central Asian countries as well, for whom, joining the free trade area could also be an option in the future.[21]

Expanding multilateral trade has been high on the agenda of the SCO as well. The political declaration at the founding summit in 2002 underlined the participants' intention to step up negotiations on creating favourable conditions for trade and investments, and to develop a long-term programme for multilateral economic cooperation. According to the document, projects in improving transportation, power generation, water use, and energy will be given priority. Similar urgency was expressed in the prime ministerial meeting of the member states on 23 September 2004 in Bishkek, where a joint communique and several agreements highlighted not only cooperation in the field of security but also in economic sphere. According to the Chinese prime minister, economic cooperation will focus on energy, transportation, telecommunication, and agricultural sectors.[22]

Geopolitical factors indicate a high priority for economic and trade contacts between Central Asia and China, argues Xing. Their economic structures are complimentary. The opening of the 'second Eurasian land-bridge' and the improvement of transport connections have provided a solid material basis for improving relations. This land-bridge is an important route for China to be the link of the Central Asian states with the Pacific. Increased cooperation with China and the Pacific states would enable the Central Asian states to join the 'dynamic Asian heartland', i.e., the emerging 'Pacific economic ring'. China provides not only a large market, but the projected oil and gas pipelines to China would further boost the economies of Central Asia.[23]

In short, beginning with confidence-building measures along the border, Central Asia-China relations have grown from strength to strength. Fight against international terrorism and religious extremism have brought these countries closer, and the Shanghai Cooperation Organisation has transformed itself into a regional forum for security and economic cooperation. There are bound to be some misgivings, especially on the Central Asian side. Given past relations including border disputes as well as uneven economic and military might, Central Asians would be more comfortable with another major power balancing China's increasing influence in the region.

Iran-Central Asia Cooperation and Regional Stability

The creation of five independent states in Central Asia brought new challenges and opportunities for Iran. Iran had historical and cultural ties with the region since ancient times. Its geographical location close to the region has its advantage. It shares Caspian Sea with Kazakhstan and has a long border with Turkmenistan. According to Abbas Maleki, the disintegration of Soviet Union led to the formation of a new security complex in Central and West Asia of non-Arab states. This complex includes Iran, Afghanistan, Caucasian states and Central Asia. This provides Iran a historical opportunity to break out of the unstable and troublesome Arab-dominated West Asian sub-system to a new sub-system. Iran saw the merits in the new security complex, which includes countries with historical and cultural affinities and can fulfil Iran's aspiration for leadership.[24]

The military-industrial complex of Kazakhstan and Uzbekistan, producing communication devices and aircrafts, such as Mig-29 and IL-76, could supply Iran with military hardware. Some have even suggested that a special dimension to Iran's interest in this region might include search for nuclear capability.[25]

Central Asia's large market for items such as foodstuff, agricultural products, consumer goods, electronics and vehicles, etc., and need for modernisation of industries created opportunities for Iran. Oil and gas industry of Iran could take advantage of energy resources in countries like Kazakhstan, Turkmenistan and Uzbekistan, which can also benefit from shortest access to international markets through Iran's Persian Gulf ports. The transportation time could even be shortened by swap arrangements with Iran. For poor countries like Tajikistan and Kyrgyzstan, which lack oil and gas resources, Iran could be an alternative source of energy.[26]

A more pragmatic policy towards the region was initiated during the visit of President Rafsanjani in 1993, when religion occupied a very small part of the discussion, and more emphasis was laid on peace, stability and cooperation, especially in the economic field. Iran came to appreciate the need for peace and stability in Central Asia, which, if threatened, could affect Iran's own national security.[27]

Iran's Role in Regional Peace

After initial attempt to use radical Islamic forces for spreading its influence in Central Asia, Iran played a constructive role in the security of Central Asia. As a result, Iran's relations with Russia and Central Asian states improved since the mid-nineties. Iran has not developed much military-security ties with the Central Asian republics. However, it has played an active role in conflict resolution and mediation, especially in the case of Tajikistan.[28] Iran became a key supporter of the UN-backed mediation efforts and was instrumental in securing the acceptance of the Islamist-led United Tajik Opposition (UTO) to a ceasefire in 1994. Eventually, Tajik President Rakhmonov visited Tehran in 1995, and the final peace accord was signed in 1997, for which Iran received a lot of international goodwill.

The success of the Taliban in neighbouring Afghanistan drew Iran closer to countries that were threatened by the Taliban brand of radicalism. Following the killing of 10 Iranian diplomats in the Afghan town of Mazar-e-Sharif in August 1998, Iran started troop mobilisation and military manoeuvres involving nearly 70,000 revolutionary guards and 200,000 regular troops close to Afghan border. Like Tajikistan, Iran too was host to a huge number of refugees (estimated to be about 1.5–2 million) pouring in from Afghanistan. Apart from being a country that was directly affected by the civil war in Afghanistan, Iran also had to take into cognisance the persecution of Shia minority under the Taliban rule. Together with Russia, Iran became a major sponsor of the Northern Alliance and, after the ouster of the Taliban from power, Iran also played a constructive role at the Bonn Conference that discussed the future set-up in Afghanistan. Its role in conflict resolution in Tajikistan and support to anti-Taliban coalition—the Northern Alliance—has endeared it to countries such as Tajikistan and Uzbekistan.[29]

Cooperation in the Energy Field

Iran had limited success with multilateral regional organisations like ECO to improve relations with Central Asia. Competition with Turkey affected its efforts to economically integrate Central Asia with Iran. Both formed regional groupings to counter each other's influence.

Iran initiated the Caspian Sea Council while Turkey formed the Black Sea Common Market. Another organisation formed in April 1992, Caspian Sea Littoral States Cooperation Organisation (CSLSCO), which includes Iran, Russia, Kazakhstan, Turkmenistan and Azerbaijan (Caspian littoral states), has not made much headway. On the other hand, Iran has achieved relatively better success in its bilateral dealings with Central Asian countries.

A series of bilateral agreements were signed with Turkmenistan in 1994 regarding rail connectivity, freight transport, custom arrangement, and border trade. The following year, Turkmenistan agreed to market its natural gas to Europe through Iran by constructing a pipeline from Korpeje (Turkmenistan) to Kurt Kui (Iran). This pipeline has been operational since December 1997. Another agreement was made in 1999 for export of Turkmen oil to the Persian Gulf through Iran. Kazakhstan has been exporting its oil to the Persian Gulf by a swap arrangement with Iran. This arrangement, agreed to in 1999, allows for a million ton of Kazakh oil to be delivered to the northern port of Iran for the equivalent amount of Iranian oil to be delivered to a Persian Gulf port for Kazakhstan, which is to be exported outside.[30]

The visit of President Khatami to the region in 2002 resulted in a number of agreements. These included improvement of the transport infrastructure in Uzbekistan to facilitate transit of goods to China from the Persian Gulf, opening in future of a trade centre in Kyrgyz capital Bishkek, and focussing on Iran as an export route for Kazakh energy.

Iran's image as a radical Islamic country and US hostility to the Islamic republic has handicapped Iran's advantage as an immediate neighbour (bordering Turkmenistan) located between the Persian Gulf and the Caspian Sea. The advantage of a potential transit country for Central Asian energy, and US effort to bypass Iran further, underlines Iran's need to go beyond the Islamic ideology and look for allies. US military presence in Afghanistan and Central Asia has added to Iran's security worries. However, some experts are of the view that Iran is going to play a positive role in Central Asia, and focus on developing political and economic ties with the region. Hoping to play an important role in future Caspian energy development, Iran's interest in the stability of the Central Asian region is going to outweigh any political role based on Islamic ideology, or ethnic ties.[31]

India-Central Asia: Strategic Interests

For reasons dictated by geography, India's strategic concerns are tied up with the regions bordering its north and northwest. India, thus, has a vital interest in the security and political stability of Central Asia, which can also be a future source for India's rising energy requirement. Accessing the oil and gas from Central Asia remains a major focus. Second, India as an extended neighbour of Central Asia has strong geostrategic and economic interests in this region. Any geopolitical changes in the region inevitably extend their impact on several states in the neighbourhood, including India. As an emerging regional power in South Asia, India is naturally interested in any changes occurring within or close to the region, which may have implications for its own security. Peace and stability in Central Asia is vital for India's security. Conversely, Central Asian security is critically linked to peace in Afghanistan and the Indian subcontinent. For example, the coming of Taliban to power in Afghanistan in 1996 posed a serious threat to the security of the Central Asian states, as well as India.

The common threat of terrorism resulted in a growing convergence of perspectives on the need to devise ways to combat this menace. India, realising that Central Asia held the key to the two of its major worries—Pakistan's expanding influence over Afghanistan and beyond, and, the threat of a growing belt of fundamentalism sponsoring cross-border terrorism—chose to cooperate closely with the Central Asian states. It provided financial assistance to the anti-Taliban Northern Alliance led by Ahmad Shah Masood that enabled the Alliance to acquire weapons and ammunitions. The diplomatic support was not confined to just maintaining the Embassy of Afghanistan in New Delhi, representing the Rabbani leadership (ousted by Taliban). In all diplomatic forums, India condemned the Taliban and played a crucial role in the campaign against international recognition to the Taliban, which was recognised by only three states till the end. India played host to the families of the anti-Taliban leadership.[32]

The defeat and ouster of Taliban has put on hold Pakistan's hopes of achieving some strategic edge over India. The positive development has been the weakening of the destabilising forces that were unleashed since the Taliban takeover, threatening countries such as

India, China, Russia and the Central Asian states. The informal alliance of India and Central Asian countries that had developed in the course of sustaining the United Front (Northern Alliance) contributed substantially to the campaign against international terrorism.

Given the still unstable situation in Afghanistan, the need for continued cooperation between India and Central Asia is very critical. Even after the ouster of the Taliban from Afghanistan, India neither feels totally secure or comfortable about the reports of continuing attempts to destabilise Afghanistan, despite US presence in both Pakistan and Afghanistan.[33] Indian policy makers believe that Pakistan still continues with its policy of what India's former foreign secretary described as 'sustainable terrorism' and the international community has been unable to address to India's concerns.[34] To ensure its own security, India would need to focus on greater involvement in the Central Asian region.

Stability and Reconstruction in Afghanistan

Central Asian states and India have a big stake in ensuring economic reconstruction, inter-ethnic harmony, and stability in Afghanistan. As a sign of the importance that India attaches to Afghanistan, New Delhi has converted to grant the $100 million loan it had earlier extended to Karzai government. Ultimately, the stability of the post-Taliban set-up in Afghanistan can improve the security scenario in Central Asia as well as India.

India has reportedly renegotiated the use of Farkhor in Tajikistan as a base for assistance to Afghanistan. Earlier it had built a military hospital and an airstrip there to help the Northern Alliance. The hospital was shifted to Kabul after the fall of Taliban. India signed a bilateral agreement during Indian defence minister's visit to Dushanbe in April 2002. According to the agreement, 'India will train Tajik defence personnel, service and retrofit Soviet and Russian military equipment and teach English to army and airforce personnel'.[35] There are suggestions that the base in Farkhor is a sign of India joining the 'new great game' of scramble for Central Asia's oil and gas reserves and of India's intention to have a ring of bases around Pakistan. It is, however, difficult to imagine that India has the financial ability and military strength to think in terms of joining the 'great game' and compete with powers such as the United States, Russia and China in projecting its power beyond its own borders. Indian official sources have denied any such grand ambition.

Stephen Blank thinks that India's present policies are oriented to play a larger role throughout Asia in both defence and economics by establishing strategic partnership with the key players.[36] He also suggests that beyond purely economic and military links, India has upgraded its military profile in Central Asia to the extent of acquiring an air base at Ayni in Tajikistan. This, he underlines, 'testifies to India's new interest in capability for power projection missions as well as its ability to threaten Pakistan from the rear and deny it a strategic hinterland'.[37]

Such views seem to exaggerate India's capabilities and ambitions. India has not so far done anything to suggest expansionist or hegemonic designs in the region. The situation in Afghanistan is yet to be stable, and India feels the urgency of providing economic and other developmental as well as humanitarian assistance to Afghanistan. Given the present India-Pakistan relations, access to Afghanistan is not possible for India through Pakistan. As a result, it has chosen the Central Asian route and that too through Tajikistan, the most reliable and close ally during the Taliban days in power. The facility provided by Tajikistan has enabled India to remain involved in the developmental process in Afghanistan and help it meet many of its socio-economic challenges. During his visit to Central Asia in February 2003, then India's External Affairs Minister Yashwant Sinha made India's involvement with the region clear by stating, 'We are not in Central Asia to replace anyone. We see Central Asia as part of India's extended neighbourhood and our presence there is to promote a mutually inclusive relationship'.[38]

As recognition of India's positive role in the region, President Nazarbaev even has been persuading India to join the Shanghai Cooperation Organisation (SCO). During the February 2002 visit of Nazarbaev to India, the Joint Declaration stated that India's membership in SCO 'would add to the strength of that organisation'.[39] Similar sentiments were expressed at the time of the then Prime Minister Vajpayee's visit to Kazakhstan in June 2002, during which a protocol on military-technical cooperation, and an agreement on setting up an India-Kazakhstan Working Group for joint fight against terrorism and other crimes were signed.

Economic Relations

India's relations with Central Asia have, in general, lacked much economic thrust. Some token assistance was provided in the initial period in the form of credit lines to encourage imports by Central Asian states. Not much investment was done in the region. Civil war in Tajikistan and Afghanistan scared away investors from the subcontinent. The level of interaction between the two regions has not been encouraging, though there have been many visits by dignitaries, delegations and signing of memoranda of understanding.[40]

The difficulties in economic relations mainly stemmed from relatively lower level of market economic reforms and unstable investment climate in Central Asia for Indian entrepreneurs. Incidentally, these problems have not come in the way of China's official trade with the region, which stood at $1.818 billion in 2000, as compared to India's $124.79 million in 2003.[41]

In recent years, India has shown some urgency for greater involvement in Central Asia. Contacts are being made with the military-industrial complex in successor states for supply of military hardware. Uzbekistan, for example, was commissioned by India in 2001 to build six IL-78 aircraft for mid-air refuelling.[42] The joint declaration signed by then Indian Prime Minister Vajpayee and Tajik President Rakhmonov during the former's visit to Tajikistan in November 2003 made a pointed reference to 'steady progress in defence exchanges and the intent to intensify relations in this area'. Indian airforce engineers are repairing and upgrading the runway at Ayni. Tajik president Rakhmonov said that Indian military transport aircraft had participated in military exercises in Tajikistan and declared, 'I would like to state for the record that we will continue military cooperation between the two countries in all areas'.[43]

Kazakhstan has shown a great deal of inclination for intensifying ties with India and has allowed India to invest in its oil sector. It has given special attention to defence cooperation between the two countries. India and Kazakhstan have established a forum not only to cooperate on fight against terrorism, but also for 'early action' finalising agreements in military and technical cooperation. This cooperation envisages joint production of military hardware such as torpedoes and heavy machine-gun barrels. Kazakhstan also cooperated in India's space programme by allowing the launch of Indian satellite from its territory (Baikanour cosmodrome operated by Russia). In return, it is said, India agreed to train Kazakh pilots.[44]

Possibilities of Cooperation between China, Iran and India

There has been a great deal of improvement in bilateral relations between China, Iran and India that can help in strengthening security and stability in the Central Asian region. All the three countries link their own security to that of the Central Asian states and Afghanistan. At many levels they are cooperating among themselves to harmonise their interests in the region in ways that would meet the needs of the Central Asian countries. This perspective was underlined during President Khatami's visit to China, when the two countries expressed their desire to cooperate in developing regional transport (including pipeline) infrastructure to link West and East Asia. China, in Tehran's perception, could become an additional counterweight to the United States in Central Asia. According to Herzig such strategic consid- erations could have been behind Tehran's decision to award a con- tract for the construction of the Neka–Tehran pipeline to a Chinese consortium.[45]

Similarly, Iran has improved cooperation with India, helping the latter's trade access to Central Asia through a rail link between Iran and Turkmenistan. This has helped India bypass the Pakistan and Afghanistan route. A tripartite agreement among India, Iran and Turkmenistan was signed on 22 February 1997 at Teheran on inter- national transit of goods. This enabled goods from India to reach Turkmenistan through Iranian port of Bander Abbas and from there by road and rail. India and Russia are developing a new transit route through Iran to Novorossisk for transport of goods between India and Russia.

India is also seeking access to Central Asia through the Iran- Afghan route and has already held talks with Iran and Afghanistan for developing the Iranian port of Chah Bahar as the nodal point of a new trade corridor in Afghanistan. Since Afghanistan and Tajikistan are neighbours, the extension of this route to Central Asia from the former can expand Indo–Central Asian trade ties. Given the nature of tension in Indo-Pakistan relations, India continues to show reluc- tance in depending on energy through pipelines across Pakistan, though talks with Iran for such a pipeline have gained momentum recently.

During Iranian President Khatami's visit to New Delhi in January 2003, the two sides announced transport projects that would deepen energy cooperation between Central Asia, Iran, Afghanistan and the Indian subcontinent. India has agreed to build a road link from Zaranj to Delaram on the Iran–Afghanistan border that would connect all the major cities of Afghanistan. This road also links up further north with Central Asia. Zaranj has road link with the newly developing port complex at Chah Bahar on the coast of Iran. Iran undertook to upgrade this link.[46] 'As India discovers the opportunities for a "forward Policy" in Central Asia, if only in a commercial and diplomatic sense, developing road and rail access to Afghanistan through Iran has become a matter of high national priority', according to C. Raja Mohan. Indo-Afghan trade has also faced difficulties due to lack of transit route option through Pakistan. As a result, the sea and land route through Iran is being opted.[47]

India can also search for the option of overland access to Central Asia through the Xinjiang region of China by joining the highway built by the Chinese in Aksai-Chin territory linking Tibet with Xinjiang, argues Devendra Kaushik, an eminent expert on Central Asia. The distance from the city of Kharog in Tajikistan to Karachi port in Pakistan is about 3,200 km, while the distance from Kharog to Kandla port in western India through Ladakh works out to about 3,800 km. This will need much less investment and would require a link road from India–Pakistan line of actual control (LOAC) to Tibet-Xinjiang road, according to Kaushik.[48]

China has the advantage of being on the border of three Central Asian states and has a highway that links Central Asia through Xinjiang with Tibet and Yunan provinces. This route can provide landlocked Central Asian countries an outlet to the Indian Ocean. It has also been reported that Central Asian states are less keen on any route or pipeline that runs through Pakistan, but does not access the Indian market.

For example, according to Pakistan daily, *The Dawn*, an agreement was signed in 1995 between Pakistan, China and Uzbekistan to establish a land route by extending Karakoram Highway through Northern Areas to connect the Central Asian States (via Gilgit). This could promote trade and tourism between the member states, and was to be implemented in 1999. According to reports, the Uzbek government, however, agreed to honour the road project on the condition that a similar road link from Uzbekistan to India should be provided through Pakistani territories. Since Pakistan was reluctant to include India in the trilateral plan, the parties could not develop a consensus to implement the project, and eventually it was scrapped.[49]

Both India and China need to ensure their energy security. Sources report that the confirmed oil deposits in the Central Asian region are 13–15 billion barrels, which is 2.7 per cent of all the confirmed deposits in the world. The region also has around 270–360 trillion cubic feet of confirmed deposits of natural gas, which constitutes around seven per cent of world deposits. Another view is that the actual reserves of oil in the Central Asian region are in the range of 60–140 billion barrels. For India, especially, this energy resource can be of use if it can be reached through a viable route.[50]

India-China relations have improved in recent years and there are new possibilities for expanding economic cooperation between the two. The decision to open the Nathu La pass (linking Tibet in China with Sikkim in India) for cross-border trade and the continuing discussions on border demarcations are positive indicators. Opening up of the Ladakh–Aksai Chin areas for trade and accessibility to markets in both countries, as well as in Central Asia can be explored.

India and China have been experiencing the problem of religious extremism and terrorism, that intensified in the nineties. Both sides agreed to coordinate their efforts on this front and set up a joint working group to combat terrorism in January 2002. India and China share ideas about the structure of the international system. Both were critical of NATO military action in the Balkans and share ideas on multipolarity. In March 2002, Chinese leadership talked of a 'co-operative partnership' with India. A month later, India backed China at the Human Rights Conference in Geneva. The development of joint security interests (against terrorism) and joint visions of the structure of the international system (multipolarity) have brought the two states closer.[51]

India has the advantage of being politically close to the Central Asian states. Geographically disconnected, India has obviously no border disputes or any legacy of hostility with Central Asia. It was, in fact, more closely associated than China with the war against the Taliban. The closeness of India to two important frontline states for combating international terrorism—Tajikistan and Afghanistan— should prompt China to seek greater Indian cooperation in this respect. India can provide China the comforting cushion against any encirclement by the West, or the Jihadi elements. The proximity of China to Central Asia and India, its infrastructure and economic profile could be of immense help to India. They can mutually benefit from Central Asian engagement, and should coordinate their efforts to acquire greater leverage in the region.

Conclusion

After the 11 September 2001 terrorist attacks in the United States, security scenario in Central Asia changed significantly. Russia and USA are militarily present in the region, and are the main guarantors of security in Central Asia. Nevertheless, positive roles played by some Asian powers like China, India and Iran make them attractive partners of Central Asian states in meeting some of the security challenges in the region. Their role may not be in terms of overt and overwhelming military support but would remain important all the same. Through confidence-building measures, assisting in conflict resolution, technical-technological help, providing access to sea and cheaper markets and consumer goods, the above three Asian powers can help improve the security scenario in Central Asia.

However, the new context has implications for China, Iran and India. The competition for access to Central Asian energy resources is going to be intense between Russia and the United States. The US is seeking to bypass Russia, Iran and China for transit of Caspian oil to international markets through an alternative cheaper route from Azerbaijan to Turkey through Georgia (Baku-Tblisi-Ceyhan pipeline). This could jeopardise the energy security of Asian powers like India and China. These countries need to evolve multiple strategies for security and economic cooperation in Central Asia, including trilateral framework involving the three.

India's Central Asia policy should have a strategic vision to—(a) ensuring its access to energy resources, (b) containing and eliminating international terrorism emanating from the region, (c) deepening India's involvement in Central Asia and Afghanistan and denying strategic depth to any potential adversary. To achieve these objectives, there have to be strategies and choices that will advance India's interest in the region, without harbouring any ambition to project its power, or engaging in a game of encirclement of any other neighbour.

India should simultaneously concentrate on enlarging its economic profile in the region. It needs to increase its investments in Central Asia to create a viable infrastructure to access the resources in the region. Without strong trade and economic relations, it may be difficult to sustain India's strategic and security objectives in the region.

Notes and References

1. Mathew Edwards, 'The New Great Game and the New Great Gamers: Disciples of Kipling and Mackinder', *Central Asian Survey*, vol. 22, no. 1, March 2003.
2. Established in 1969, OIC has 56 member countries in Asia and Africa with its headquarter in Jeddah, Saudi Arabia. Its objective is to strengthen Islamic solidarity and cooperation in economic, social and cultural spheres. ECO was established in 1985 by Pakistan, Iran and Turkey. Afghanistan, Azerbaijan and the Central Asian states joined the organisation in 1992.
3. According to Shireen Hunter, Iranian Islamic model or West's promotion of the Turkish secular-democratic model did not have any chance to succeed simply because they did not have the resources to permeate the region. 'Iran's Pragmatic Regional Policy', *Journal of International Affairs*, vol. 56, no. 2, 2003, p. 134.
4. Edmund Herzig, 'Iran and Central Asia', in Roy Allison and Lena Johnson (eds.), *Central Asian Security: The New International Context*. Brooking Institution Press, Washington DC, 2001, p. 176.
5. Guangcheng Xing, 'China and Central Asia', in Roy Allison and Lena Johnson (eds.), *Central Asian Security: The New International Context*. Washington DC, 2001, pp. 158–59.
6. Gerald Segal, 'China and the disintegration of Soviet Union', *Asian Survey*, vol. 32, no. 9, 1992.
7. Werner Gumpel, 'Economic and Political Development in the Central Asian Turkish Republics', *Eurasian Studies*, vol. 1, no. 2, 1994, p. 16.
8. Ma Jiali, 'Central Asia: Geostrategic Situation and Big Powers' policies', *Contemporary Central Asia*, vol. 3, no. 1, New Delhi, 1999, p. 45.
9. Ibid.; However, with Tajikistan dispute remains over an area of about 20,000 sq. km. in the mountainous region of Pamir. Guangcheng Xing, 'China and Central Asia', p. 154.
10. Guangcheng Xing, 'China and Central Asia', p. 160.
11. Olga Oliker, 'Conflict in Central Asia and South Caucasus: Implications of Foreign Interests and Involvement', in Olga Oliker and Thomas S. Szayna (eds.) *Faultlines of Conflict in Central Asia and the South Caucasus*. Rand, Santa Monica, 2003, p. 216; Werner Gumpel, 'Economic and Political Development', p. 16.
12. Olga Oliker, 'Conflict in Central Asia', p. 215.
13. Ma Jiali, 'Central Asia: Geostrategic Situation', p. 45.
14. Ibid., p. 45; Antoine Blua, 'Central Asia: 'Shanghai Six' Form Charter As International Organization', *RFE/RL*, Prague, 7 June 2002.

15. Vladimir Radyuhin, 'Shanghai Group Comes of Age', *The Hindu*, 11 January 2003; The regional anti-terrorist structure opened in Tashkent on 17 June 2004.
16. James P. Dorian, Brett Wigdortz and Dru Gladney, 'Central Asian and Xinjiang China: Emerging Energy, Economic and Ethnic Relations', *Central Asian Survey*, vol. 16, no. 9, 1997, pp. 461–86.
17. Svante E. Cornell and Maria Sultan, 'The Asian Connection: The New Geopolitics of Central Eurasia', *Caspian Brief*, December 2000. http://www.cornellcaspian.com/pub/0011centraleurasia.pdf
18. Breffni O'Rouke, 'China's Growing Regional, European Links Seen as Benefiting Central Asia', *RFE/RL Central Asia Report*, vol. 5, no. 4, 3 February 2005.
19. The fact that China may be importing 3 million barrels of crude oil per day by 2010 makes it necessary for cross-border cooperation in this sector. James P. Dorian, Brett Wigdortz and Dru Gladney, 'Central Asian and Xinjiang China', pp. 461–86.
20. Werner Gumpel, 'Economic and Political Development'. Recently construction of a 988 km. oil pipeline from Atasu in Kazakhstan to Atashankou in China began on 28 September 2004. Expected to be completed in 2005, the pipeline will cost $700 million and carry 10 million tons of oil a year initially. *RFE/RL Newsline*, vol. 8, no. 185, Part I, 29 September 2004.
21. Breffni O'Rouke, 'China's European Links'.
22. *RFE/RL Newsline*, vol. 8, no. 183, Part 1, 24 September 2004.
23. Guangcheng Xing, 'China and Central Asia', pp. 158–59.
24. Abbas Maleki, 'Relations between Iran and Central Asian republics', *Central Asia and Caucasus Review*, vol. 1, no. 1, 1992, p. 9.
25. Roy Allison, 'Military Forces in the Soviet Successor States', *Adelphi Papers-280*, October 1993, pp. 15, 59; Adam Torock, 'Iran's Policy in Central Asia', *Central Asian Survey*, vol. 16, no. 2, 1997, p. 185.
26. Abbas Maleki, 'Relations between Iran and Central Asian republics'.
27. Edmund Herzig, 'Iran and Central Asia', pp. 176–78.
28. Among many agreements Iran signed with the Central Asian states, only two relate to security—one for military and border cooperation with Turkmenistan signed in 1994, and the other a letter of understanding on defence cooperation signed with Tajikistan in 1997. Beyond these there have been some limited initiatives with Turkmenistan on cooperation and sharing of intelligence to tackle the drugs trade and transnational crime. Ibid., p. 187.
29. Ibid., pp. 186–87.
30. Abbas Maleki, 'Relations between Iran and Central Asian republics'.
31. Olga Oliker points to the silence on the part of Iran to Uzbekistan's persecution of Islamic groups and Persian-Speakers as an indication of Iran's shifting focus from ideology to economic opportunities and regional stability. 'Conflict in Central Asia and South Caucasus: Implications of Foreign Interests and Involvement', in Olga Oliker, 'Conflict in Central Asia', pp. 209–12; Shireen Hunter suggests that Iran should come to terms with reality and must reach a modus vivendi with the US to achieve its goals in Central Asia, despite the growing volume of trade between Iran and the region—from $74 million in 1994 to $430 in 2000 with Turkmenistan, from $220 million in 2000 to $500 million in 2002 with Kazakhstan. Shireen Hunter, 'Iran's Pragmatic Regional Policy', pp. 146–47.

32. India reportedly supplied the United Front with high altitude warfare equipment, worth about $8–10 million between 1999–2001. Apart from these there were defence advisers and helicopter technicians. Rahul Bedi, 'India dabbles in the new "great game", *Jane's Intelligence Review*, June 2002.

33. According to Firdous Syed, President, Kashmir Foundation for Peace and Development Studies, Kashmir, more than half the Taliban core survived the US assault and continues to be active in parts of Afghanistan and in the Federally Administered Tribal Areas (FATA) in Pakistan. *The Hindu*, 5 October 2002.

34. Indian Foreign Secretary Kanwal Sibal's press conference on 4 October 2002, *The Hindu*, 5 October 2002.

35. Rahul Bedi, 'India dabbles in the new "great game"'.

36. Stephen Blank, 'India and Central Asia: the Return of Strategy', *Central Asia-Caucasus Analyst*, 11 September 2002.

37. Stephen Blank, 'India's Continuing Drive into Central Asia', *Central Asia-Caucasus Analyst*, 14 January 2004.

38. *Tribune News Service*, 1 February 2003, Chandigarh.

39. Rahul Bedi, 'India and Central Asia', *Frontline*, vol. 19, no. 19, 14–17 September 2002.

40. India announced a credit line to different Central Asian republics worth 5–10 million each during former Prime Minister Narshimha Rao's visit to Central Asia in 1991–92. Two credit lines of $10 million each were extended to Uzbekistan in 1993 and again in 1999. India opened credit lines to Turkmenistan worth $10 million in 1993 and extended another credit line of the same amount in 1997.

41. IMF, *Direction of Trade Statistics Quarterly*, no. 2, March 2002; *Export-Import Data Bank*, Directorate General of Foreign Trade, Ministry of Commerce, Government of India, 2004.

42. Dietrich Reetz, 'Flash Points South and Central Asia: Strategic Aspects of a Historical Relationship', in Erich Reiter and Peter Hazdra (eds.), *The Impact of Asian Powers on Global Developments*, Physica-Verlag, Heidelberg, 2004, p. 22.

43. *India Discussion Forum*, www.indolink.com, 14 November 2003.

44. Dietrich Reetz, 'Flash Points South and Central Asia', p. 22.

45. Edmund Herzig, 'Iran and Central Asia', p. 192.

46. C. Raja Mohan, 'India, Iran Unveil Road Diplomacy', *The Hindu*, 26 January 2003.

47. C. Raja Mohan, 'India and Afghan Railroads', *The Hindu*, 20 February 2003.

48. Devendra Kaushik, 'The New Geopolitics of Central Asia, Russia, China and India', *Contemporary Central Asia*, vol. 3, no. 2, 1999, p. 19.

49. *The Dawn*, 22 March 2003; Tajikistan linked its city of Kharog in the Pamir region with Karakoram highway in 1999. Other states of Central Asia are taking keen interest in this route, which can link Central Asia with Sea at Karachi. Devendra Kaushik, 'The New Geopolitics', p. 19.

50. Alim Jone, 'The Energy Security Challenges and Resource: Transport Corridors', Paper Presented at India-Central Asia Seminar in New Delhi on 11–12 September 2000.

51. Christian Wagner, 'Indo-Chinese relations', in Erich Reiter and Peter Hazdra (eds.), *The Impact of Asian Powers on Global Developments*. Physica-Verlag, Heidelberg, 2004, p. 110.

9

JAPAN'S EXPANDING SECURITY PERSPECTIVES IN THE ASIA-PACIFIC

K.V. Kesavan

Japan's security perspectives are changing incrementally within the framework of its Constitution. Despite the fact that more than 58 years have passed since its enactment, Article Nine of the Constitution still provides a formidable barrier to the Self-defence Forces (SDF) assuming a role in any collective security arrangement with the United States. Yet it has been possible for the Japanese government to gradually expand the parameters of SDF activities by means of pragmatic, but highly contested interpretations of the Constitution. The present strategic dilemma of Japan lies in its efforts to find a balance between its rapidly expanding security needs, and the limitations laid by its Constitution.

International relations have witnessed a sea-change since the end of the Cold War in that the old ideological rigidities that characterised the bi-polar world have become irrelevant. New factors have now come to influence nations in the conduct of their foreign and security policies. To be sure, military strength continues to be still a major determining factor, and military spending and weapons modernisation have been on the upswing in the Asia-Pacific region. Nuclear proliferation issues coupled with the spread of missile technologies have deepened the security concerns in the region. There are unresolved territorial issues that could suddenly trigger tensions among countries in the region. But the concept of security itself has assumed a multi-dimensional character. It is now increasingly defined in nonmilitary terms. Issues such as resource scarcity, technology transfer, trade, investment, environment, sea-lane security, etc., have assumed new significance. It is relevant to note that Japan was one of the earliest countries to think in terms of what it called comprehensive security even during the Cold War period. Since the end of the bi-polar era, Japan has laid utmost importance on it because it believes that the world has now entered a period of closer interdependence.

Low Cost, Low Risk Policies

How has Japan conducted its foreign policy to ensure its national interests? It is well known that Japan has pursued its diplomacy with utmost caution and circumspection with an eye on the fulfillment of its national interests. As one writer has stated, Japan has been doing 'defensive driving' in that without being either aggressive or reactive, it has kept its direction and destination in clear focus.[1] It has pursued its goals single-mindedly with low cost and low risk.

Japan's Security Policy

Japan's security policy is predicated on the following three principles: (a) reliance on its alliance with the US; (b) development of its own effective defence capabilities; and (c) maintenance of good and cooperative relations with the countries of the Asia-Pacific region.

(a) Reliance on the US: End of Ideology

The end of the Cold War removed the ideological hold over Japanese politics, and the subsequent decline of the Liberal Democratic Party (LDP) from 1993 onwards created an unprecedented fluidity in Japanese politics. But there was no threat to the continuance of the security pact with the US either from the end of the Cold War or from the decline of the LDP. Despite the fact that there have been several coalition governments since 1993—some included the socialists and one led by them—alliance with the US has continued to be the core element in Japanese diplomacy. There is hardly any political party which is inclined to categorically denounce Japan's alliance with the US. Both the Japan Communist Party and the Democratic Socialist Party are making desperate efforts to survive in the face of rapidly moving domestic political scenario in the direction of a bi-party system. The last two elections—the lower house election in November 2003 and the upper house election in July 2004—clearly demonstrated the strong trends towards a two-party system in Japan. The Democratic Party (Minshuto) fully endorses the need for continuing the alliance with the US though it opposes some aspects of the conduct of the alliance relationships like Japan's dispatch of military contingents to Iraq, the realignment of US military bases in Japan, etc.

A great beneficiary of the Cold War, Japan took a fairly long time to set its diplomatic sails to the new winds. Several developments during the nineties, such as the Gulf war and its aftermath, exposed Japanese diplomacy to serious difficulties and subjected Japan-US relations to severe strains. Criticism of Japan's checkbook diplomacy, and its lack of sensitivity to the post-Cold War security imperatives, was loudly heard in the US during the Gulf war 1990–91. The war forced Japan to come out of its vacillation and face the hard realities of the newly emerging global security environment. The political shift from a single party monopoly of power to a coalition situation complicated the bilateral relations with the US. Issues such as political reforms, international peace-keeping bill, the economic recession following the burst of the bubble, etc., led to prolonged confusion and uncertainty in policy making. The international peace-keeping bill passed in 1992 after an unusually prolonged debate was meant to assuage the feelings of the US which was unhappy about the failure of Japan to participate in the Gulf war. Many in the government wondered whether it would be possible to convince the public about the relevance of the alliance to the unfolding post-Cold War era.

Though several official meetings at the highest levels took place thereafter to redefine the importance of the bilateral security alliance, the summit meeting held between President Clinton and Prime Minister Hashimoto Ryutaro in April 1996 was a landmark in the post-Cold War bilateral relations since, for the first time, it clarified the future direction of the bilateral security relations. The two leaders unmistakably reiterated that the alliance remained 'the cornerstone for achieving common security objectives and for maintaining a stable and prosperous environment for the Asia-Pacific region as we enter the 21st century'. The summit gave a new momentum to bilateral cooperation. It was immediately followed by several significant developments. The defence guidelines of 1978 were revised to make them more relevant to the needs of the uncertain post-Cold War period.

Another important development related to the revision of the National Defence Programme Outline (NDPO) of 1976. The NDPO had been formulated at the time of the Cold War. Though Japan's defence capabilities had grown significantly since then, a new policy outline that would reflect the post-Cold War situation was needed. In 1996, a new NDPO replaced the earlier one, and clearly highlighted the new responsibilities of the SDF. The three main principles of the 1996 Outline can be stated as follows:

- Though the Cold War had ended, a great deal of uncertainty and fluidity continued to mark the security situation in the East Asian region, thanks to a range of issues like tension in the Korean peninsula, the Taiwan issue, unresolved territorial questions, religious fundamentalism, terrorism, and so on. It would be, therefore, essential for Japan to continue to maintain a basic and standard defence capability on the assumption that efforts for stabilising international relations would continue to be made.
- Alliance with the US would continue to be the main core element of Japan's security policy.
- While the essential mission of the SDF would be the defence of Japan, it would be called upon to play a role in the government's efforts to create a more stable security environment in the East Asian region.[2]

Japan's Expanding Security Role

Even prior to the formulation of the 1996 Outline, the need for involving the SDF, at least in the UN peace-keeping operations, was increasingly felt thanks to the severe criticism that Japan faced at the time of the 1990–91 Gulf war. The international peace-keeping law, which was passed in 1992 following a vexatious and prolonged parliamentary debate, was meant to assuage the US in particular. But since then, Japan has made significant contributions to the UN peace-keeping operations in Cambodia, Mozambique, Rwanda, Golan Heights and Eastern Timur.

Anti-terrorism Activities

Following the 11 September 2001 terrorist attacks on the US, Japan quickly passed the Anti-terrorism Law which markedly expanded the role of the SDF. The Law authorised the government to dispatch SDF vessels to the Indian Ocean to provide supplies to US and British ships involved in the war against Afghanistan. One major reason for Japan's prompt action was to avoid the earlier diplomatic embarrassment it had faced in the 1990–91 Gulf war when Japan, despite its big economic aid package of $13 billion, received no appreciation from the coalition forces involved in the war. While passing the bill, the Japanese government made it clear that its assistance was meant to pursue the objectives as spelt out in the UN resolutions and that Japanese assistance would be rendered only in non-combat areas. The government sent 17 vessels altogether for assisting the US and British vessels. Later, the Japanese government sent aegis destroyers, along with supply vessels, in order to tighten the security. The inclusion of aegis destroyers provoked a serious controversy in the Diet. The September 11 attacks, for the first time, raised the important question of how to ensure internal security against potential terrorist activities. The Japanese government amended the SDF Law enabling the SDF units to safeguard SDF installations, as well as American military facilities in Japan. The September 11 incident also triggered the government to move in the direction of undertaking an emergency legislation against armed attacks. The subject of how to respond to situations of armed attack against the country was debated extensively in the Japanese Diet during 2002–03, and bills were passed on the subject after reaching an agreement with the opposition parties.[3]

Japan and the War in Iraq

Following military action against Iraq by the US, Britain and other countries, Japan extended full support to the coalition forces. But the fact that the US and Britain decided on military action without a proper mandate from the UN Security Council put the Japanese government in a very delicate position. The media reported that 80 per cent of the Japanese people seriously doubted the wisdom of Bush administration's policy in Iraq. Confronted by this unhelpful situation, Prime Minister Koizumi sought to justify his support to the US on the ground that public opinion might not be always correct.[4]

But the Iraq issue polarised Japanese politics from the beginning, and figured very prominently in the two major national elections—the House of Representatives election held in November 2003, and the House of Councilors election, held in July 2004. The opposition parties, in particular, the Minshuto, utilised the Iraq question fully to prop up its election fortunes. They argued that Japan's dispatch of its military personnel to Iraq constituted a serious infringement of Article Nine of the Constitution which prohibits Japan to have the right to collective self-defence. But Koizumi asserted that Japan's assistance was confined only to the economic reconstruction of Iraq and that the Japanese military personnel would be dispatched only to non-combat areas. For the opposition parties, however, the whole of Iraq constituted a combat area, and the spread of violence, including regular kidnapping and murder of Japanese journalists and diplomats, clearly supported their apprehension. The deepening crisis situation in Iraq, accompanied by so many horror stories about the conduct of the US military personnel, did very little to support the position of Koizumi. Discussion on the Iraqi situation became more intense on the eve of the upper house election scheduled in early July 2004. When the US decided to hand over sovereignty on 30 June, the question of maintaining a multilateral force in Iraq after that date was discussed. The way Koizumi announced Japan's decision to join the multilateral force at the time of the G-8 conference held in Georgia, US, surprised even many of his own party colleagues. The opposition parties were quick to pick up the issue and attacked Koizumi for announcing a major political decision without discussing it in the Japanese Diet. Later, when the opposition closely questioned him as to who would command the Japanese self-defence forces under a multinational framework, he tried to maintain that the Japanese forces would work under their own command. When further pressed to state whether he had any guarantees to that effect, he asserted that he had verbal assurances from both the US and Britain to that effect. Far from convincing the people of the correctness of Koizumi's decision, it aggravated the heat of the discussion on the constitutionality of Japan's participation in the multinational military operations in Iraq. During the upper house election campaign, he strongly justified his decision on the ground that he could not discharge his functions if he was to discuss with the Diet and the opposition parties first. He also accused the *Asahi Shimbun* and the *Mainichi Shimbun* of pursuing 'anti-American' policies in criticising Japanese participation in the multinational force in Iraq. In a well reasoned editorial, the *Asahi* explained the reasons why it had to oppose the war in Iraq and the dispatch of SDF troops to that country. The *Asahi* maintained that the joining of the SDF personnel in the multinational force amounted to a major change of policy that had important bearings on the Constitution and the foreign policy of the country. It argued that changes of such magnitude could not be made without discussing them at the Diet first. It concluded by cautioning Koizumi, 'Good relations with the United states are important for Japan. But there are many ways to ensure that this continues. If the prime minister overreaches in his efforts to pander to the Bush administration, he will create an Americanophobic atmosphere among the people.'[5] The Iraq issue along with the slow pace of his structural reforms greatly undermined the position of Koizumi. That the ruling coalition suffered serious setbacks in both the lower and upper house elections could be attributed to Iraq to a considerable extent.

Debate on Constitutional Revision: Right to Collective Self-defence

Though discussions on constitutional reforms have been going on for a long time, they have assumed considerable relevance particularly in the post-Cold War period. For one thing, the functions of the SDF have been consistently expanding following the passing of the international peace-keeping law in 1992. Counter-terrorism measures, Japan's support to the US in its war against Iraq, China's growing military strength, and North Korea's nuclear weapons and missile technology programmes have added a new urgency to the issue, and made it increasingly hard for Japan to operate within the constraints of its Constitution. Two parliamentary commissions on constitutional reforms have been discussing a wide range of issues and they have already published interim reports. Final recommendations of these commissions are expected to be ready by 2005. In the last two parliamentary elections to the lower house and the upper house, constitutional reforms formed an important subject of the political campaign.

All major political parties now understand that the time has come for them to squarely address this issue instead of treating it as a political sacred cow. On 22 June 2004, the Democratic Party released an interim report on constitutional revision which suggests that Japan has a 'limited right' of self-defence. The report has suggested that Japan should establish a reserve force for the United Nations so that it can contribute to global peace. The report further says that Japan can exercise the right of self-defence only under the United Nations.[6] But still opinion within the party on the subject is sharply divided since the party has a large number of erstwhile socialists who continue to cling on to their earlier strong support for retaining Article Nine of the Constitution. According to Minshuto President Okada Katsuya, Japan does not enjoy the right to collective self-defence. Strongly opposed to the increasing tendencies on the part of the US to undertake unilateral military action, he fears that the exercise of collective self-defence could risk Japan being involved in a rash war. He has cautioned, 'If the notion of collective self-defence becomes widely accepted, there is a strong possibility that Japan will have to join wars waged by the United States in other countries'.[7] Okada has contended that Article Nine could be revised only to enable Japan to participate in a military action under the auspices of the UN. But Okada's views are contested so strongly by several members within the party that the party's secretary general Fujii Hirohisa has called those views as purely 'personal', and do not reflect those of the party. A party heavyweight and a staunch supporter of constitutional revision, Ozawa Ichiro has criticised Okada on the ground that Japan can participate in any UN-sponsored military action under the terms of Article Nine of the Constitution without any amendment. He fears that the views of Okada are 'tantamount to saying that Japan is prohibited from using force (for UN sponsored action) under the current constitution'.[8]

In January 2004, the LDP at its annual convention decided to release its proposals for constitutional revisions in 2005. But within the party, there is a multiplicity of views expressed on the subject. The party has set up a research commission under the chairmanship of Yasuoka Okiharu to make recommendations by the end of 2004. Opinions within the party differ on whether to clearly spell out Japan's right to collective self-defence. But there is also an apprehension expressed by some members that if there is no restriction placed on Japan's right, then it will be obliged to support US military operations anywhere in the world. They fear that this could create serious problems for Japan. Further, many believe that it is necessary to give constitutional recognition to the SDF as a military force. They feel that once this is done, the question of exercising the right of collective self-defence will become automatically possible.[9] Though Koizumi has often expressed his strong views on the need for Japan to exercise the right to collective self-defence, given the sensitiveness of the issue, it will not be easy for the LDP to mould a consensus on the question. Further, any speedy move on the question will have a serious impact on its political alliance with the New Komeito Party, which is strongly opposed to incorporating the right of collective self-defence in the Constitution. The Japan Communist Party (JCP) and the Social Democratic Party of Japan (SDPJ) are equally opposed to any change, though their political clout in the legislative sphere is too negligible.

Pressures from the US

The US has long been interested in seeing that Japan undertakes more 'tangible' responsibilities under the alliance. To be sure, American leaders are pleased with the contributions of Japan, and appreciative of the assistance extended by Tokyo in combating terrorism. But at the same time, they also understand how the present Constitution adversely impacts on the bilateral security cooperation. Richard Armitage, US Deputy Secretary of State stated in July 2004 that Article Nine of the Japanese Constitution was an 'obstacle' to the bilateral alliance. He further said that Japan's claim to a permanent membership of the UN Security Council could also be hampered by Article Nine since permanent members were required to use military force on certain occasions for the benefit of the world.[10] On 12 August, Secretary of State Colin Powell more or less reiterated these views by stating that Japan would have to examine Article Nine if it wanted to become a permanent member of the Security Council.[11]

Despite the willingness of the political parties to discuss the question of constitutional revision, it still continues to be politically very sensitive. Further, the procedures involved in the process of amending the Constitution are too complex requiring a prolonged period of consensus building. Unless the LDP and the Democratic Party work out some minimum acceptable formula, there is very little prospect of any amendment taking place. But given their basic differences on the issue, a common formula may well be elusive in the near future.

The Expanding Role of the
US Military Bases in Japan

Since 11 September 2001, the US government has been restructuring its military bases all over the world. The main objective of the ongoing restructuring exercise is to strengthen the ability of US military forces to respond effectively to any emergency situations. In the case of American bases in Japan, the US government took the first step in October 2003 by integrating the US bases in Yokohama, Aomori and Misawa Navy's patrol and reconnaissance air wings. Their main function is to monitor North Korea's nuclear and missile development, as well as the activities of Chinese naval ships. Under the new scheme, several military bases are being designated for joint use by both SDF and the US force. The Air Self-defence force of Japan (ASDF) and the US force are now jointly using the air base in Misawa. Similarly, the US Marine corps and the Japanese Ground Self-defence Force (GSDF) are using training ranges in Shizuoka and Hokkaido. Further, the ASDF is permitted to use the US Air Force's Kadena base in Okinawa. The ASDF's Air Support command and Air Defence Command are now being shifted to Yokoto Air Base of the US.[12] As part of this realignment plan, the US also wants to transfer its Army First Corps Headquarters from Washington state to Camp Zama in Kanagawa prefecture.

The realignment programme has understandably provoked a debate within Japan. The opposition parties have expressed their concerns that the plan to transfer the Army's first headquarters from Washington to Camp Zama would involve Japan more deeply in the US global military strategy. In fact, even within the government, there is a basic difference between the foreign ministry and the defence agency. The former is wary of the relocation plans as they would take the bilateral defence cooperation beyond the terms spelt out in Article Six of the bilateral security pact, and involve Japan in the broader US global strategy against 'the arc of instability' running from North Korea to the Gulf area. Article Six of the security pact states: 'For the purpose of contributing to the security of Japan and the maintenance of international peace and security in the Far East, the United States of America is granted the use by its land, air and naval forces of facilities and areas in Japan.' The ministry would like to take the traditional line that the treaty is meant to protect the security of Japan and the Far East. But the Defence Agency tends to take a softer view of the realignment plan as an opportunity to alleviate the burden borne particularly by the Okinawans. The proponents of the relocation plan contend that the US marines, based in Okinawa and the US aircraft carrier USS Kitty Hawk based at Yokosuka Naval base, have been very often deployed to areas that do not come under the definition of the Far East clause. They point out that it is nothing but a 'fiction' to insist that Tokyo should not permit the US military stationed in Japan, to undertake missions that have no direct relevance to the security of Japan, or of the Far East.[13]

The crux of the problem involved in the bilateral relations is that as the US global strategy expands, it expects Japan to come out of some of its self-imposed taboos. Though the security alliance is bilateral, it has several multilateral aspects too, but Japan with its many domestic and external constraints is unable to fully respond to the demands of the US. In the past, the US seemed to be satisfied only with Japan's generous financial contribution to bear some of the expenditure involved in the maintenance of the US bases in Japan. But since 11 September 2001, the whole scenario has changed in the sense that the US now insists on what reciprocal measures Japan can adopt for safeguarding American security. Though the Koizumi government has strongly supported Bush, the real problem stems from the dichotomy that the US, which is the only superpower now, is not operating in a unipolar world. When the US resorts to unilateral military decisions, it is very difficult for Japan to follow suit given its domestic compulsions.

(b) Development of its Own Defence Capabilities

While keeping the bilateral alliance as its anchor, Japan has been developing its own defence capabilities over the years. Under two NDPOs, Japan has carried out several mid-term defence build-up programmes that have modernised the self-defence forces, and equipped them with sophisticated weapons. Defence spending in Japan has always been constrained by a traditional dislike for military forces as well as inter-ministerial bickering. It has been hovering around 1 per cent of the country's GNP which still makes Japan among the topmost spenders on defence.

Currently, two major developments that could change the complexion of the self-defence forces are under discussion. The first one relates to the need for formulating a new defence programme outline by the end of 2004. It is now felt that since the September 11 terrorist attacks have altered the global security scenario, the 1996 NDPO needs to be replaced by a new one that addresses effectively the threats posed by terrorism and the proliferation of nuclear weapons and missile technologies. A high level advisory council of experts, appointed by Koizumi, has submitted a set of far-reaching recommendations for the government's consideration for their incorporation in the new defence programme outline under way. Some of the recommendations are as follows:

(a) The council has stated that the 1996 NDPO's objective of maintaining a minimum standard defence force has become outmoded since the nature of the new threats has become diverse and complex. It has therefore emphasised the need for the government to develop a multifunctional, flexible defence force to tackle the new threats stemming from terrorism, and the potential North Korean ballistic missiles. It has referred to the rapid rise of China, and how it could impact on the security situation of East Asia. In this context, the council has suggested that Japan should even consider the option of pre-emptive strikes in case of threats to its sovereignty.

(b) The council has stressed the need for Japan to seriously contemplate on the question of exercising its right to collective self-defence. This issue, as noted earlier, has been heatedly debated by political parties in the context of constitutional revisions.

(c) The council has urged the government to treat the future role of the SDF in peace-keeping as a key factor in Japan's security strategy.

(d) Another recommendation of the council relates to the need for strengthening the position and powers of the national security council on the lines of its American counterpart.

(e) The council has also recommended that the 1996 US-Japan joint statement should be replaced by a new one that would explain the objectives of the bilateral alliance in the changing security context. It wants the government to make the alliance more effective. It further believes that the government should pursue seriously the present exercise on the restructuring of American forces abroad since it provides an opportunity for comprehensive strategic negotiations with the US.

(*f*) Finally, the council has called upon the government to do
away with the existing ban on the export of Japanese military
technologies to other countries. It fears that the continuance
of the ban could hamper Japan's effective participation in any
joint programme on missile technology, particularly with the
US.[14]

Second, in response to North Korea's launching of Rodong-I and
Taepodong-I missiles, Japan has decided to develop a missile system
of only defensive nature. The system is supposed to stop those
incoming missiles that target Japan. Although a sum of more than
$900 million has been set apart under the 2004 fiscal year, opinion
on the effectiveness of such a system is sharply divided. If Japan were
to intercept any North Korean missile, the time at its disposal to do
so would be minimal, and therefore, its system would have to be very
efficient. Even though the plans are at the preliminary stage, China
and North Korea have expressed their serious objections. Apart from
their misgivings, the final cost of developing a full-scale missile
defence system could be staggeringly high, and given its present
economic situation and the external pressures, Japan will think many
times before launching the plan.

(c) Good Relations with Neighbouring Countries

Japan believes that its security interests will be best served by maintaining good and cordial relations with the countries of its immediate
neighbourhood. Having suffered the traumatic experiences of atomic
bombs, Japan has long been a strong advocate of nuclear non-
proliferation. It is a party to the Nuclear Non-proliferation Treaty
(NPT) and the Comprehensive Test Ban Treaty (CTBT). Having
stood by its three non-nuclear principles, it is anxious that the Asia-
Pacific region should be free from the threats of nuclear weapons.
It has always shown its deep concerns about the Chinese nuclear
weapons. But what now worries Japan most is North Korea's development of nuclear weapons and missile programmes. It considers
North Korea as constituting a direct threat to its security. North
Korea is the only country with which Japan does not have normal
diplomatic relations. The end of the Cold War raised the prospects
of normalisation, and several rounds of talks were held between the
two countries during the early nineties. But it became clear that their

positions diverged sharply on issues like Japan's compensation for its colonialism, and North Korea's obligation to accept International Atomic Energy Agency's (IAEA) inspection of its nuclear installations. In addition, North Korea's missile tests in 1994 aroused the concerns of Japan, which was now more keen to cooperate with the US in getting Pyongyang committed to non-proliferation. It was around this time that US was directly negotiating with North Korea on the nuclear issue. The Democratic administration under President Clinton considered that Pyongyang's nuclear programme, which included the production of plutonium, posed a threat to the regional security balance in East Asia. In 1993, North Korea threatened to withdraw from the NPT regime, but decided to 'suspend' its decision until after negotiations with the US.

KEDO, Japan and North Korea

In October 1994, both the US and North Korea signed an agreement by which the latter agreed to freeze its nuclear programmes in exchange for two light water reactors. A multinational body called the Korean Energy Development Organization (KEDO) was founded with the US, Japan, South Korea as members. Finding the KEDO a good mechanism for dismantling North Korea's nuclear programmes, Japan supported it by agreeing to provide $1 billion for constructing the light water reactors. Subsequently, when negotiations started between the US and North Korea, sharp contradictions between the two came to the surface. While the US insisted on Pyongyang's elimination of its nuclear weapons and missile programmes, North Korea wanted the US military forces to withdraw from Northeast Asia. Further, the continuous launching of missiles by North Korea, and its export of missile technology to Iran and Pakistan further vitiated the negotiations. There was no further progress in the negotiations during Clinton's tenure.

Bush Administration, Japan and North Korea

The Republican administration under President Bush, from the beginning, adopted a hard-line policy calling North Korea a rogue state, and a member of 'the axis of evil'. In the initial period, relations between the two reached a new low and North Korea abandoned its commitment to KEDO, and withdrew from the NPT regime. Further, it also openly admitted that it had a nuclear weapons programme.

More recently, the US has adopted a multilateral approach to negotiate with North Korea. The six-nation mechanism involving China,
Russia, Japan, South Korea, the US and North Korea seems to have
created some confidence in the minds of North Korean leaders.
Although a few rounds of talks have taken place, it will take a long
time before the multilateral mechanism achieves any substantial
results. Japan has fully supported the six-nation talks by actively
coordinating with other member countries.

Koizumi's Diplomacy and North Korea

The year 2002 witnessed a major breakthrough in Japan-DPRK (The
Democratic People's Republic of Korea) relations due to the initiative
taken by Koizumi. In order to put an end to the prevailing stalemate
in the bilateral relations, he went to Pyongyang in September 2002,
and held a summit meeting with Kim Jong II. The resultant Pyongyang
Declaration constitutes a good framework for the future direction of
bilateral relations. Expressing Japan's apologies for the sufferings
caused to the Korean people during its colonial rule, Koizumi assured
that Japan would extend economic cooperation to North Korea. Kim
on his part, admitted for the first time, that the DPRK had abducted
Japanese nationals and expressed his sincere apologies. He further
assured that he would take all appropriate steps to ensure stability
and security of the Northeast Asian region by resolving the nuclear
and missile issues. Although in October, North Korea released a
few abductees, there were fresh revelations about the existence of
more abductees, and Japan wanted a thorough investigation into the
question. On 22 May 2004, Koizumi undertook another trip to
Pyongyang. Unlike the earlier summit, there was no joint statement
this time. But both leaders reiterated their commitment to the
Pyongyang Declaration of September 2002. Soon after, preliminary
official level talks were started to prepare the ground for full-scale
normalisation dialogue. But they floundered on the question of
DPRK's refusal to address the abduction issue satisfactorily.

Within Japan, public opinion on Koizumi's North Korean policy
is heatedly debated. Opposition political parties accuse him of showing his weakness to North Korea which has not given full details of
the Japanese nationals, who are still missing. They suspect that some
of them could be still alive languishing in North Korea. As of now,
the nuclear issue and the abduction question continue to affect the
prospects of normalisation of relations between the two countries.

Relations with China

Japan–China relations have steadily expanded, especially in the economic sphere, in the last more than 30 years. Japan is the biggest trading partner of China. China is also fast replacing the US as Japan's biggest trading partner. In 2003, trade between the two countries reached a record figure of $133.6 billion. A marked increase in Chinese domestic demand in automobiles, electronic goods, mobile phones, etc., has been responsible for this unprecedented surge. Japanese private investment has also grown making Japan the third biggest investor in China. But perhaps more than trade and investment, Japan's ODA (Official Development Assistance) has contributed a great deal for strengthening the bilateral relations. China remained as the biggest recipient of Japanese economic assistance for a long time. But now, since China has become an economic power, there is a debate in Japan on the advisability of continuing to assist it. There are strong voices raised by official and non-official elements that ODA to China should not only be reduced but also subjected to stricter conditionalities. Already China has ceased to be the biggest aid recipient in the last two years.[15]

Sino-Japanese relations continue to be influenced by historical legacies even though the current Chinese leadership hails from the post-war generation. China feels quite uncomfortable about the expanding security role of Japan under its alliance with the US. Beijing suspects that Japan is using terrorism as an excuse for dispatching its self-defence forces beyond its shores. It has taken strong exception to issues like Koizumi's visits to the Ysukuni shrine, school textbooks, etc. In recent months, there is a serious controversy over the exploitation of the natural resources in the exclusive economic zones around the Senkaku islands. Japan believes in a policy of engagement with China. It wants China to be integrated closely with the regional and global economic and security forums. It has strongly supported China's participation in the World Trade Organization and the ASEAN Regional forum.

Japan and the ARF

Japan's relations with Southeast Asia have diversified in the post-Cold War period. Japan has worked hard to bring all Southeast Asian countries within the framework of the ASEAN, which now has 10 members. In a way, the earlier vision of Fukuda Takeo has materialised.

Japan had always been concerned that the security situation in the Asia-Pacific region was complex in view of the new threats like terrorism, religious fundamentalism, nuclear proliferation and so on. Japan worked cautiously and behind the scene to create a security body for the region. In 1994, the ASEAN Regional Forum (ARF), the only security forum in the region, came into existence. In the initial period, China had many misgivings about the aims of the new body. But now, China has accepted it and takes a fairly active role in its deliberations. The ARF is still young, and cannot claim any great achievements to its credit. Its confidence-building measures have, however, gone a long way in easing tension among its members. Of course, in order to become an effective forum, it has to graduate quickly to the next stages of preventive diplomacy and conflict resolution. The coming decade will be crucial for the ARF to prove its effectiveness. In the meantime, as multilateral arrangements, the ARF and the ASEAN + 3 promote dialogue and transparency among member countries. It is relevant to note how Japan has used the ARF to take measures for ensuring the security of the sea-lanes in the region. Japan has also provided economic assistance for the deepening of the Malacca Strait, and cooperated with other countries to combat piracy and terrorism in the Indian Ocean.

Successive prime ministers of Japan have understood the importance of the Southeast Asian region and made their contributions to forge closer relations. In this connection, one should note the efforts made by Koizumi. In January 2002, he visited many ASEAN countries and enunciated the so-called Koizumi doctrine which emphasised the importance of 'acting together and advancing together'. He called for a comprehensive economic partnership with the ASEAN countries, and intensive security cooperation between the two. Koizumi signed the first free trade agreement with Singapore to be followed by similar agreements with other ASEAN countries. He envisaged the building of an East Asian Economic Community including the ASEAN, Japan, China and Korea. In the meantime, China has also signed a similar free trade agreement with the ASEAN, which will come into effect after 10 years. In addition, China overtook Japan in signing a treaty of amity and cooperation with the ASEAN countries. In December 2003, after initial vacillation, Japan also signed a declaration on accession to the treaty of amity and cooperation.[16]

Notes and References

1. Susan Pharr, 'Japan's Defensive Foreign Policy and the Problems of Burden-sharing', Gerlald Curtis (ed.), *Japan's Foreign Policy After the Cold War: Coping with Change*. New York, 1993, pp. 235–36.
2. See National Defense Program Outline FY 1996, Ministry of Foreign Affairs, Tokyo, p. 3.
3. Katahara Eiichi, 'Japan', Charles E. Morrison (ed.), *Asia-Pacific Security Outlook*, 2004, Japan Center for International Exchange, Tokyo.
4. *Asahi Shimbun*, Tokyo, 8 March 2003.
5. See editorial, *Asahi Shimbun*, 6 July 2004.
6. *Yomiuri Shimbun*, Tokyo, 23 June 2004.
7. *Asahi Shimbun*, 28 June 2004.
8. *Daily Yomiuri*, Tokyo, 2 August 2004.
9. *Daily Yomiuri*, 24 October 2004.
10. *Yomiuri Shimbun*, 23 July 2004.
11. *Daily Yomiuri*, 14 August 2004.
12. *Yomiuri Shimbun*, 23 August 2004.
13. See Okazaki Hisahiko, 'Japan Must Keep US Military Ties', in *Daily Yomiuri*, 17 October 2004.
14. See 'Takinodanryoku teki boeiryoku o teigen', *Yomiuri Shimbun*, 5 October 2004; See also its editorial, 'Aratana Boeiryoku kochi ni do ikasu'.
15. See the editorial, 'Tai-Chu yenshakkan wa uchikiru toki da', *Yomiuri Shimbun*.
16. See East Asian Strategic Review, 2004, Tokyo, The National Institute for Defense Studies, pp. 142–45.

10

Is Human and Gender Security Relevant for Asia?

Anuradha M. Chenoy

Introduction

The history of most Asian states shows the recurrence of armed conflicts ranging from territorial, ethnic, religious ones to class and caste based. Of the current armed conflicts worldwide, almost 40 per cent are in Asia, and most of these remain unresolved for decades. These conflicts have been viewed within the traditional security discourse, and the states involved have attempted to manage these through the concerns of national security. This paper argues that these conflicts have some common indicators that point to a set of reasons for the conflicts that relate to wider issues of identity and rights, and therefore, it is pertinent to look at these conflicts through a rights-based framework. The two rights-based frameworks that come close to understanding these issues are the human security concept and the feminist understanding of armed conflict. This paper examines the relevance of these frameworks to conflict resolution in Asia, and the lacunae within these.

Of these Asian conflicts, most have ethnic origins that took on a secessionist character. Two are struggles against occupation—one is opposition to a military government, and the other for economic and political change, and some are related to territorial disputes. Besides these armed conflicts most Asian states have had a history of inter-community/sectarian violence, gender and caste/class based violence and unrest.[1]

An analysis of the conflicts in Asia shows some common indicators. Most conflicts are rooted in civil society, and extend into social and political institutions. For instance, one would find class, caste, ethnic, religious, gender based biases, practices and policies in most social, economic and political institutions. These practices extend to social interaction, employment, cultural practices and laws that can be subliminal or overt, but are nonetheless present. Political parties reflect and use these divisions in different ways. Right wing parties often base themselves as representative of one (religious) group, specifically in opposition to the 'other', and use this as a primary method of mobilisation. They create a threat perception of the minorities as 'outsiders' whose loyalty to the nation is suspect. The Right wing parties, groups and fundamentalists homogenises multiple traditions to conform to a unilateralist vision that they alone would interpret, and by doing so, divide on communal or ethnic bases, civil society and the polity. Centrist parties while contesting such views, often do not mobilise sufficiently against such trends, remain divided on their strategies and tactics and fear political defeat if they do not succumb to 'majoritarian' or populist politics. The Left parties and groups in most Asian states are deeply divided, and thus not a major force. In states where they link up with specific social movements, they have some say in mainstream politics. Some sections of the extreme left in some Asian states are involved in armed movements.

The states in Asia have been far from neutral in most of these conflicts. An analysis of any conflict in Asia reveals how the regime in power has used conflicts for serving its interest. For example, by constructing a nationalism based on 'majority' politics and attempting to isolate the minorities; or using a minority primarily as a vote bank; or using religion or language to homogenise people for electoral purposes; or use one religion/ethnic group against another, etc. In all these conflicts the state has resorted to tactics of majority militarist nationalism and sought legitimacy by evoking images of threat perceptions, territorial disintegration, and 'national honour'.

In all these conflicts the state has used the armed forces to control and manage the conflict. They have treated dissent and dissatisfaction of a group against state policies as law and order problems, and attempted to use one faction against the other or repress the conflict,

before trying to look for a negotiated solution. Most states in Asia
have attempted negotiations primarily after much bloodshed and
terror, or after intervention from 'outside powers'. (Thus conflicts
like Cambodia, East Timor, Sri Lanka, Georgia, Palestine, etc., have
all seen international pressure.)

All these states have promulgated highly draconian national security laws and legislation. In all the regions of armed conflict emergency provisions like special powers for the armed forces and
paramilitary are operational. Armed forces have special rights like
conducting searches without warrants, destroying shelters that could
be hideouts, granting wide discretionary powers to even junior officers, disallowing assembly or meetings of large numbers of people,
and giving immunity to officers who have committed human rights
violations. All these states show a record of systematic human rights
violations, especially in the region of conflict.

All states have seen increases in their military budgets, the number
of armed forces, acquisition of weapons.[2] In three of the Asian states
official expenditure on military as percentage of GDP is higher than
that on the expenditure on education and health combined. Two
states are openly nuclear, and two are known to have nuclear
programmes. There is evidence of increasing militarisation of all
these states.

All these indicators reveal that these states use militarist responses
to ethnic/identity movements and that the policies of militarisation
led to greater emphasis on defence expenditures and the use of
militarist values in resolving essentially civil disputes. Such policies
have led to a spiral of violence in these societies, and a reenforcement
gender stereotypes, caste and class hierarchies as they legitimise
aggressive nationalism and force.

The ethnic/secessionist/anti-state movements in all these states
have many common features. Most of these anti-state movements
begin as demands for justice or social change and are often based
on ethnic sub-nationalism that incorporate ethnic-nationalist myths,
symbols and strategies. Most of these movements have a number of
factions and different strategic perceptions, tactics and goals, and
some of these groups have used violence against each other. Many
of these movements have sections that use violent strategies, labelled
as terrorism. Many of the movements are hierarchically organised,
based on military principles and are 'underground'. Most use women
cadre in their operations, most of whom are support cadres and lower

in the hierarchy. Thus, many ethnic secessionist and anti-regime/ state movements valorise force, often because of the failure of other methods. The use of violence however, has its own logic that leads to militarisation of these movements with all its problems.

These kinds of approach to security, where both the state and anti-state movements are highly militarised, have implications for civil society that has been felt and documented all over Asia. In all these conflicts the largest number of people who have been killed, hurt, or maimed have been civilians. Non-combatants get marked as support-ers, and are subject to army grilling and searches, and women are especially targeted for abuse. All these conflicts have generated large numbers of internally displaced persons and millions of refugees.

Six of the states engaged in armed conflicts are very low in the Human Development Index (HDI) and six fall in the medium HDI scale. The Gender Development Index Ranking for five of these states is amongst the lowest in the World. Women have been subject to violence and degradation on the basis of 'honour'. Women have been disproportionately affected by these conflicts, the largest num-bers of those displaced and made refugees (70 per cent) have been women. In most Asian countries, women loose their status in society as widows as the rehabilitation packages for women in all these conflicts have been lesser than those given to men, and in many instances, women have not personally benefited from compensation since this has been taken over by the extended families. Since women symbolise the honour of their community they loose their autonomy during such conflicts since there is an attempt to keep them 'secure' at home. On the other hand, women who 'belong' to the 'enemy' are raped, since this violates the 'honour' of the entire community. All the Asian conflicts, as those elsewhere, have witnessed rape and sexual abuse of women as a method of punishment for the entire community.

Children have been caught in the crossfire in all these conflicts and have been killed, maimed, traumatised, and militarised. In many of the Asian conflicts there have been reports of kidnappings, use of child soldiers, etc. Conflicts orphan children, keep them away from schools, traumatise, and dehumanise them, and instill militarist values within them. In most conflict regions counter-insurgency measures are carried out. These measures are aimed at destroying the infrastructure support base of terrorists. This has generally meant that the homes, workplaces, farms of ordinary people in these regions get destroyed, or marked as enemy territory. Thus infrastructure in conflict region is often destroyed.

All these indicators show that Asian states need to re-examine their security strategies. States that use primarily state-centred and militarist methods of security have failed to solve conflicts with just resolutions, they have only 'managed' or controlled conflicts temporarily with the use of force. Several paradigms of security that differ from traditional security have been advocated ranging from comprehensive security, non-traditional security and human security. Constructivist theorists, feminists and others have levelled critiques of the traditional security.

The human security concept is based on the premise that human rights and needs are necessary for security and that conflicts occur when rights are denied and needs repressed, as our examples from Asian states show. The human security approach has evolved with the human development approach, and has been brought together by the United Nations Commission on Human Security.[3] Human security seeks to compliment state security by broadening and democratising security since issues like identity politics, or the neglect of social justice can become the central issues of national security, just as many inter-ethnic rivalries or sectarian conflicts have become.

Traditionally, states had a monopoly over security, and in many cases, this concern got mixed with regime security. States are concerned primarily with preserving their territory and sovereignty, and furthering their perceived national interests.[4] If this status quo is intact, they consider themselves secured. Human security argues that people's security should be a critical part of the states concern without diluting state interests. The people-centred approach, thus, is a radical departure from traditional security conceptualisation. The human security concept, however, assumes that women's security will follow 'naturally' if human security is accepted by states. This paper argues that gender needs to be designed and mainstreamed into the human security discourse, in the absence of which, it would remain marginal.

In national security and international relations discourses gender issues are either taken for granted, ignored, or problematised.[5] This is because a fundamental premise of international relations theory continues to be the Realist theory that sees the international political system as anarchic, and thus values the need for military force as a currency of power. Once power is based on force, values associated with masculinity get privileged, and whoever exercises power, (men or women) valorise these values. Further, Realism argues that international relations remain disconnected from domestic issues, and thus ignores the vital issues such as identity politics, internal institutions, and politics on external relations. The human security approach broadens the realm of security to include almost all the needs of society from democratic and economic to identity and cultural aspirations. It recognises the implications of gender and takes serious account of gender discrimination, the need for gender equity, and the implications of gendered violence. But in this conceptualisation, gender is subsumed under the larger problem of people and since feminists argue that the concept of power is gendered, especially at times of armed conflict, then any approach that seeks security needs to recognise this.

Women's security is not guaranteed either at peace or war times.[6] Women's insecurity can come from within the family, from community conflict, from state or interstate sources. This insecurity is largely invisible in the private sphere and gendered in the public sphere.[7] Further women's insecurity does not have to be measured merely in terms of violence or the absence of it. This insecurity is linked to her identity, her roles, status and being.

Structural discrimination against women remains in most societies (in different degrees and with cultural and economic variations), and is linked to the perceptions about women's roles. Patriarchal ideologies give less value to feminine roles and identity in comparison to masculine ones. This gendered valuation of roles and identity is part of all structures of society, state and the international system, more so in authoritarian, militarist and fundamentalist systems, and wherever there is the absence of democratisation and feminisation. Women remain largely absent from most spheres of public policy making, and this ensures the domination of agendas that exclude them. This results in routine (domestic) violence and intersects with structural violence. Violence from routine and structural conflict remains hidden because it does not fit the state-centric criterion.[8] Nor do policy strategies aimed at preventing and mitigating violent conflict adequately address the impact on women, who remain in the private sphere.

At times of insecurity and armed conflict, institutional structures break down and are overtaken by militarised ones, patriarchal controls increase, and gender differences are essentialised. Women's insecurity during armed conflicts is different than that of men. The public language and practice of politics and media becomes a weapon of conflict and terms such as 'manhood', 'brotherhood', 'martyrdom', 'honour' and 'sacrifice for motherland' dominate the discourse.[9] Masculinity and force are associated with power just as femininity is associated with the powerless, with weakness and peace. Further, power implies control over others. The enemy 'other' (or 'them') is demonised and homogenised, just as the 'us' is homogenised and glorified with militarist values. Masculinity intersects with militarist values and becomes the base for a militant approach. Issues like honour, national glory, victory are mixed with valour, revenge, retribution and power. Thus feminine and feminist values are marginalised. These militarist and gendered values are part of all armed conflicts.

In such circumstances, women's identities are constructed to intersect with the needs of militarised nationalism. Women get bracketed to either the nation or their relatives like 'mother of the nation', 'rape victim', 'martyrs mother', 'half widow' or 'war widow', that symbolises shared victimisation and solidarity that feeds into generating retribution and nationalism. In the case of all recent armed conflicts, women have been constructed as cultural symbols. They are signifiers of the 'honour' of their community, family and nation and stereotyped as the feminine 'other'. They are then either seen as subjects to be protected and confined to the private sphere, behind veils and walls (from Kashmir to Afghanistan) or violated as symbols of the enemy 'other'.[10] This signification makes women into targets of gendered crime like rape and forced prostitution.[11] Female relatives of offenders or the 'other side' are targeted by conflicting sides, and by state agencies to collectively punish the other side. While abuse against men gets publicity, all sides have a conspiracy of silence against abuse of women.

Women get little independent status since their agency is undervalued and restricted to their body, which like their identity, is held hostage to militarist values and they are subject to greater control then at normal times. Conflicts are structurally gendered, and this is the reason why women are primary victims and treated as part of the infrastructure, no matter what and how many roles they play.[12] Thus guaranteeing 'peoples security' does not guarantee women's security. In dealing with the gendered structures of security, the approach should be engendered.

Traditional security considers threats to security mainly from other states, from the military and from non-state actors (such as terrorists). Human security argues that since most current conflicts occur because of internal reasons, it is these issues that need to be addressed. A deconstruction of recent armed conflicts in Asia establishes that when community rights related to religious, ethnic, race or political issues, remain unresolved, or are denied rights or justice, they develop movements that can take on sub-nationalist and secessionist aspirations. In many cases, states create insecurities for people when they do not follow rule of law and civil and human rights.[13] States vary along the continuum from authoritarian to democratic systems, and within this continuum, the level and depth of democracy varies. Many democracies, especially in the Third World, continue to have a strong militarist or authoritarian presence and people and groups are marginalised because of gender, ethnic or communal lines. This leads to intractable conflicts like those we witness in Asia where the state has not been neutral, but a party to the conflict.[14] The human security approach argues that internal threats arise when communities that have a sense of nationhood are denied rights, suffer poverty, inequity, injustice; or when majority and minority group interests clash. It is thus in the interest of state security that human rights are guaranteed.

Threats from militarism, patriarchy, chauvinism, sectarianism, poverty, and denial of rights affect women differently than men. Women's identity as 'belonging' to fathers/husbands/sons and their signification as cultural symbols of their community/nation, remains constant before, during and after wars. These ideologies combine with militarism and patriarchy to restrict women. Women's value is reduced to her chastity and her role to the private sphere. Thus for example, dress restrictions and behaviour codes for women remain, whereas none of these are applicable to men. (Afghanistan, Iraq, Kashmir and northeast India are all conflict zones that enforced dress codes.) After armed conflicts are over, men are rehabilitated and get back to work and routine, while women continue to be insecure, subject to control by men brutalised by war, by militarised institutions, as all post-conflict situations from Afghanistan, Iraq, the northeast India and elsewhere show. Therefore insecurity threats are gendered and influenced by class and strategic location. Violence against women is just one manifestation of these gendered structures.

In addressing security, gender issues tend to be papered over if they are not specifically highlighted.

In case of traditional security, diplomacy is carried out on a state-to-state basis, and because the interest of the state is at stake, national security issues are privileged agenda. States emphasise the use of force to ensure security. Internal security is perceived as law and order maintenance, and movements that go against state/regime interests are repressed and labelled anti-national. National security acts are used to protect states' interests even if they trample rights. Conflicts are usually managed through control, compromise, or sheer repression. States use military methods of counter-insurgency that are designed to destroy infrastructure. In all current armed conflict zones, there is little to distinguish between war and civilian zones. The conflicts and anti-insurgency operations enter homes, schools, and private spheres.[15] Most of the methods used by conflicting sides are gendered, and women face the consequences differently than men. Here, rape is a weapon of war, revenge and retribution. No laws for privacy are respected, and women are punished for being relatives of suspects.[16] National Security Laws are a common method of ensuring state security, many of which violate normal constitutional procedures, and are known to abrogate civil and political rights.

Human security argues for rule of law based on secular and consent based constitutions, negotiated settlements and institutionalisation, and greater use of international law for conflict resolution. It makes a plea for divided sovereignty, where the international community can intervene in cases of genocide and armed conflicts within states. It argues for increasing democratisation, decentralisation, peoples' intervention on foreign policy and security; introduction of creative concepts like divisible sovereignty, shared territoriality; non-violent resolution. It supports a greater role of the United Nations in intervening in cases of prolonged armed conflict.

Gendered security argues for a further feminisation of the human security approach. Legal experts and international lawyers have shown that most domestic and international law needs to be gender sensitive. The 'neutrality' of legal institutions invisibilises gender biases inherent in them. Many constitutions over the world provide for equality to all, yet the interpretation of laws however, do not give women the same rights as those of men. Traditions, customary laws, social customs and culture back these inequalities, which take much longer to change even after laws have been enacted. (All South Asian states show this dichotomy.) It has been repeatedly shown that negotiated settlements exclude women's issues, since they are always relegated to a 'later' day solution. For example, while the violation of women's rights was a reason for regime change of the Taliban, women in post-Taliban Afghanistan, still feel insecure and unsure of equal rights either in society or before law. Women's movements are still struggling that women's rights are included in human rights.

In traditional security, state actors (dominantly male elite) retain exclusive privilege since national security is considered too sacrosanct to be transparent or subject to public debate or action. In some instances, there is token or real presence of women who are trained to become advocates of militarist and state ideologies. When security issues are debated publicly, women take on roles related to motherhood. For example, the US election of 2004, where security is a major issue, the concept of 'national security moms' has been popularised in the public discourse, to show the security concerns for women.[17] But here too, women are clubbed with children, and as primarily mothers, rather than equal citizens.

Conflict prevention and capacity-building strategies target mainly official authorities, not the communities (and community leaders), individuals at risk. This also means that protecting and assisting people in internal conflicts is seen primarily from the perspective of national sovereignty—and the principle of non-interference—instead of from a perspective of responsibility shared by states. State-centred security tends to reflect the concerns of a narrow policy making elite, which are likely to exclude the views of women, minorities—ethnic and religious, marginalised communities. This exclusion itself eventually leads to movements that threaten the security of states. In current circumstances, more states are threatened from within than externally. This is especially true of almost all of Asia today. Human security pleads for the active participation of people at all levels of the security discourse. It perceptively argues that without the agency of people, the grass-roots issues of safety cannot be resolved.

Popular mandates and representative institutions continue to reflect gender imbalance. Contemporary peoples' institutions, whether they are parliaments, non-governmental organisations, public institutions, or international organisations have little gender balance. Women's agency and capabilities for peace and conflict resolution remains unutilised. In many conflicts, women play a role in bringing peace in civil society. They use their power of bereavement and the agency of motherhood to talk of peace, as the mother's movements in several conflicts like Sri Lanka, Naga Mothers, Meira Peibis of Manipur have demonstrated. These movements have had their limitations. They have used their gendered and symbolic values for intervention, had factional links, and setbacks, but have still worked as civil society initiatives.

In all the conflicts in South Asia, where peace talks have been attempted (Sri Lanka, Kashmir, Nepal, Nagaland), women are absent from the negotiating table. This is because peace is between the states and opposing militant forces. Civil society representatives and women are left out of the main negotiations, which results in a militarised or partial peace, where crucial sections of society feel excluded. Thus, unless special provisions are made for gendered agency there is little likelihood of change.

The goals of traditional security are to protect states' national interests by maintaining the territory, sovereignty, and ensuring hegemony of states. Though the traditional methods of security laid a clear emphasis on state security and took a militarist stance, the more democratic and 'stable' states were able to resolve conflicts through providing social justice and building institutions for negotiation between communities. This meant widening the concept of security to bring in different points of view, including especially that of women to enable a gender balance and make security sensitive to people. This method assists national security, whereas militarist methods may well undermine it.

Human security discourses argue that security can be empowering if it is linked to human rights and human development. The convincing argument is made that states that do not accept these social ethics cannot protect people from critical and pervasive threats and situations.[18] In many countries that accept the conception of 'peoples rights', women's rights are still not included in democratic and human right discourse. For instance, in India and elsewhere, equality is a constitutional right, yet, women do not have equal rights under law to their family inheritance. In the US women still do not get the same wages as men for the same amount of work. The goals of human security will be further widened, if special efforts are made to include women, and marginalised at all levels of institutions and policy planning.

Security Arena

States that practice traditional security use the instrumentality of regional and collective security. The arena of traditional security has extended to regional military organisations like NATO, joint military exercises and global coalitions against terrorism. Globalisation has increased this interconnection to global elite connections. Human security also focuses on the interconnectedness of globalisation and advocates the strengthening of international organisations like the United Nations, and supports international peace and social movements. A gendered arena would mean a linking of women's issues with peace and other social movements so that all their problems are joined in a common rainbow alliance. It means a feminisation of the peace and social movements, since women's issues often remain purely the concern of women.

In all states that use primarily traditional security, defence expenditures remain high. Acquisition of missile technologies and weapons are a goal, and there are increases in military, paramilitary and private armies.[19] Economies of countries with long unresolved armed conflicts suffer greatly.[20] Very often, they have uneven development, with an advanced military complex and poor consumer and social sectors. Further, their economies and social systems are militarised.

Human security clearly shows the need for equity based development, and favours increased social sector spending on health and education. The experience of many African and Asian nations shows, however, that development does not mean gender balanced development. The development decades left out many sections of society and especially women. As the 'Human Security Now', Report (2003) shows, women own 2 per cent of the land globally. Thus, unless special provisions are made for women's economic rights, and efforts are made to change economic and inheritance laws in favour of women, gender inequity will continue.

Traditional security and national security discourses are based on realist and neo-realist theories on the models outlined by philosophers like Machiavelli, Thomas Hobbes, developed by Clausewitz, and re-worked by the founders of Realism like Morganthau, and later, Waltz. All these theorists saw the international system as essentially anarchist, and states had to further their interests by increasing their power and might. The power of states could be curbed by a balance of power, and by some international institutions backed by a collective of powerful states. The most powerful states in the international system accept and propagate this theory since international anarchy serves to further their goal and hegemony. The understanding of power in this paradigm is power over the other.[21] This 'other' is constantly being constructed and demonised, and may be another state, community, race, religious or political group, or gender.

Many Western states have through long processes of democratic cultures, used the capabilities and gendered approaches to resolve internal conflicts, but traditional and militarist security continues to be part of their foreign policy agenda. Since the end of the Cold War, practitioners and academics alike have called into question this militarised conception of security and offered alternative views. The clearest opposition has come in the form of the human security approach that views security much more than the absence of violence. It encompasses human rights, good governance, access to education and health care, opportunities and choices to individuals. It advocates poverty reduction, freedom from want and fear. It is thus not just about protecting, but about empowering.[22] At the same time however, human security also accepts a neutral identity when it comes to gender, which leads it to subsume women under the paradigm of the universal man.[23]

Human security is rooted in democratic theory, as is gender equality. Women have had to struggle for equality, these struggles have a greater chance of success within democracies. Greater democracy is associated with a robust civil society. Democracy and civil society re-enforce each other, weakening one impacts negatively on the other. Women have the potential to be leaders and activists in civil society, if given the opportunity.

Feminists support the human security approach, but want to engender it because experience has shown that the concept of 'people' still leaves out women, especially those at the margins. Further, as feminist theory shows, while structures and institutions remain patriarchal, women who are part of these processes also accept patriarchal and nationalist regimes. It is only the women's movements, the feminists and others who oppose patriarchy and want to change the basis of power, who question traditional security and patriarchy. Feminists thus argue for both a gender balance as well as a feminisation of security.

The human security approach establishes that conflict data has been state centred and not people centred. These omissions have far-reaching implications, as violence remains hidden when it does not fit into the state centric approach. The strategies to prevent and mitigate conflict then do not adequately address communities at risk, but rather official authorities. The national sovereignty perspective is restrictive rather than allowing for shared responsibility.[24] A gendered approach would take the argument further to show that the most invisible group in conflicts, till date, have been women. There is little data and limited analysis of the gendered nature of conflicts, or even the implication of wars on women. Wars have been fought, chronicled and analysed by men. Human security, even when people oriented, will have to be engendered to correct this vision.

Human security has been recognised by important sections of civil society as a necessary and interconnected step towards guaranteeing security, and as a precondition for ensuring rights and social justice. International organisations like the UN, international social movements like the World Social Forum, several heads of states, and multilateral and regional organisations have accepted and propagated this concept. Women's insecurity is a major concern of international organisations and states. Women's groups and social movements have emphasised this, and it has been recorded by the UN resolution 1325. There is, thus, a clear and unambiguous logic and necessity of merging these two concepts. Historical experience has shown that human security needs to be engendered because women's security cannot be subsumed under peoples' security since women have special needs and have been marked as special targets. Women's security has to be simultaneously located with, and not follow after people's security. Women have the experience of their rights being shelved for decades, as nationalist struggles showed, where women's rights were reserved for 'later' days, and in some cases, remain waiting.

Women's security needs to be defined and measured in different national, regional and local situations. Gendered Human Security Indicators similar to the Gender Development Index that is used in the Human Development Reports can be evolved to highlight women at risk. These will point to marginalised communities at risk. These indicators will identify trends and share comprehensive cross-regional information and analysis to promote an understanding of the gendered nature of conflicts. These indicators will reveal the politicised experience of women's subordination and gender roles, and the myths and beliefs around these roles at times of conflict to show how they influence and shape conflict. Feminist analysts have related the roles, experience, needs and capabilities of women and men in conflict, and shown the gendered aspects of causes (both the structural and macro and subjective or micro) of war.[25] The gendered nature of power at the site of every human interaction, as suggested by analysts, need to be measured at different points, specific to regional conflicts, before, during and after armed conflicts.[26] This is necessary for revealing the extent of damage to civil and political society that such insecurity causes. Such analysis helps design pre-emptive steps and policy to end gender insecurity.

Conclusion

Hundreds of thousands of deaths, millions displaced and made refugees, child soldiers, women raped and humiliated, inter-community violence, increased defence expenditure at the cost of social and developmental sectors—this is what conflicts have done to our societies. Women's experiences as peacemakers, and the internationally vibrant women's movements has shown how women have practically used the gendered human security approach in their day-to-day civil society interventions in conflict situations. Women invariably combine the political, the social and the personal in their politics, and as flexible organisers at the grassroots level, will be the most effective propagators of such security concepts. The success of concepts, like human security, rests with civil society activists, NGO's and social movements. A robust civil society is more effective in influencing foreign policy where a human security perspective is operative rather than where traditional security predominates.

It is evident that the concept of human security is a necessary and empowering idea with the potential to improve the terms of human existence when accepted by states. However, this idea remains incomplete because as our arguments have shown, the concept of peoples' security will allow for the repetition of gendered structures at times of peace and conflict. These gendered structures are part of the chain that links to other conflicts and joins the spiral of violence. For human security to be complete in itself, it is necessary to engender the human security concept and to use it in Asia.

Notes and References

1. The ethnic conflicts with some secessionist character are—Ache (and earlier East Timor) in Indonesia; Moro in Philippines; the Naga, Manipur, and other Northeast Indian ethnic conflicts and Kashmir conflicts in India; the Tamil Tigers in Sri Lanka; the separatist conflicts in Thailand. Two are struggles against occupation: Palestine and Iraq; one is opposition to a military government: Myanmar; and one for economic and political change: Nepal; two territory based: India-Pakistan and North and South Korea. Afghanistan continues to have armed conflicts in several regions. This data is available from web sites like: The Carnegie Commission on Preventing Deadly Conflicts, Carnegie Corporation of New York, http://wwwics.si.edu; The World's Armed Conflicts site http://www.jmk.su; also www.ploughshares.armedconflicts2003 (International Peace Research Institute, Oslo).

2. See Tables in 'Armaments, Disarmament and International Security', SIPRI Yearbook, Oxford University Press, SIPRI, Stockholm, 2003, pp. 341–42.

3. Commission on Human Security: Human Security Now, United Nations, New York, 2003; Ramesh Thakur, 'A Political Worldview', Security Dialogue, vol. 35, no. 3, September 2004, p. 347.

4. Kanti Bajpai, 'The Idea of Human Security', International Studies, vol. 40, no. 3, 2003, pp. 195–228. Also Liota, P.H., 2002. 'Boomerang Effect: The Converging of National and Human Security', Security Dialogue, vol. 33, no. 4, September 2004, pp. 473–88; Lloyd Axworthy, 'A New Scientific Field and Policy Lens', Security Dialogue, vol. 35, no. 3, September 2004, p. 348.

5. Cynthia Cockburn, 'The Gendered Dynamics of Armed Conflict and Political Violence', Caroline O.N. Moser and Fiona C. Clark (ed.), Victims, Perpetrators or Actors? Gender, Armed Conflict and Political Violence. New Delhi, Kali for Women, New Delhi, 2001, p. 13.

6. Surveys show that up to 80 per cent of women worldwide suffer domestic and other violence. 'One In Three Women Worldwide Could Suffer Violence Directed At Her Simply Because She Is Female', UNIFEM, 24 November 2003, http://www.unifem.org/press releases.

7. 'Sexual Assault Statistics', www.stopfamilyviolence.org. The International Convention on the Elimination of All Forms of Discrimination against Women (CEDAW). http://www.unifem.undp.org/CEDAW/

8. Francine Pickup, Susanne Williams and Carol Sweetman, Ending Violence Against Women: A Challenge for Development and Humanitarian Work, London, Oxfam, 2001, p. 78; Also, 'Rape So Common In D.R.C., It Is Considered Combat Injury', UN Wire, 27 October 2003. http://www.unwire.org /UNWire/ 20031027/449_9787.asp.

9. In all these conflicts the state has resorted to tactics of majority militarist nationalism and sought legitimacy by evoking images of threat perceptions,

territorial disintegration, and 'national honour'. See Human Development
Report, UNDP, New York, Oxford, 2003.

10. Cynthia Enloe, 'All the Men are Militias, All the Women are Victims: The Politics
of Masculinity and Femininity in Nationalist Wars', in Lois Lorentzen and
Jennifer Turpin, edited, *The Women and War Reader*. New York, 1998, New
York University Press, pp. 50–62. Also, Anuradha M. Chenoy, *Militarism and
Women in South Asia*. 2002, Kali for Women, New Delhi, 2001, pp. 31–33.

11. Meredeth Turshen, 'The Political Economy of Rape: An Analysis of Systematic
Rape and Sexual Abuse of Women during Armed Conflict in Africa', in Caroline
O.N. Moser and Fiona C. Clark (ed.), *Victims, Perpetrators or Actors? Gender,
Armed Conflict and Political Violence*. New Delhi, Kali for Women, New Delhi,
2001, pp. 55–57. Jefferson, LaShawn R., 'Human Rights Watch World Report
2004, In War as in Peace: Sexual Violence and Women's Status', January 2004,
http://www.hrw.org/wr 2k4/15.htm. 'Gender Aspect of Conflict and Peace'
http://www.un-instraw.org/en/research/gacp/index.html

12. Women have been disproportionately affected by these conflicts, the largest
numbers of those displaced and made refugees (70 per cent) have been women.
In most Asian countries women loose their status in society as widows; rehabilitation packages for women in all these conflicts have been lesser than those
given to men and in many instances, women have not personally benefitted from
compensation since this has been taken over by the extended families. All the
Asian conflicts as those elsewhere have witnessed rape and sexual abuse of
women as a method of punishment for the entire community. See the yearly
Amnesty International Reports, 1998–2003, London, 1998–2003.

13. Carnegie Commission on Preventing Deadly Conflicts, Carnegie Corporation
of New York, http://wwwics.si.edu

14. The World's Armed Conflicts site http://www.jmk.su

15. For example hundreds of schools in the Ache conflict in Indonesia were
destroyed during counter-insurgency operations; bridges and buildings in northern
and eastern Sri Lanka were targeted during counter-insurgency measures. The
Kashmir conflict has seen the destruction of hundreds of public institutions,
etc.

16. Anuradha M. Chenoy, *Women and Militarism in South Asia*. Kali for Women,
New Delhi, 2002, p. 138.

17. Frank Gaffney Jr., 'They May be President Makers: Both Bush and Kerry are
Tailoring the Campaigns to Appeal to Women', *Washington Times*, 28 September 2004.

18. Commission on Human Security: Human Security Now, United Nations, New
York, 2003.

19. The Federation of American Scientists, The Arms Sales Monitoring Project.
http://www.fas.org

20. Most states with prolonged armed conflicts fall very low in the Human Development Index, and some fall in the medium HDI scale. For example, 43 per cent
of states in the bottom half of the Human Development Index in the year 1994–
2003, were at war. Human Development Report, Oxford University Press,
UNDP, New York, 2003.

21. Eisler, Riane, 'Work, Values and Caring: The Economic Imperative for Revisioning
the Rules of the Game', Centre for Partnership Studies, Pacific Grove, CA, 2003.

22. Commission on Human Security: Human Security Now, United Nations, New York, 2003.
23. Gunhild Hoogensen and Svein Rottem, 'Gender Identity and the Subject of Security', Security Dialogue, vol. 35, no. 2, pp. 55–171.
24. Commission on Human Security: Human Security Now, United Nations, New York, 2003.
25. Tatjana Sikoska and Juliet Solomon, 'Introducing Gender in Conflict and Conflict Prevention: Conceptual and Policy Implications', paper for UNU, INSTRAW, Santo Domingo, 14–16 December, 1999.
26. Caroline O.N. Moser and Fiona C. Clark (ed.), Victims, Perpetrators or Actors? Gender, Armed Conflict and Political Violence. New Delhi, p. 16.

11

Economic Developments and Regional Economic Trends in Central Asia: Emerging Asian Linkages

Gulshan Sachdeva

In this paper an attempt has been made to understand contemporary economic trends in the Central Asian region. While discussing the nature and characteristics of Central Asian economies, the paper also deals with broad trends in their foreign trade, investment inflows, as well as regional economic initiatives. It is shown that although Russia is still an important partner, Central Asian countries have strengthened their economic relationship with many Asian countries. A special section also analyses the current status of Indo-Central Asian economic relations. Major economic trends, as well as certain recommendations for Indian policy makers are summarised in the concluding section.

Since 1992, the five Central Asian countries (Kazakhstan, Kyrgyz Republic, Tajikistan, Turkmenistan and Uzbekistan) are witnessing transformation of their economic systems. All these countries have moved along this transformation to varying degrees. Despite having a very complex legacy (of central planning, dissolution of the USSR, distorted economic structures, ethnic problems), the region has made some progress in market reforms. Due to certain specific features (natural resources, strategic location, political systems and background of political elite), the region has used both standard as well as non-conventional strategies of economic transformation. The

Soviet era leaders in more or less non-competitive regimes have tried to pursue economic stability, while securing their own dominance in the new political system. They have also tried to learn a few lessons from the Chinese model of development.

After the failure of centrally planned system in the former Soviet bloc, countries in the region started their journey towards a market economy. Even in countries which still consider themselves socialist or communist, like China and Vietnam, the mechanism of economic coordination has shifted to a great extent from bureaucratic coordination to market allocation of resources.[1] Most of the earlier writings on transformation asserted that there was no theory to guide the practical process of transition, only theories of socialism and capitalism. Most of the earlier reform deliberations within these countries had also been confined to improving 'market socialism'.

From the vast literature on transition, soon a consensus on the new paradigm started emerging. Although there was some confusion even in the Western thinking,[2] and it may be almost an impossible task to capture the complex analytical framework of transformation, it is not that difficult to cobble together from a few key writings a workable 'model' of the transformation. Kornai[3] highlighted two changes that were needed: *forcing a move from a seller's market to a buyer's market* (via price liberalisation) and *enforcing a hard budget constraint* (via privatisation and ending various government support mechanisms). Blanchard[4] defined the process of change as comprising two elements: *reallocation of resources from old to new* (via closures and bankruptcies and establishment of new enterprises) and *restructuring within surviving firms* (via labour rationalisation, product line change, and new investment). The policy actions needed to put in place are outlined in many works,[5] and are well exemplified by Fischer and Gelb.[6] The key measures of reforms were (*a*) macroeconomic stabilisation; (*b*) price and market liberalisation; (*c*) liberalisation of exchange and trade system; (*d*) privatisation; (*e*) establishing a competitive environment with few obstacles to market entry and exit; (*f*) redefining the role of the state.[7] The 1996 World Development Report[8] argued that building on early gains of transition would require major consolidating reforms, strong market supporting institutions, a skilled and adaptable work force, and full integration with the global economy. It also recognised that while initial conditions were critical, decisive and sustained reforms were important for recovery of growth and social policies designed to protect the most vulnerable sections. It emphasised that investing in people is the key to growth. Recently, the World Bank has highlighted the key role of the entry of new firms, particularly small- and medium-size enterprises in generating economic growth and employment.[9] It calls for *encouragement strategy* which has to be accompanied by a *strategy of discipline*. It also calls for the need to develop or strengthen the legal and regulatory institutions to oversee the management and governance of enterprises, both those in the private sector and those remaining in the state sector. It recognises that winners from the early stages of reforms may oppose subsequent reform steps when these reduce their initially substantial but potentially temporary benefits or rents. The early winners may also capture the state, and force the economy into low level reform equilibrium.

As a result of all these policy prescriptions and later empirical findings,[10] a new branch—*economics of transformation*—came into existence to deal with these economies. In recent years, research in transition economies has moved from purely *economics of transformation* to *political economy of transformation*. The theory of political economy of transformation in transition economies belongs to more fundamental research in recent years to integrate the political process into the analysis of economic problems.[11] Central Asian economic transition has, however, many dimensions. Apart from managing the challenges of transition, the region also faces the challenge of development.[12] As a result, the region is facing both the dilemmas simultaneously—the dilemma of the *political economy of transformation*, as well as that of *developmental economics*.[13]

In the early years, the break-up of the Soviet Union hit the region very badly for many reasons. Trade and transit was interrupted with new borders, increased transportation costs, illegal check-points, and collapse of traditional markets. Industrial and agricultural production was hurt due to disruption in access to inputs and markets. There was loss of subsidies for budgets, enterprises and households, which were paid earlier directly or indirectly through social payments, as well as through prices below the market rate on transport and energy. There was also loss of administrative structures and skilled labour as traditional Soviet administration collapsed, and many Russians left the region. The access to secure water and energy resources was also lost in the region, which was key for the agriculture, industry and household requirements. Countries in the region were left with large environmental burdens (including the Aral sea ecological disaster, as well as industrial, nuclear and biological waste). Above all, there were also ethnic tensions and civil war (especially in Tajikistan).[14] All these were added complications to the 'normal' transformational problems faced by any country moving from a centrally planned economy to a market economy.

Despite a common historical and cultural background, including more than seven decades of Soviet legacy, the five Central Asian republics have had different abilities to cope with the transformation challenges.[15] As a result they have adopted different strategies. Even through a quick view at the vast transformation literature, one could find 'early and late reformers', as well as 'radical' and 'gradualist' reformers in Central Asia. The transition strategies adopted by these countries have also been influenced greatly by the political environment in the region and in their particular countries. Uzbekistan adopted a gradual and cautious approach to market reforms, while Kazakhstan and Kyrgyz Republic followed a relatively more aggressive approach. Turkmenistan and Tajikistan have cautiously joined later. These different policies have led to different macroeconomic outcomes, as well as different policy environments.

Progress with Transition

The countries of Central Asia in the first decade of their transformation displayed some common trends and some significant variations. However, output decline in all the countries in the region was very deep and longer. Recovery in some of the countries was further derailed with the fiscal financial crisis in the Russian Federation in 1998. According to the World Bank data, Central Asia had an average of seven years of declining output, resulting in loss of almost 41 per cent of the initial measured output. With the base year of 1990, even at the end of the decade, Central Asia had recovered only 75 per cent of its starting GDP values. The highest loss of output was in Kyrgyzstan and lowest in Uzbekistan. This 'transformation recession' is now over. Some of the countries in the region are now on a path of recovery.

Overall, the success on market-oriented structural and institutional reforms has shown mixed progress in Central Asia. According to different methodologies and classifications developed by major

Table 11.1
Growth in Real GDP in Central Asia, 1990–2002

Country	1990	1991	1992	1993	1994	1995	1996	1997	1998	1999	2000	2001	2002	GDP in 2002 1989=100
KAZ.	−0.4	−11.0	−5.3	−9.3	−12.6	−8.2	0.5	1.7	−1.9	2.7	9.8	13.2	7.6	84
KYR.	3.0	−5.0	−19.0	−16.0	−20.1	−5.4	7.1	9.9	2.1	3.7	5.1	5.3	2.0	71
TAJ.	−1.6	−7.1	−29.0	−11.0	−18.9	−12.5	−4.4	1.7	5.3	3.7	8.3	10.3	7.0	56
TURK.	2.0	−4.7	−5.3	−10.6	−17.3	−7.2	−6.7	−11.3	5.0	16.0	17.6	12.0	13.5	96
UZB.	1.6	−0.5	−11.1	−2.3	−4.2	−0.9	1.6	2.5	4.4	4.1	4.0	4.5	2.5	105

Source: European Bank for Reconstruction and Development (EBRD).

multilateral organisations, as well as other independent agencies to measure reform progress in transition economies, Kazakhstan and Kyrgyzstan have progressed much faster. Similarly, Uzbekistan and Turkmenistan have been classified as countries which have achieved less progress in establishing market institutions. According to widely used indicators developed by the European Bank for Reconstruction and Development (EBRD), level of reforms concerning prices, foreign exchange and external trade, privatisation, enterprise reforms and banking sector is high in Kazakhstan and Kyrgyz Republic. In some cases it is comparable to Russia and Poland. Tajikistan has also made significant progress in price reforms, external sector reforms and small privatisation. The level of reforms in Uzbekistan and Turkmenistan is low, particularly in the external sector and enterprise, and banking sector reforms. Except Kazakhstan, other Central Asian countries are quite low in Euromoney risk ratings. Kazakhstan's rating has improved consistently, while ratings of Kyrgyzstan has gone down in recent years. Overall there has been very little improvement for the region.[16]

Transformation in Agriculture

The Central Asian region entered the transition with a common institutional and organisational heritage in agriculture. Most of the agricultural land in the region was cultivated collectively in collective and state farms that managed thousands of hectares and employed hundreds of member-workers. Though essential dimensions of transition in agriculture in former socialist countries include abolition of central planning, reduction of government interventions, elimination of price controls, development of functioning market services, emergence of rural credit institutions, technological improvements, new capital investment patterns and agricultural labour adjustments, still the most controversial component of agricultural transition in the region has been land reforms, i.e., establishments of private property rights in land, and restructuring of traditional socialist farms. During the Soviet period, only one form of land ownership was recognised. All lands were owned by the state, while farm enterprises were given land use rights. As a result, the first step in market-oriented reform in all the former Soviet republics is to give up this exclusive ownership

Table 11.2
Progress with Transition—EBRD 2002 Indicators
(Average Transition Score from 1 to 4)

Country	Enterprises				Markets & Trade			Financial Institutions & Infrastructure		
	Private Sector Share (% of GDP Mid-2001)	Large Privatis-ation	Small Privatis-ation	Govern-ance & Enterprise Restruc-turing	Price Liberalis-ation	Trade & Foreign Exchange	Compet-ition Policy	Banking Reform and Interest Rate Liberalis-ation	Security Market & Non-Bank FIs	Infrastr-ucture
Kazakhstan	65	3	4	2	3	3+	2	3–	2+	2
Kyrgyz Rep.	60	3	4	2	3	4	2	2+	2	1+
Tajikistan	50	2+	4–	2–	3	3+	2–	2–	1	1+
Turkmenistan	25	1	2	1	2	2–	1	1	1	1
Uzbekistan	45	3–	3	2–	2	2–	2	2–	2	2

Source: Transition Report 2002, EBRD.

of land and transfer it to private ownership. Kyrgyzstan has allowed private landownership. Kazakhstan restrict private ownership to household plots up to one hectare only, whereas Tajikistan and Uzbekistan retain full state ownership of land. Turkmenistan is an interesting case. Its post-Soviet Constitution, adopted in May 1992, recognised private ownership of land. However, the property rights of private landowners are restricted to the most basic right to usufruct. Private owned land might not be sold, given away as gift, or exchanged. So rights of private landowners are in fact similar to Uzbekistan and Tajikistan. Countries also differ in attitudes towards land transactions. Land use rights are secure in Kazakhstan and Tajikistan. Kyrgyzstan and Turkmenistan recognise land rights, but severely restrict transactions in land. Restructuring strategy in the region is through allocation of 'paper shares'. Like in many other CIS countries, transformation in agriculture mechanism prescribed re-registration of former collective, or state farms in new organis-ational forms, such as limited liability companies, an agricultural co-operative, a joint stock company, an association, etc. The immediate outcome of the strategy has been retention of former collective structures as new organisational forms. The process has resulted in (a) corporate units created by reconfiguration of shares inside the former collective shell; (b) successor farm (stay as is) created by keeping the share in the former collective; (c) individual farms established by withdrawal of shareholders.[17] Despite all these changes, in reality, very little has changed in the form of farm restructuring in Central Asia.

External Economic Relations

Central Asian economies inherited state-controlled foreign trade, which was subordinated to the central planning. In this situation price signals played very little role in allocation of resources. Foreign trade was, in fact, the responsibility of the Gosplan, the state foreign economic commission, the ministry of foreign economic relations and many other specialised foreign trade agencies. Individual enter-prises had very little role in conducting foreign trade.[18] Within the integrated economic structure of the Soviet Union, Central Asian region has strong dependency on imports of energy, food and

Table 11.3
Characteristics of Land Relations in Central Asia

	Potential Private Ownership	Transferability	Privatisation Strategy	Allocation Strategy	Farm Organisation	Composite Land Policy Index*
Kazakhstan	Household plots only	Use rights transferable; buy and sell of private plots dubious	None	Shares	Corporate-renamed collectives + individual	5.4
Kyrgyzstan	All land	5 year moratorium on land transactions	Distribution/ conversion	Shares	Corporate + individual	5.4
Tajikistan	None	Use rights transferable	None	Shares	Corporate-renamed collectives + individual	2.5
Turkmenistan	All land	Use rights non-transferable	None; virgin land to farmers	Leasehold	Corporate-renamed collectives + individual	4.0
Uzbekistan	None	Use rights non-transferable	None	Leasehold	Corporate-renamed collectives + individual	0.6

Source: Zvi Lerman, Csaba Csaki and Gershan Feder, *Land Policies and Evolving Farm Structures in Transition Economies.* Washington DC, 2002.
* On the scale of 0 to 10; Land policy index 10 corresponds to ideal market conditions, 0 to no market attributes.

consumer goods. The production structure of the region was heavily oriented towards agriculture and mineral extraction. Because of lack of diversification and high import dependency, these countries were vulnerable to adverse trade shocks.

External economic reforms in the region have covered five areas— liberalisation of foreign trade prices, reform of the trade system, market diversification, phasing out of barter trade and currency reforms.[19] Progress on these reforms has varied across the region. Although the role of state in foreign trade has been reduced throughout the region, progress has been more pronounced in Kazakhstan and Kyrgyzstan. Uzbekistan and Turkmenistan are more gradual with foreign trade liberalisation, particularly in the foreign exchange market. In the last one decade, exports have grown and significant diversification of trade has taken place.

The Central Asian experience with external trade could be classified in distinct phases. The first phase between 1991 and 1994 was a period of adjustments to the shocks of sudden dissolution of the USSR and sharp fall in mutual trade. During this period, all regional economies (except Turkmenistan), incurred sizeable and persistent external current account deficits. The main reason for this were: (a) the inherited economic structures (agricultural, industrial and households sectors) were highly energy intensive; (b) the demand for investment goods to replace this structure was high; (c) imports demand for Western consumer goods was very high.

The second phase was between 1995 and August 1998. During this period attempts were made to keep reasonable trade relations with traditional partners, and to enlarge trade ties with the rest of the world. In the third stage, which starts from 18 August 1998, the region faced many negative impacts of Russian and Asian economic crises. With the sharp devaluation of Russian rouble, competitiveness of Central Asian commodities in traditional markets was affected. However, many of the negative impacts are eased since 2000 with strong recoveries in Russia and Central Asia.

Share of trade within CIS countries has declined in the region. However, as a result of some regional trade initiatives, (discussed in the following pages), mutual trade in the region was increased, particularly in the initial years of transition. Since 1994, the share of trade with the non-CIS countries has been growing fast in both exports and imports. In the last few years about 70 per cent of Uzbekistan's trade has been with non-CIS countries. Although Russia is still an important partner at the regional level, the geographical distribution of trade has shifted from CMEA to EU (Germany, UK), East Asia (China, South Korea, Japan), North America (USA), and Middle East (Iran, Turkey). China has been able to make some significant trade partnership with Kazakhstan and Kyrgyzstan. The commodity structure of Central Asian exports mainly consists of mineral resources and agricultural raw materials. The main exports has been oil and gas products, ferrous and non-ferrous metals and grain in Kazakhstan; cotton fibres, gold, natural gas and non-ferrous metals in Uzbekistan; gold, tobacco and wool in Kyrgyzstan; aluminium and cotton fibres in Tajikistan; and natural gas, cotton fibres and oil and oil products in Turkmenistan. Import composition in the region has been changing. In the initial years imports consisted mainly of food products and other consumer goods. This structure of imports has been changing in favour of machinery, equipment, etc.

Regional Cooperation Initiatives

Due to landlocked location and remoteness from major world markets, small domestic markets, rational use of water and energy resources and to integrate themselves with the global economy, the Central Asian countries have taken many regional and international trade and other economic co-operation initiatives. It is realised that developing regional markets would save large transport costs, exploit scale economies, and yield gains from trade, including those based on resource complementarity.[20] In the past, however, the development of regional cooperation involving all five countries in the region has been difficult at the political level. Two big countries, Kazakhstan and Uzbekistan, have competed for the position of regional leader. As a manifestation of its declared policy of neutrality, Turkmenistan has resisted participation in many regional forums.

All central Asian republics are important members of the Commonwealth of Independent states (CIS). On the economic affairs, the CIS has not implemented a customs Union or a free trade area covering all member states. In 1995, Kazakhstan and Kyrgyzstan formed a Customs Union with Belarus and Russia. Tajikistan later joined this union in 1999. In October 2000, the Customs Union was transformed into Eurasian Economic Community (EEC). Its

Table 11.4
Kyrgyzstan, Direction of Trade (million US dollars)

Exports	2000	2001	2002	3 Year Average (%)
Total	501.9	476.1	480.5	
1. Germany	144.6	94.5	2.4	16.4
2. Russia	65.1	64.6	69.5	13.6
3. Switzerland	34.0	124.2	144.1	15.3
4. Uzbekistan	89.4	47.9	28.6	11.3
5. Kazakhstan	33.4	39.0	34.6	7.3
6. China	44.1	19.4	38.2	7.0
7. UK	18.7	14.1	0.9	2.3
8. USA	2.9	7.1	30.5	2.8
9. Tajikistan	7.4	6.7	7.1	1.4
10. Turkey	7.2	13.8	18.6	2.7

Imports	2000	2001	2002	3 Year Average (%)
Total	554.3	464.4	592.7	
1. Russia	132.5	85.1	106.5	20.1
2. Uzbekistan	75.2	66.8	70.0	13.2
3. Kazakhstan	57.5	81.9	119.6	16.1
4. USA	53.8	26.7	43.4	7.6
5. China	36.9	48.6	59.3	9.0
6. Germany	25.1	24.3	28.9	4.9
7. Turkey	26.7	15.8	17.9	3.7
8. S. Korea	6.9	7.8	7.1	1.4
9. Canada	11.3	10.9	10.2	2.0
10. Turkmen'an	18.8	9.0	3.6	1.9

Table 11.5
Kazakhstan, Direction of Trade (million US dollars)

Exports	2000	2001	2002	3 Year Average (%)
Total	9,138.0	8,646.8	9,930.4	
1. Russia	1,783.9	1,748.4	1,743.6	19.1
2. Bermuda	1,358.1	1,221.2	1,325.3	13.7
3. Italy	891.9	970.9	600.9	9.0
4. China	670.3	655.5	832.8	8.0
5. Germany	566.6	509.6	905.9	7.0
6. Switzerland	497.6	407.3	422.0	4.7
7. UK	231.0	295.0	47.2	2.1
8. Ukraine	268.5	490.5	532.3	4.6
9. Netherlands	240.0	144.9	123.6	1.4
10. USA	211.0	159.1	316.6	2.4

Imports	2000	2001	2002	3 Year Average (%)
Total	5,051.7	6,362.8	6,809.1	
1. Russia	2,459.8	2,890.9	2,686.9	44.5
2. Germany	333.7	471.4	624.5	7.7
3. USA	276.9	341.6	665.2	6.9
4. UK	219.4	246.3	152.0	3.5
5. Turkey	142.6	131.3	142.5	2.3
6. Italy	155.0	266.1	206.0	3.4
7. China	154.0	169.2	244.3	3.0
8. Ukraine	79.8	154.9	168.1	2.2
9. S. Korea	82.5	106.5	115.6	1.7
10. Japan	105.5	140.2	103.1	1.9

Table 11.6
Tajikistan, Direction of Trade (million US dollars)

Exports	2000	2001	2002	3 Year Average (%)	Imports	2000	2001	2002	3 Year Average (%)
Total	784.3	651.6	536.6		Total	675.0	687.5	704.5	
1. Netherlands	178.2	194.4	2.8	17.7	1. Uzbekistan	185.6	150.7	163.6	24.2
2. Uzbekistan	97.8	87.2	94.7	14.5	2. Russia	105.1	129.4	88.0	15.6
3. Russia	258.8	104.7	64.4	20.4	3. Switzerland	0.6	2.1	2.1	0.22
4. Switzerland	72.2	52.2	54.1	9.0	4. Kazakhstan	82.4	89.1	96.7	13.0
5. Turkey	58.4	75.1	81.5	11.4	5. UK	86.9	2.5	1.2	4.5
6. Latvia	0.0	11.7	12.7	1.4	6. Turkmenistan	29.3	62.3	67.6	7.7
7. Iran	12.5	29.9	24.8	3.6	7. Ukraine	0.0	63.6	69.0	6.3
8. Hungary	1.0	38.8	65.8	6.1	8. Azerbaijan	63.1	33.5	36.4	6.5
9. Italy	21.4	5.8	18.9	2.4	9. Romania	41.0	10.9	11.8	3.1
10. Belgium	5.1	6.0	5.0	0.8	10. Iran	7.6	10.0	10.6	1.3

Table 11.7
Turkmenistan, Direction of Trade (million US dollars)

Exports	2000	2001	2002	3 Year Average (%)
Total	2,505.2	1,132.4	1,218.9	
1. Russia	1,029.3	35.5	23.4	15.4
2. Iran	242.0	241.0	199.9	15.8
3. Ukraine	164.9	182.1	197.6	12.9
4. Germany	404.8	5.8	10.5	5.8
5. Turkey	186.0	65.2	70.8	5.8
6. Azerbaijan	37.1	122.9	133.4	7.7
7. Switzerland	91.9	0.8	0.8	1.3
8. Afghanistan	38.0	42.0	45.5	3.0
9. Tajikistan	29.1	56.7	61.5	3.9
10. Kazakhstan	5.3	70.5	76.5	4.2

Imports	2000	2001	2002	3 Year Average (%)
Total	1,787.8	1,557.5	1,432.5	
1. Ukraine	214.3	235.7	255.8	15.0
2. Turkey	253.3	115.8	125.7	10.1
3. Russia	254.5	153.4	152.3	11.6
4. USA	62.8	273.4	51.9	8.2
5. UAE	146.6	158.2	168.2	10.0
6. Germany	52.6	140.6	173.9	8.0
7. Iran	90.9	98.1	104.3	6.2
8. France	75.7	50.5	67.6	4.0
9. Japan	144.4	35.9	6.0	3.6
10. Uzbekistan	35.3	38.8	42.1	2.5

Table 11.8
Uzbekistan, Direction of Trade (million US dollars)

Exports	2000	2001	2002	3 Year Average (%)
Total	2,135.3	2,028.1	1,900.0	
1. Russia	602.0	527.2	327.8	23.8
2. Tajikistan	168.7	137.0	148.7	7.5
3. Italy	172.8	155.2	157.7	8.0
4. Ukraine	161.8	178.0	193.2	8.8
5. S. Korea	94.5	124.3	134.9	5.9
6. Germany	67.6	56.4	44.2	2.8
7. Kyrgyzstan	68.4	60.7	63.6	3.2
8. Kazakhstan	66.6	72.9	79.1	3.6
9. Poland	36.7	82.3	89.3	3.5
10. Turkey	78.0	32.8	35.6	2.4

Imports	2000	2001	2002	3 Year Average (%)
Total	2,078.1	2,303.4	2,370.1	
1. Russia	301.9	400.2	486.9	17.5
2. S. Korea	253.5	380.3	412.7	15.4
3. Germany	233.3	227.2	211.4	10.0
4. USA	182.7	162.5	151.9	7.4
5. Ukraine	125.4	138.4	150.3	6.1
6. Tajikistan	107.6	95.9	104.1	4.5
7. Turkey	90.9	98.7	107.1	4.4
8. Kazakhstan	153.1	163.7	177.6	7.3
9. France	73.4	118.8	42.8	3.5
10. Kyrgyzstan	98.3	52.7	31.5	2.8

Source: Asian Development Bank Databank.

objectives include broadening of the coordination of economic, social, industrial and financial policy of member countries.

In 1994, Kazakhstan, Kyrgyzstan and Uzbekistan also formed the Central Asian Union (CAU). The aim was to create a single economic region with improvements in payments arrangements and reduction in tariffs among member countries. In 1995, the principle of free trade among member states was approved. A Central Asian Bank for Cooperation and Development was also created. In 1998, Tajikistan also became member of this grouping. During the same year, the organisation was renamed as Central Asian Economic Community (CAEC). In 2001, the CAEC was transformed into Central Asian Cooperation Organisation (CACO). Russia, Ukraine, Georgia and Turkey have been given observer status in CACO. Kazakhstan, Kyrgyz Republic, Tajikistan, Turkmenistan and Uzbekistan, all five, have joined the Economic Cooperation Organisation (ECO), which also includes Afghanistan, Azerbaijan, Iran, Pakistan and Turkey. The main objective of ECO is to develop and improve economic infrastructure and transportation system in the region. All five have also become members of the Organisation of Islamic Conference (OIC), an intergovernmental organisation with 56 members, established in 1971 in Saudi Arabia. Its aim is to promote Islamic solidarity by improving cooperation in the political, economic, social and cultural and scientific fields. Uzbekistan also became member of the GUUAM Group in 1999, a sub-regional formation of Georgia, Ukraine, Azerbaijan, and Moldova and Uzbekistan. The Group was formally founded as a political, economic and strategic alliance designed to strengthen the independence and sovereignty of these former Soviet Union republics. Some scholars have analysed GUUAM as a product of the clash in American-Russian interests in the region. It was also considered an organisation to counterbalance EEC and to reduce Russian economic and political control in this region. In June 2002, however, Uzbekistan withdrew from the organisation.

Kyrgyzstan has become member of the WTO, and all others have shown interest in becoming its member. The European Union (EU) has granted Central Asian countries access to Generalised System of Preferences (GSP). It allows tariff reductions on manufactured products and certain agricultural goods. To encourage regional cooperation in the region, in 1997, Asian Development Bank initiated a programme called Central Asia Regional Economic Cooperation (CAREC). The operational strategy of the CAREC is to finance infrastructure projects and improve the policy environment for promoting cross-border activities in the areas of trade, energy and transportation. The United Nations also started a Special Programme for the Economies of Central Asia (SPECA) in 1997. The objective of the programme is to strengthen regional cooperation in order to both stimulate their economic development and facilitate their integration into Europe and Asia. Another international initiative to promote poverty reduction, growth and debt sustainability in seven low income CIS countries is also in operation. The seven CIS countries are: Armenia, Azerbaijan, Georgia, Kyrgyz Republic, Moldova, Uzbekistan and Tajikistan. Along with these seven CIS countries, the initiative brings together the four sponsoring organisations: ADB, EBRD, IMF and IDA (WB), and a group of bilateral creditors/donors. Currently, 24 countries participate in the CIS 7 Initiative, and in addition, several organisations/countries hold the observer title. These include Canada, China, EU, OECD, Islamic Development Bank, France, Germany, Italy, Japan, Russia, Turkey, UK and USA. At the technical level, some other regional initiatives include the Inter-governmental Commission on Central Asian Sustainable Development, the Inter-State Water Commission, the Central Asians Energy Advisory Group and regional Electricity Grid. The following table summarises the major regional economic cooperation initiatives in Central Asia.

As a result of these initiatives, the Central Asian countries have made some modest gains. In the beginning of transition, mutual trade among Central Asian countries played an important role. Although regional trade has clearly developed in Central Asia, its growth has been uneven at best. The potential for expanding intra-regional trade remains considerable. Despite the common interest toward increasing trade, all the countries in the region have trade-restricting policies and practices. There are the barriers of tariffs, public policies, procedures and regulations, and weak financial systems. Some other policy-related constraints to trade include import quotas, export licensing requirements and transport restrictions. Arbitrary and often corrupt bureaucracies throughout the region administer regulations that are archaic and frequently conflicting. There are slow, difficult border procedures, multiple cargo inspections within a single country and prohibitions that prevent vehicles from transporting goods between countries. Other barriers to trade include transit fees and the costs of dealing with corrupt border officials and local police. Trade is also restricted by such practices as requiring importers to register

Table 11.9
Regional Economic Initiates in Central Asia

Country	CIS	EEC	CACO	ECO	OIC	CAREC (ADB)	SCO	CIS-7 Initiative
Kazakhstan	X	X	X	X	X	X	X	
Kyrgyzstan	X	X	X	X	X	X	X	X
Tajikistan	X	X	X	X	X	X	X	X
Turkmenistan	X			X	X			
Uzbekistan	X		X	X	X	X	X	X

CIS—Commonwealth of Independent states (with Armenia, Azerbaijan Belarus, Georgia, Maldova, Russia, Ukraine).
EEC—Eurasian Economic Community, ex Customs Union (with Russia and Belarus).
CACO—Central Asian Cooperation Organisation, ex Central Asian Economic Community.
ECO—Economic Cooperation Organisation (with Iran, Pakistan, Turkey and Afghanistan).
OIC—Organisation of Islamic Conference (total 56 members, established in 1971).
CAREC (ADB)—Central Asia Regional Economic Cooperation (with Azerbaijan, Mongolia and Xinjiang Autonomous Region of China; Turkmenistan is also expected to join soon).
SCO—Shanghai Cooperation Organisation (with Russia and China). SCO began as a forum for discussing border delineation issues. As a result of threat of terrorism in the region it has lately focussed more on security issues. Economic cooperation is also envisaged among members.
CIS-7—An International initiative to promote poverty reduction, growth and debt sustainability in seven low income CIS countries: Armenia, Azerbaijan, Georgia, Kyrgyz Republic, Moldova, Uzbekistan, Tajikistan.

contracts and currency conversion restrictions. In no country is there a healthy financial system that provides modern services to facilitate trade. Most of the trade is, in fact, conducted through inefficient cash transfers or barter.[21]

In the last two years, Chinese have cited strengthening cooperation in energy as a key factor for promoting the SCO's objectives. To meet its growing demand for energy, China has seriously focussed Central Asia and the Caspian region. China National Petroleum Corporation (CNPC) has acquired oil concessions in Kazakhstan and Azerbaijan. So far the major deal has been CNPC's acquisition of a 60 per cent stake in the Kazakh oil firm Aktobemunaigaz.[22] Earlier, there was also some discussions of a possible oil pipeline from Kazakhstan to China. CNPC now says that it would only be considered if reserves were sufficient, and it was economical. In March 2003, a Chinese company pledged $615 million to British Gas for roughly 8 per cent of the Kashagan oilfield, in the Kazakhstan section of the Caspian Sea. In May 2003, the consortium partners in the Kashagan oilfield exercised their rights to block the sale. After a few months, CNPC acquired 35 per cent of the North Buzachi oilfield from Saudi oil company Nimir Petroleum. Later, CNPC took full control of the field by buying the remaining shares from Chevron Texaco. In addition, the Chinese are also discussing several pipeline projects, including the China-Atasu-Alashankou oil route, and a gas link to Turkmenistan via Kazakhstan. In June 2003, it was also announced that China's Shengli oil company had signed an $80 million deal with the Azerbaijani state oil company, SOCAR, to develop the Pirsaat field, located south of Baku.[23]

India's major initiative in the region so far has been Indian-Iranian cooperation in building North-South trade corridor. The main transport projects undertaken under this programme will be development of a new port complex at Chah Bahar on the coast of Iran, from where a road goes north to the border with Afghanistan. India will build a link from Zaranj on the Iran-Afghan border to Delaram, from where all major cities in Afghanistan and further north Central Asian republics are connected. Another transport project involves the linking of the Chah Bahar port to the Iranian rail network which is connected to Central Asia and Europe.[24] When materialised, this initiative means speedy flow of goods, especially energy, from Central Asia to Iran to India. Still the shortest route from India to the Central Asian republics is through Pakistan and Afghanistan.

It is evident from the earlier analysis that most of the regional initiatives in Central Asia are either groupings to recreate lost linkages among the former Soviet republics or initiatives by multilateral organisations to strengthen regional linkages in the areas of trade, energy, water resources, infrastructure and communications. These are largely affairs within the former Soviet space. Other countries like China, Iran, Turkey, Pakistan and Afghanistan have also been able to create some formal structures for closer interactions, which will become useful in the long run. India is totally absent from any meaningful regional economic initiative. India should now seriously pursue extending SAARC to Afghanistan and the Central Asian region. Because of the past result of the SAARC, if Central Asians are not interested in this grouping, then India should seriously consider creating another independent organisation involving India, and some of the countries in the region.

Foreign Investment

During the first half of the nineties, Central Asia was considered highly risky because of breakdown of the trade and payments mechanisms and economic decline. As a result, the region had to depend on official bilateral and multilateral sources for financing new projects. Later, there was marked increase in private capital flows in the form of commercial bank lending and FDI, particularly in the traditional export-oriented, resource based industries. All countries in Central Asia have tried to encourage FDI flows through far-reaching reforms in their foreign investment laws.[25] Table 11.10 shows that these flows have grown (with some disruptions during the 1998 crisis in Russia). On the whole, however, apart from Kazakhstan's oil and gas sector, the FDI flow has been low in large measures because of foreign investment climate. Turkmenistan has received about US $1 billion since independence, primarily in the oil sector. Kyrgyzstan has received some modest FDI flows, connected largely to gold mines project. There has been some improvement in FDI flows to Uzbekistan in the last few years. The United States has been the major investor in the region which has been followed by Europe. Some modest investments have been made by Chinese (in oil sector) and South Korean companies.

India and Central Asian Economic Linkages

During the Soviet period, all contacts with the republics of the USSR were through Moscow only. The nature and character of the then Indo-Soviet trade and economic relations largely determined these relations. In the post-socialist period, like other CIS countries, economic relationship with the Central Asian region has also declined considerably. The official two-way annual trade between India and the region has been about US $100 million in the last few years. Apart from Kazakhstan and Uzbekistan, economic relations with other countries are minimal. This relationship is also restricted mainly to traditional items. The main commodities being exported from India are pharmaceuticals, tea, readymade garments, woollen goods, leather goods, jute, cosmetics, cotton yarn, machinery, machine tools, rice, plastic products, machinery and instruments,

Table 11.10
Inflows of Foreign Direct Investment in Central Asia 1992–2002 (million US dollars)

	1992	1993	1994	1995	1996	1997	1998	1999	2000	2001	2002
Kazakhstan	100	228	635	964	1,137	1,321	1,151	1,468	1,245	2,835	2,583
Kyrgyzstan	–	10	38	96	47	83	109	44	–2	5	5
Tajikistan	9	9	12	20	25	30	24	21	22	9	36
Turkmenistan[a]	11	79	103	233	108	108	64	80*	100*	100*	–
Uzbekistan[a]	9	48	73	–24	90	167	140	121	75	83	–

Source: United Nations Economic Commission of Europe.
[a] Net of residents' investments abroad.

electronic goods, chemicals, etc. Imports from the CAR are restricted to raw cotton, Iron and steel, zinc, etc.

Table 11.11
India-Central Asia Trade, 1996–97 to 2002–03 (million US dollars)

	1996–97	1997–98	1998–99	1999–2000	2000–01	2001–02	2002–03
Kazakhstan	16.96	51.16	50.43	40.65	64.12	53.09	59.61
Kyrgyzstan	0.98	10.80	8.81	15.61	22.02	11.52	15.13
Tajikistan	1.53	1.12	3.04	4.72	4.10	2.56	8.73
Turkmenistan	1.65	1.70	2.03	6.03	3.83	6.30	15.70
Uzbekistan	10.74	20.3	14.50	22.91	19.98	23.80	25.62
Central Asia	31.86	85.08	78.81	89.92	114.05	97.27	124.79
% of Total Indian trade			0.104	0.103	0.119	0.102	0.109

Source: DGFT, Ministry of Commerce, Government of India.

Table 11.12
Indian Exports to Central Asia, 1996–97 to 2002–03 (million US dollars)

	1996–97	1997–98	1998–99	1999–2000	2000–01	2001–02	2002–03
Kazakhstan	4.39	15.13	38.0	27.19	50.08	45.70	46.88
Kyrgyzstan	0.98	10.79	8.70	13.80	17.59	10.95	14.67
Tajikistan	0.73	1.12	0.51	2.38	3.55	1.22	8.65
Turkmenistan	1.38	1.68	1.93	5.64	2.71	4.35	10.29
Uzbekistan	8.14	17.59	12.83	9.94	9.39	6.53	5.08
Central Asia	15.62	46.31	61.97	58.95	83.33	68.78	85.57

Source: DGFT, Ministry of Commerce, Government of India.

Table 11.13
Indian Imports from Central Asia, 1996–97 to 2002–03 (million US dollars)

	1996–97	1997–98	1998–99	1999–2000	2000–01	2001–02	2002–03
Kazakhstan	12.57	36.03	12.43	13.45	14.04	7.39	12.73
Kyrgyzstan	–	0.01	0.10	1.82	4.43	0.56	0.47
Tajikistan	0.80	–	2.53	2.33	0.54	1.34	0.08
Turkmenistan	0.27	0.02	0.11	0.38	1.12	1.95	5.40
Uzbekistan	2.60	2.71	1.67	12.97	10.58	17.27	20.54
Central Asia	16.24	38.77	16.83	30.96	30.72	28.50	39.22

Source: DGFT, Ministry of Commerce, Government of India.

To give impetus to bilateral trade, economic and scientific cooperation, bilateral inter-governmental Joint Commissions have been set up with the countries in the region. A number of high level visits have also taken place.[26] India has also extended credit lines ranging from $5 million to $10 million to almost all countries in the region. It has signed many agreements with these countries for technical, economic cooperation under International Technical and Economic Cooperation (ITEC). So far about 1,000 candidates from the region have come to India in various disciplines, such as diplomacy, banking, finance, trade, management and small industry promotion. ONGC Videsh has also been active in Kazakhstan. Despite all these developments, economic linkages between India and the region have been much below its potential. The main reasons are lack of information and connectivity. Lack of economic and financial sector reforms in the region could also have discouraged many Indian companies.

Cooperation in the energy sector is an obvious potential area. Since this region has great tourism potential, cooperation in the tourism-related services would also be useful. Information technology is another area where Indian services could be in great demand, particularly when this region is undergoing a major transformation in the financial and other sectors. There is great scope for cooperation as some of these countries are blessed with high quality human resources. Indian consultancy companies could also play a very major role in the ongoing modernisation process in the region. Another area of major interest to Indian businesses would be to take part in the continuing privatisation process in the region. Compared to Russia and other east European countries, the region is still in the middle of privatising their huge state sectors. This could provide a huge opportunity for India as is shown by an NRI company Ispat International which has bought the 6.5 million tonne capacity Karaganda steel plant, a linked power plant and 15 coal mines in Kazakhstan. This deal has become one of the major success stories in the region. Ispat could turn around this loss making plant into a profit making venture. It has a workforce of 67,000 local workers. Some other Indian companies like Punj Lloyd have also participated in oil pipeline projects in Kazakhstan.

Conclusion

Despite having a very complex legacy, the Central Asian region has made some progress in market reforms. The region has used both

standard, as well as non-conventional strategies of economic transformation. It has been successful in some economic stability. However, success with structural and institutional reforms is mixed. The
inflation has been reduced, GDP is rising, and production and trade
has been diversified. Yet reforms have not been consolidated, and the
region is still vulnerable to external shocks. The FDI in the region
has been mainly concentrated in the energy sector, and only
Kazakhstan has been able to attract significant FDI. Most of the
regional economic arrangements in the region are either grouping to
recreate lost linkages among the former Soviet republics, or through
initiatives undertaken by multilateral organisations strengthening
regional linkages in the areas of trade, energy, water resources,
infrastructure and communications. Although Russia is still an important economic partner, countries in the region have tried to
strengthen its relationship with many Asian countries, particularly
with China, Iran, South Korea and Japan.

India's economic relationship with the Central Asian region has
declined considerably in the post-socialist period. The official two-
way annual trade between India and the region has been about US
$100 million in the last few years. The main reasons have been lack
of information, connectivity and economic decline of the region, and
lack of economic and financial sector reforms in some of the countries. As these economies have picked up in the last few years, this
is the right time to give a big boost to economic relations. Since
economic reforms are well under way in Kazakhstan, Indian companies should particularly focus on this country to expand into the
region. To begin with, however, a strong network of information
regarding Central Asian economies is a must. India is also totally
absent from any of the regional economic initiative. India should now
seriously pursue the incorporation of the Central Asian region within
SAARC. Going by the past record, if Central Asians are not interested
in this grouping, then India should seriously consider creating another independent organisation involving India and some of the
countries in the region.

Notes and References

1. Grzegorz Kolodoko, *Ten Years of Post-Socialist Transition: The Lessons for Policy Reforms*. Policy Research Working paper no. 2095, Washington DC, The World Bank, 1999.

2. Peter Murell, 'The Transition According to Cambridge, Mass', *Journal of Economic Literature*, vol. 33, no. 1, 1995, pp. 164–78.

3. Janos Kornai, 'Transformation Recession: The Main Causes', *Journal of Comparative Economics*, vol. 19, no. 1, 1994, pp. 33–63.

4. Oliver Jean Blanchard, *The Economics of Post-Communist Transition*. Oxford, Clarendon Press, 1997.

5. Oliver Blanchard, Kenneth A. Froot and Jeffery D. Sachs (eds.), *The Transition in Eastern Europe*. 2 volumes, Chicago, University of Chicago Press ,1994; Paul Marer & Salvatore Zecchini (eds.), *The Transition to a Market Economy*. 2 volumes, Paris, OECD, 1991.

6. Stanley Fischer & Alan Gelb, 'The Process of Socialist Economic Transformation', *Journal of Economic Perspectives*, vol. 5, no. 4, 1991, pp. 91–105.

7. Some of this literature survey has been taken from Oleh Havrylyshyn, Thomas Wolf, Julian Berengaut, Marta Castello-Branco, Ron van Rooden, and Valerie Mercer-Blackman, *Growth Experience in Transition Countries, 1990–98*, Occasional paper no. 184, Washington DC, IMF, 1999.

8. The World Bank, *From Plan to Market: World Development Report 1996*. New York: Oxford University Press, 1996.

9. The World Bank, *Transition: The First Ten Years: Analysis and Lessons for Eastern Europe and Former Soviet Union*. Washington DC, The World Bank, 2002.

10. Stanley Fischer and Ratna Sahay, *The Transition Economies After Ten Years*, IMF Working paper 00/30, Washington, IMF, 2000; *UN Economic Survey of Europe*, from various issues 1990–91 to 2001, Geneva; UNECE.

11. Gerard Roland, 'The Political Economy of Transition', *Journal of Economic Perspectives*, vol. 16, no. 1, 2002, pp. 29–50.

12. This point was discussed first by Joseph E. Stiglitz in the context of Chinese economic transformation. See Joseph E. Stilitz, 'Whither Reform? Ten Years of the Transition', *Annual World Bank Conference on Development Economics 1999*, 2000, pp. 27–56. Also see Laszlo Csaba, *Transition, Development, EU Integration*, Discussion paper no. 8, Frankfurt, FIT, 2001.

13. Gulshan Sachdeva, 'Economic Transformation in Central Asia', *International Studies*, Sage, vol. 34, no. 3, 1997, pp. 313–28.

14. See Johannes Linn, 'Central Asia: Ten Years of Transition', Talking points for Central Asia Donors' Consultation Meeting, Berlin, Germany, 1 March 2002. www.worldbank.org.

15. For details, see Gulshan Sachdeva, 'Understanding Central Asian Economic Models' in Nirmala Joshi (ed.), *Central Asia: The Great Game Replayed: An Indian Perspective*. New Delhi, New Century, 2003.

16. See various issues of *Euromoney* for country risk ratings.

17. For details, see Zvi Lerman, Csaba Csaki and Gershan Feder, *Land Policies and Evolving Farm Structures in Transition Economies*. Washington DC, The World Bank, 2002.

18. For a comprehensive analysis of external economic relations in a socialist economy, see chapter 14 in Janaos Kornai, *The Socialist System: The Political Economy of Communism*. Oxford, Clarendon Press, 1992.

19. For details, see Jimmy McHugh and Emine Gurgen, 'External Sector Policies', in Emine Gurgen and others, *Economic Reforms in Kazakhastan, Kyrgyz*

Republic, Tajikistan, Turkmenistan and Uzbekistan, IMF Occasional paper no. 183, Washington, International Monetary Fund, 1999, pp. 35–47.

20. See Renata Dwan and Oleksandr Pavliuk, *Building Security in the New States of Eurasia: Subregional Cooperation in the Former Soviet Space.* London, M E Sharp, 2000; R. Sampat Kumar, 'Central Asian Economic Integration: Emerging Trends', *Economic and Political Weekely,* 2 May 1998, pp. 1013–17; Heribert Ddeter, 'Regional Integration in Central Asia: Current Economic Position and Prospects', *Central Asian Survey,* vol. 15, nos. 3–4, 1996, pp. 369–86.

21. Asian Development Bank website, www.adb.org.

22. Country Analysis Brief on China, American Energy Administration Country Analysis Brief on China, http://www.eia.doe.gov/emeu/cabs/china.html, 27 June 2005.

23. Ted Weihman, 'China Making Diplomatic Push in Central Asia', Eurasinet.org, 6/09/2003.

24. For details, see C. Raja Mohan, 'India, Iran Unveil Road Diplomacy', *The Hindu,* 26 January 2003; Sudha Ramachandran, 'India, Iran, Russia Map out Trade Route', *The Asia Times,* 29 June 2002 and Stephan Blank, 'The India–Iranian Connection and its Importance for Central Asia', Eurasianet.org, 3/12/03.

25. Details about FDI laws could be found in Jimmy McHugh, 'Capital Flows and External Debt' in Emine Gurgen and others, *Economic Reforms in Kazakhstan, Kyrgyz Republic, Tajikistan, Turkmenistan and Uzbekistan,* IMF Occasional paper no. 183, Washington, 1999, p. 54.

26. For details of these visits, see S.D. Muni, 'India & Central Asia: Towards a Cooperative Future', in Nirmala Joshi (ed.), *Central Asia: The Great Game Replayed: An Indian Perspective.* New Delhi, New Century, 2003.

12

STRUCTURAL IMPERATIVES
AND ASIAN SECURITY

Rajesh Rajagopalan

The stability of the Asian region will depend upon a number of factors, including the state of bilateral ties between the major powers in the region. But an often overlooked perspective is the structural one: how will the structure of the international system affect the Asian balance? what are India's options given such structural imperatives? A structural perspective necessarily looks at the placement of the great powers within the international system and draws conclusions about their potential behaviour on the basis of such placement. It is, of course, 'potential' behaviour, as a number of scholars have pointed out; structural theories are notoriously poor at explaining particular behaviour.[1]

What does such a comprehensive structural overview reveal about India's options in Asia? There are two ways of looking at India's relations with the major powers in Asia. One is to look at these relations from the perspective of bilateral politics, as being determined by common interests, and the result of the effort and investment each side is willing to devote to that relationship. If the state of relations with the major powers were to be solely determined by these factors, we should then attempt to find such areas of common interests with these powers and work hard to develop these relations. This is the premise of New Delhi's policies towards the major powers; this is also the premise of much writing on India's bilateral relations with the major powers. The effort to build a 'natural alliance' with the US, and the effort to promote closer economic relations with China and the other major powers are good examples of this tendency.

But common interests should not be the starting point in determining the quality of our relations with the major Asian powers. Rather common interests are themselves determined by the structure of power in the international system. The correct question to ask of India's relations with the major Asian powers is not 'how to build common interests with a major Asian power' but rather 'what are our common interests given a particular configuration of power in Asia'. Trying to build common interests in a manner that ignores the imperatives of the existing configuration of power would be at the least futile and in extremes, potentially dangerous. A good example is India's attempt to build a united front with China in the immediate aftermath of independence based on a shared history and perceived interest in anti-colonial resistance, ignoring the possibility that the balance of power in Asia suggested competition rather than cooperation between New Delhi and Beijing. Though not all efforts have to end as disastrously as that one, it would be fruitful to examine what strategic possibilities are available within a particular pattern of power relations.

In the international system, at any point of time, the nature of the great power system frames the strategic choices of all states, including that of the great powers.[2] But the type of great power system is particularly important for weaker states in the international system, such as India, because their margin for error is so much lesser. Throughout the history of interstate relations, this structure was characterised either by the dominance of a single great power (unipolarity), or a rough parity between more than two major powers (multipolarity). For brief periods, as during the Cold War, the international system was dominated by two great powers. Such configurations of great power politics do not *determine* the strategic and foreign policy choices that states make, but it *limits* the menu of policy choices that they can prudently take.

India's relations with the major powers have been and will be framed by the nature of the international system. Put another way, it is not just the amount of effort New Delhi puts on bilateral relations with the major powers that will determine the state of these relations, though that could be one factor. The state of our relations with the major powers will also be determined by the nature of the distribution of power in the international system. We need, therefore, to examine these international systemic imperatives first before discussing the specific issues that animate our relations with some of the major powers. Before attempting to build natural alliances, we need to ask who our potential natural allies are.

International Structural Imperatives

By international systemic factors I mean the state of the global balance of power and the nature of the international system that gives rise to such configurations of powers as bipolarity, multipolarity and unipolarity. The nature of these systems exert a certain amount of influence on the strategic policy choices of the states in that particular system. But we should be careful not to confuse such effects with the specifics of the foreign policies of particular great powers. For example, in a bipolar world, the two polar powers face certain strategic compulsions because they are the polar powers. These compulsions are different from the one that a polar power faces in a multi-polar world. Similarly, other states face different compulsions in different types of international systems. The pressures that an India or a Pakistan faces in a bipolar world are different from the pressures that they face in a unipolar world, or what they might face in a multipolar world. Polarity exerts a force on international politics in a manner that is not well recognised by policy makers, but which is critical.

Examining such (international systemic) pressures on national policies and on the outcomes of inter-state relations is different from examining the foreign policies of the great powers or the policies of the regional actors. Indeed, these policies themselves can be seen as the consequences of international systemic pressures (among other things). Another way to state this is to say that international systemic factors is, in a methodological sense, analogous to domestic political or bureaucratic political factors in foreign policy decision-making. It is well understood that foreign policy decisions and international political outcomes are influenced both by domestic politics and the bureaucratic decision-making process of particular states. International systemic factors similarly exert influence on both political decision-making and on international outcomes. But while the impact of domestic politics and bureaucratic and decision-making processes on the making of foreign policy is well recognised, no such attention is paid to international systemic factors.

The importance of the effect of the international political system is easily illustrated. For example, the transformation of the global order from bipolarity to unipolarity has been considered to be an important development in the international system since the end of the Second World War. The impact of this transformation on global politics has been much in debate.[3] This is a change at the international systemic level—a change from an international system in which two powers dominated, to one in which one power alone dominates. The imperatives of state behaviour are different in a unipolar world as compared to a bipolar or a multipolar one.

But how so? To answer this question, one must move away from the specifics of national interests as perceived by the polar powers in the two systems and discuss how the nature of the international system (i.e., whether it is bipolar, multipolar or unipolar) affects states, as well as international political outcomes. A multipolar world is populated by many powers of roughly equal strength—no one or two powers dominate the international system. In such an international system, the possibility of shifting alliances between the three or more powers in the system prevents clarity about who would be the adversary and the ally. This leads to loose alliances, where the loyalty of allies are always suspect, where defection is a constant threat, and where allies today might be adversaries tomorrow. The possibility of such shifting alliances lead to constant tension between the powers, increasing insecurity for all. The miscalculations inherent in such multipolar systems—the favourite example being Europe prior to the First World War—results eventually in systemwide war, or a war that includes all the major powers in the system, such as the Napoleanic wars and the First and Second World Wars. In a multipolar world, in short, states are highly insecure, suspicious of the fidelity of their allies, and in constant search for new alliances. The consequences for the international system are increasing instability and eventual war. But a multipolar system will increase the strategic choices that weaker states, such as India, will have. There will be a number of great powers in the system, which would permit greater choices in strategic partnerships. On the other hand, such a system would also increase instability, and enhance the possibility of a wider, systemwide conflict that can drag in unsuspecting weak powers. The chaos of such a system would present great opportunities for weaker states such as India, but that chaos will also bring great dangers.

In bipolarity, by contrast, the management of the global conflict is far easier because there are only two dominant powers. Because these two powers are far more powerful than any other power, only they can threaten each other. None of the other powers in the system pose a significant threat to the polar powers. Moreover, because of their dominance over all others, allies are less important, and the shifting of allegiances by the other powers are less catastrophic to the global balance. Such shifts are unlikely to lead to systemic war. This does not mean that there are no dangers in a bipolar world. The danger, however, is 'over-reaction', the endowment of importance to allies who, even if they shift allegiances, are unlikely to shift the global balance very much. Nevertheless, the two polar powers compete for such allies, one of the consequences being regional conflicts and competition. On the other hand, such crises are unlikely to result in systemic war, thus making bipolarity relatively more stable than multipolarity.

What are the consequences of bipolarity for states such as India? In a bipolar order, the two polar powers are likely to find themselves on the opposite side of every regional conflict because even regional conflicts with local causes are seen as having larger global consequences. The loss of a Vietnam or an Afghanistan, both weak states that would have added little to the overall strength of either the US or the Soviet Union, were nevertheless seen as critical to the fate of the Cold War. But bipolarity also has its advantages for weaker states: alliances in a bipolar system are likely to be more solid and longer-lasting than those in a multipolar world, and there is less fear of shifty allies and shifting alliances. When allies do shift their allegiances, as happened in the Horn of Africa, new alliances are immediately formed with the old adversaries. But such shifts have been relatively rare. In essence, bipolarity encourages long-lasting alliances and stable relations, while providing a modicum of autonomy for weaker states because they tend to be pampered by their great power patron. The constant confrontation between the polar powers permits considerable freedom of action for weaker states, who, as the superpowers constantly complained during the Cold War, play off one polar power against the other.

A unipolar world is an unusual and rare system, and its consequences are still being debated. The dominance of a single power can ensure peace (though this will be a peace on terms acceptable to the sole power), but this will be an unsatisfactory peace for many of the other major powers in the system. However benign the sole polar power is, its dominance will cause a certain amount of dissatisfaction, which can lead other powers to challenge the dominance of the unipolar power.[4] But, on the other hand, other powers will also face contradictory pulls—there will be incentives to make peace or 'bandwagon' with the sole polar power, if only because it might be futile to resist, but there will also be incentives to join other dissatisfied states to try to balance the polar power.

Unipolarity is not friendly towards weaker states in the international system. The empirical evidence itself is strong: the frequent hopes among middle and weaker states over the last decade that a multipolar world could be fashioned even within the current international system reflect both a certain amount of naiveté (because polarity is determined by the distribution of power, which cannot be created artificially) and a considerable amount of distress at the loss of their relative autonomy under the bipolar structure. The reasons are not difficult to understand. In unipolarity, bandwagoning with the unipolar power becomes the preferred strategy for most states in the international system. The polar power thus faces a veritable feast of alliance choices, while all others have only a solitary option— the polar power. The competition amongst regional powers to bandwagon with the polar power might appear ungainly—witness India and Pakistan competing for American support—but there is eminent sense in it. This is not to suggest the US, as the polar powers, has to make no choices; indeed its strategic choices can help or hinder the formation of countervailing alliances.[5]

It is true that unipolarity will not last; international systems never do. Changes in relative power are inevitable, and as they change, so will the current unipolar system. But such changes typically are slow because the basis of the change in power equations—the economic and military capability of states—takes time. Moreover, the US is so far ahead of all others today that the possibility of one or more major powers catching up with the US in the near future seems relatively remote.[6]

In short, the nature of the international system is important because it shapes the strategic choices of states. It would be unnecessary to bandwagon with a great power in the bipolar world; it would be futile, foolish and even dangerous to attempt balancing the hegemonic power in a unipolar world. In the current unipolar world, the preceding discussion suggests the sensibility of attempting to bandwagon with the hegemonic power; it also points to the practical difficulty of doing that when all other powers are also competing to do so. The following section examines how the logic of unipolarity will impact on Asian security.

Unipolarity and Asian Security

How does unipolarity affect Asia? Asia, in many ways, is the fulcrum of the global balance: it is the fastest growing region in the world, and thus the most unstable. This instability should not be confused with chaos; what I mean to suggest by 'instability' is that there is the possibility of increasing competition in Asia, primarily as a consequence of the changing nature of the distribution of wealth across the continent. The changing distribution of wealth leads to changing distribution of power; wealth is the most important ingredient of power. Such changes provide both opportunities and constraints, even to those whose wealth and power are increasing. This section examines briefly some of the possible dynamics that are introduced because of such changes.

Increasing power affords greater options to those who are its beneficiaries. It could even, over the long term, suggest changes in the unipolar distribution of power. But this possibility need not detain us long—it will be a while before such a radical redistribution happens, if it ever does. But short of a complete change in the nature of the international system, wealth redistribution among the major states in Asia can also lead to other, perhaps equally dramatic, effects.

Rapid economic growth is likely to create at least three new powers in Asia: China, Japan and India. A number of common interest, most importantly economic interdependence, unite these three; but there is also potential for severe conflict. China does not look kindly upon the possibility that Japan and India might join the ranks of the great powers, as evidenced by its discomfort at the possibility that one or both of these countries may join the United Nations Security Council as a permanent member. Both India and Japan, on the other hand, have good reasons to worry about the potential for China dominating the region, but historical and cultural factors, and distance make it unlikely that Japan and India will join together against China. Another factor unites India and Japan—

neither are likely to dominate the Asian landmass in the manner of
China, at least if current trends hold.

The picture is complicated somewhat because of two additional
factors—the uncertain trajectory of Russia and the external-balancer
role that the US plays. If Russia were to stabilise and grow rapidly,
the picture in Asia could change dramatically. India and Russia have
old and comfortable ties, and they are natural allies against China.
The US role, though, is likely to be more critical. The US role in Asia
is somewhat akin to the British 'continental commitment' in Europe
in the nineteenth century. An offshore power, its primary objective
today in Asia is, as the British objective in Europe in the nineteenth
century was, to ensure that no country dominates the continental
landmass. Britain thus always aligned with the weaker European powers against potential European hegemons, such as France in the eigh-
teenth century, Germany in the nineteenth and early twentieth century,
and Russia later.[7] Many Americans want Washington to play this role
today.

Such a role could provide clearer options to the weaker of the three
major powers in Asia, helping to strengthen their resources, and
providing a modicum of stability to the region. On the other hand,
it is not clear that the US will consistently play that role. For one,
which among the three is the potential hegemon may not always be
clear. Even if it is clear, the US may not want to risk other benefits,
including cordial ties with the most successful and wealthiest economy
in the region, for the benefit of its allies. This is particularly serious
because a potential hegemon will be aware that the US can provide
such a counter-balance, and work to ensure that Washington is given
no excuse to undertake such a role, much as Bismarck's diplomacy
did in preventing the formation of a countervailing balance in Europe
during the time he managed German grand strategy.

How will these dynamics impact on India? The following section
looks at India's relations with the most important of the major powers.
India has little choice but to bandwagon with the US, but this is easier
said than done. India also needs to balance China because China is
potentially the most serious threat that India faces. Partnerships with
Russia and Japan are essential for India but this will be difficult
without a common strategic frame, which is absent today. There are
other major powers, of course, but the ones I mentioned earlier are
the ones most likely to have the greatest influence on India. For
obvious reasons, I pay the most importance to the US.

Bandwagoning with Washington

For all countries of the world, their most important relationship is the one they have with the unipolar power. New Delhi was quick to realise the importance of the US and did manage to change tracks to emphasise ties with the US over all the other major powers. Unfortunately, though the relations did show marked improvement, there were clear limits to the possibilities of the relationship. The clearest limitation is that India needs the US much more than the US needs India. There is nothing peculiar or unique about this; it describes, as well, the relations of most countries with the US. It is pointless to blame Pakistan, or the war on terror for this—its cause lies in the nature of the unipolar system.

The Indian response to these difficulties have been to try to develop with the US a special relationship that is outside the parameters of pure national interest, somewhat akin to the relations India enjoyed with the erstwhile Soviet Union, or that the US enjoys with the UK or Israel. Indeed, by the summer of 2001, it appeared as if Indo-US relations were about to break free from the traditional, familiar 'estranged democracies' pattern.[8] There was considerable empathy in both capitals towards each other's strategic concerns, fed by a strong political commitment to improving these ties. But nearly three years after the September 11 attacks, it is clear that Indo-US ties is on its way to being another casualty of the attacks and its strategic consequences. The political commitment that was the basis of the improving relations has been steadily waning in Washington. The war on terror has taken much of the attention away from New Delhi, and to New Delhi's chagrin, it has drifted towards Islamabad.[9] But more importantly, it has left Indo-US relations once again in the hands of the bureaucrats, especially in the State Department, who are more concerned with ensuring equitability between India and Pakistan in South Asia and theological issues of non-proliferation than in improving US-India relations. And New Delhi's frustration with Washington has been growing.

The greatest continuing difference between India and the US relates to Pakistan, and its role in the war on terrorism. Though there was a strong belief in India that the US would act to curb Pakistan-sponsored terrorism against India, this has not happened. The US appears severely constrained in pressurising Pakistan on this issue. One of the constraints is that the US believes that it needs Pakistan to pursue the war on terrorism, a dependence that is unlikely to end in the near future.[10] This is a constraint that, from New Delhi's perspective, is difficult to accept. India is loath to concede the American claim that Pakistan is a 'stalwart' ally in the war on terrorism, and with some reason. Washington's own acceptance of its failure to control Pakistani actions in Kashmir, and Pakistan's complicity in the increasing violence in Afghanistan point to the hollowness of American claims. From the Indian perspective, America's frequent commendation of Pakistani cooperation in the war on terror betrays either American naiveté, or its hypocrisy.

Clearly, from the American perspective, the picture is somewhat more complex. Pakistan's strategy has made a careful distinction between terrorism directed at the US, and terrorism in the pursuit of other Pakistani objectives in India, Afghanistan and other parts of the region. Islamabad has discouraged any terrorism of the first kind, and has been quick to cooperate with the US in apprehending those that have targeted the US and extraditing them, sometimes even in contravention of domestic Pakistani law. American officials repeatedly claim that Pakistan caught over 400 terror suspects wanted by the US, including some of Al Qaeda's top commanders. Self-interest dictates that the US cannot but acknowledge such cooperation, even if such cooperation is a tactical move designed to forestall American pressures in other areas.

This Pakistani policy of discriminate terrorism has driven a wedge into Washington's war on terrorism, forcing the US to either suborn its policy to a philosophical consistency about the indivisibility of terrorism, or recognise that American security interests can sometimes trump political rhetoric. What is clear is that the US will be careful about risking Pakistani cooperation in the war that Washington is waging against its terrorists for New Delhi's sake. And, in a unipolar world, the US can easily risk India's displeasure, knowing that India will have little choice but to come to terms with it.

The nuclear issue is the second major source of disagreement between Washington and New Delhi. The salience of the nuclear issue in US-India relations has continued to wax and wane. The waning of nuclear proliferation issues began in the late Clinton administration, mainly as a consequence of the Strobe Talbott–Jaswant Singh dialogue.[11] However, the Bush administration's junking of the CTBT, and their generally lower emphasis on nuclear proliferation issues in the relationship, has been a more significant factor. But non-proliferation issues may again be beginning to cast a shadow over the relations.

There are several indicators to this. One is what New Delhi used to call the 'Trinity' issues—cooperation in civilian nuclear and space technology, and high technology trade issues. Though there has been some progress on these issues, notably the declaration of the 'Next Steps in Strategic Partnership' (NSSP), from New Delhi's perspective, the progress has been insufficient. In particular, the continuing American opposition to the transfer of civilian nuclear power plants and technology from third countries such as Russia point to the left-over influence of the proliferation fundamentalists in the Washington think-tank community, and sections of the American foreign policy bureaucracy.

On the surface, it might appear that the US–India defence relationship is the saving grace in the current scene, with US naval ships routinely calling at Indian ports, and all services conducting joint exercises and so on. Defence trade possibilities have also increased: India now requires no Congressional authorisation for purchases below US $14 million, putting India in the same category as American allies. However, there are a number of problems that afflict even this facet of the ties.

The first point to note is that India has only purchased one major defence system from the US, the Firefinder artillery locating radar. US and India are reportedly discussing the sale of P-3 Orion maritime surveillance aircraft to India, but the US is apparently unwilling to sell the latest variant (P-3C) of these aircrafts because of fears about both technology leaks, and of upsetting the military balance in the region.

In fact, concern over these two issues—technology leak from India to third countries and upsetting the military balance in the region—is continuing to be a block on robust Indo-US arms trade relationship, despite its potential. Paradoxically, the US also wants to sell India more advanced weapons than India might be willing to buy. For example, there are concerns in the US about Indian plans to put the Phalcon radars, which India is procuring from Israel, on Soviet aircraft, rather than on more advanced US aircraft. Another possibility is the sale of the US-built Patriot-3 anti-missile missile instead of the US-Israeli Arrow system.

Indeed, the tribulations of the Arrow itself are a good indicator of the state of the defence trade relations. Because the Arrow missile has significant US collaboration, Israel needs US permission to sell it to India. Despite the fact that the US is pushing missile defence, and despite the fact that Indian support for President Bush's initiative on missile defence was one of the foundations of the much improved Indo-US ties, the US has refused an Israeli request to permit it to transfer the Arrow to India. A familiar Washington coalition, made up of non-proliferation fundamentalists and nay-sayers from the State Department are behind the effort to block the Arrow sale, and, as of now, they are winning.

Indo–US relations cannot improve simply because they are 'natural allies'—that would be a rare beast in international politics. US-India ties improved dramatically in the last two years, but this was not the consequence of any great confluence of interest. It reflected, rather, the lack of any major dissonance in the relations. Nevertheless, despite the current difficulties, India has little choice but to seek closer ties with the US, fighting others seeking a seat on the same bandwagon.

Balancing China

China should be India's primary long-term concern. This is not because China is strong, and could grow stronger. A strong and stable China can be beneficial to India and to others in the region. But what is most worrying about China is what the Sinologist Alastair Iain Johnston has called China's 'parabellum paradigm'—its hardcore and sometimes crudely Realist view of the world.[12] China's role in Pakistan's development of nuclear weapons technology is a good example. Though there has been little analysis of the motives and rationale behind such a dramatic initiative, it was clearly driven by the need to balance India. It is possible that China assumed that India would develop an atomic arsenal irrespective of what China did, and that Beijing was unaware that India's nuclear weapons programme had effectively been halted after 1974. But the effect of China's policies was to force India to restart its nuclear weapons programme. There are other examples of China's pathological Realism, but the point I want to make here is simple: Chinese Realism assumes an imprudent view of possible adversaries, and there is little indication that China's view of India has changed since the fifties.

Given both China's power and the strategic culture that will direct that power, India's primary strategic concern should be to balance China. But this is a process that is delicately done. India's nuclear arsenal gives it a certain baseline power capability that China cannot afford to overlook; New Delhi should therefore be confident of handling its security concerns regarding China at the military level. At the larger strategic level, New Delhi needs to continue focussing on improving its economic power, which is the root of national power, and resolving old border disputes with China. But New Delhi also needs to pay greater attention to potential allies to balance China, such as Russia, Japan, Vietnam and South Korea.

China's potential as a possible challenger to American hegemony opens up a unique long-term opportunity for India.[13] If China should become Washington's adversary, India could have substantial gains. The common perception that great power competition would be harmful to the region and to India's interests is based more on a sense of the ethical disagreeability of such competition rather than any prudent analysis of its consequences. But we must also realise that there is little likelihood of any such competition in Asia in the immediate future, unless either China or the US is particularly strategically maladroit. Thus, though New Delhi should not miss an opportunity to benefit from such a rivalry should one come about, yet basing its policies on the hopes of such a rivalry would be rather foolish.

In the absence of such an eventuality, India has limited choices in balancing China. Its internal resources are insufficient, and there are no external sources of balancing, such as allies. India's best bet then is to build up its internal strength while waiting for an external opportunity, meantime giving China no cause to feel that its perception of an Indian threat is justified. But India should also be careful of China, understanding that the nature of the international power structure, China's strategic culture, and India's own relative weakness all make India potentially vulnerable to China.

Promoting Partnerships with other Major Powers

There are two other major powers whose roles could be potentially decisive in India's favour—Russia and Japan. Both are tremendously strong but face peculiar problems with the fungibility of their power; and importantly, India shares no conflict with either. Most importantly, both these powers share, or should, India's concern about China's rise and its consequences.[14] Both Russia and Japan have troubled histories, and this limits their freedom considerably. Japan is viewed with considerable suspicion in all of East Asia, where the scars left by the Japanese Empire have yet to heal. Many of the former republics that constituted the Soviet empire—and many of the former allies of that empire—have unpleasant memories that seriously constrain Moscow's elbowroom in its immediate neighbourhood.

India's long ties with Russia were beneficial to both powers, and the warmth in that old relationship still lingers. But Russia today has other immediate concerns, most pressingly the need to re-establish its economy and internal stability. Russia also needs peace on its borders while it rebuilds itself. Many of these factors and hard cash, besides, motivate Russian relations with China, particularly its troubling arms supply relations. Russia hopes to postpone any potential conflict until Russia is ready; China's calculus may be similar.

India has much to gain by Russia's rise, but wishing it will not make it so. Russia will remain a relatively minor power for sometime to come, but there are, nevertheless, good reasons not to discard Russia. There is a comfort in the relationship that might usefully be preserved for the future; Russia's weapons laboratories still produce some of the world's best military equipment, and Moscow is willing to sell them to India; and despite its relative weakness, Moscow still has a useful presence in places like the UN Security Council, which is beneficial to us.

Many of these advantages will be found in a close relationship with Japan too. But getting to that close relationship will be harder than in the case of Russia. Unlike Russia and India, there is no history of common perceptions on global politics between India and Japan. Indians no doubt shared in Asia's pride as one of its own stood up to the West successfully while much of the rest of Asia and Africa were under colonialism's yoke, but that past is little recalled today. Japan, on the other hand, looks to India as one of the sources of its religious and cultural heritage, but little else besides. During the Cold War, Tokyo and New Delhi found themselves on the opposite sides of the fence. There has been no indication of any great sympathy towards each other's concerns. Perhaps because of such perceptions, relations between the two powers have been, at best, correct. It appears at times that Japan and India care too little about each other to even fight. Though economic ties between the two countries have improved, there is no sign of any such movement at the political level. Whatever interaction takes place, it is many times hostile, whether it was a Cold War issue, the nuclear issue, or the question of handling China.

Building a strategic relationship with Japan under such trying circumstances is difficult, but change has to happen on both sides. India needs to see Japan as a serious player and court, rather than overlook its potential. Japan needs to be more pragmatic about India's role in Asia and the world, and more importantly, realise its own potential for a significant role in Asia, and the consequences of such a role. Because these require changes in the strategic culture of both India and Japan, it is difficult to predict if it will indeed come about.

Conclusion

Indian grand strategy has rarely been conceptualised in terms of the balance of power. Where nevertheless India behaved in a manner that might appear to indicate balancing tendencies—the Cold War alliance with the Soviet Union, for instance—these represented post-facto rationalisations of policy prescriptions that have other, rather ideological roots. But it is necessary to think in these terms; at the very least, it is necessary to understand how international systemic factors point towards certain options and discourage others. Such factors do not, and should not be the determining factor in deciding grand strategy, but they provide signposts that we ignore at our peril.

Notes and References

1. Hence, the shift towards 'neoclassical' Realism among Realist scholars. See, Gideon Rose, 'Neoclassical Realism and Theories of Foreign Policy,' *World Politics*, vol. 51, no. 1, 1998, pp. 144–72.
2. Kenneth Waltz, *Theory of International Politics*. Reading, Mass., Addison-Wesley, 1979; Robert Gilpin, *War and Change in World Politics*. New York, Cambridge University Press, 1981.

3. John Mearsheimer, 'Back to the Future: Instability in Europe after the Cold War,' in Michael E. Brown, Sean M. Lynn-Jones and Steven E. Miller (eds.), *The Perils of Anarchy: Contemporary Realism and International Security*. Cambridge, Massachusetts: MIT Press, 1995, pp. 78–129; Kenneth N. Waltz, 'The Emerging Structures of International Politics,' *International Security*, vol. 18, no. 2, 1993, pp. 44–79.

4. Kenneth N. Waltz, 'The Emerging Structures of International Politics', *International Security*, vol. 18, no. 2, 1993, pp. 44–79.

5. Christopher Layne, 'Rethinking American Grand Strategy: Hegemony or Balance of Power in the Twenty-First Century?' *World Policy Journal*, vol. 15, no. 2, Summer 1998, pp. 8–28. A recent essay by Colin Dueck provides a good review of much of this literature in 'New Perspectives on American Grand Strategy: A Review Essay,' *International Security*, vol. 28, no. 4, 2004, pp. 197–216.

6. On American dominance, see Barry Posen, 'Command of the Commons: The Military Foundations of US Hegemony,' *International Security*, vol. 28, no. 1, 2003, pp. 5–46.

7. Michael Howard, *Continental Commitment: The Dilemma of British Defence Policy in the Era of the Two World Wars*. London, Humanity Books, 1989.

8. Dennis Kux first suggested the notion of 'estranged democracies', with the connotation that this was an inexplicable estrangement. Dennis Kux, *India and the United States: Estranged Democracies*. Washington DC, National Defence University Press, 1992. See also Robert J. McMahon, *The Cold War on the Periphery: The United States, India and Pakistan*. New York, Columbia University Press, 1994.

9. On American imperatives in the war on terrorism, see Ashley Tellis, 'Assessing America's War on Terror: Confronting Insurgency, Cementing Primacy', *NBR Analysis*, vol. 15, no. 4, December 2004.

10. Ibid.

11. On the dialogue, see Strobe Talbot, *Engaging India*. New Delhi, Penguin, 2004.

12. Alastair Iain Johnston, *Cultural Realism: Strategic Culture and Grand Strategy in Chinese History*. Princeton, Princeton University Press, 1997.

13. On the debate about the future of the Asian balance of power, see Amitav Acharya, 'Will Asia's Past Be Its Future?' and David C. Kang, 'Hierarchy, Balancing and Empirical Puzzles in Asian International Relations,' *International Security*, vol. 28, no. 3, Winter, 2003 and Alastair Iain Johnston, 'Is China a status quo power?' and David C. Kang, 'Getting Asia Wrong: The Need for a new Analytical Framework', *International Security*, vol. 27, no. 4, 2003.

14. On Sino-Indian, Sino-Russian and Sino-Japanese relations, see chapters by Mohan Malik, Alexander Mansourouv and Dennis Roy in the recent volume on Asian bilateral relations produced by the Asia-Pacific Centre for Security Studies, available at www.apcss.org/Publications/SAS/AsiaBilateralRelations/AsiaBilateralRelations.html

About the Editor and Contributors

About the Editor

R.R. Sharma is the former Dean, School of International Studies and Professor of Russian, East European and Central Asian Studies, Jawaharlal Nehru University, New Delhi. He earlier served as the Vice-Chancellor of the University of Jammu (1996–2002). Professor Sharma has authored or edited a number of books including *Marxist Model of Social Change: A Study of Soviet Central Asia* (1979), *The USSR in Transition: Issues and Themes* (1985), *Asian Dimension of Soviet Policy* (edited, 1986), *New Contours of Soviet Foreign Policy* (editor, 1989), *Economic Reforms, Liberalization and Structural Change—India and Hungary* (edited, 1997) and *Reform, Conflict and Change in the CIS and East Europe* (edited, 1999). He is currently co-editing a volume on *Globalisation and Transnational Conflicts*, which will be published in early 2006 by Sage, London.

About the Contributors

Anuradha M. Chenoy is Professor at the School of International Studies, Jawaharlal Nehru University, New Delhi. She works on topics related to International Relations, Russia, Central Asia and Gender issues. She has been the Chairperson in the Centre for Russia and Central Asian Studies and Director of the Area Studies Programme of that Centre. She has been on the governing bodies of several institutions like the Indian Social Institute, Centre for Education and

Communication, New Delhi. She is the author of *Militarism and Women in South Asia* (2001), *The Making of New Russia* (2001) and the co-author of *India Under Siege: Challenges Within and Without* (1994). She has edited *Labor, Environment and Globalization: The Social Clause in Multilateral Agreements* (1967). She has been a specialist at the Expert Group Meeting of the United Nations Division for the Advancement of Women, in October 1996, at Santo Domingo, Dominican Republic, on 'Conflict Resolution: The Role of Gender' and at the UNESCO Conference on 'Women and a Culture of Peace' in Vietnam from 6–9 December 2000. She was the keynote speaker at the 56th DPI NGO Conference of the United Nations, in 2003.

Manoj Joshi is the Editor 'Views', *The Hindustan Times* and a member of the National Security Board of India's National Security Council. He has a PhD from the School of International Studies (SIS), Jawaharlal Nehru University and studied at St Stephen's College, Delhi University and the Lucknow University. He is the author of a definitive study of the Jammu and Kashmir insurgency titled *Lost Rebellion: Kashmir in the Nineties* (1999) as well as a number of articles and papers in academic studies relating to terrorism and security. He has been a Visiting Professor at the SIS and a Visiting Fellow at the Strategic and Defence Studies Centre at the Australian National University, Canberra, and the Political Editor of *The Times of India*.

K.V. Kesavan was the former Chairman and Professor of Japanese Studies, Centre for East Asian Studies, School of International Studies, JNU, New Delhi. He is currently the Visiting Professor, Kobe Gakuin University, Japan. He is the author of several books and numerous research papers on Japan's domestic politics and foreign policy. He has received the Commendation Award of the Ministry of Foreign Affairs, Government of Japan, for his contribution to the development of Japanese Studies in India.

Mahendra P. Lama is Chairman, Centre for South, Central, South East Asian and South West Pacific Studies. He is also Chief Economic Adviser to the Chief Minister of Sikkim with a Cabinet Minister rank. Central to his intellectual pursuits is development and cooperation in South Asia. While teaching economic cooperation and integration in South Asia and India's Foreign Economic Policy, he does extensive research with distinct policy slants. He was nominated by the Government of India to the Independent Expert Group set up by the South Asian Association for Regional Cooperation (SAARC) in 1997. He has extensively worked on the issues of trade, investment, migration, natural resource management, development assistance and energy cooperation in South Asia, and has produced very widely acclaimed reports on cross-border power trading among the South Asian countries. He has been Asia Leadership Fellow in Japan, Visiting Fellow, Calcutta University, Ford Foundation Fellow in Notre Dame University, USA and Visiting Professor in Hitotsubashi University, Tokyo.

Chintamani Mahapatra is currently Associate Professor of American Studies at the School of International Studies, Jawaharlal Nehru University, New Delhi. Formerly, he was a Research Fellow at the Institute for Defense and Strategic Analyses. His major publications include *American Role in Origin and Growth of ASEAN* (1990) and *Indo–US Relations in the 21st Century* (1999). He has also contributed articles to over 25 books published in India and abroad, and 50 articles to various academic journals.

C. Raja Mohan is Professor of South Asian Studies, Jawaharlal Nehru University, New Delhi. Earlier he had served as Senior Research Associate at the Institute for Defence Studies and Analyses, New Delhi and as the Strategic Affairs Editor of *The Hindu*. He is currently a member of India's National Security Advisory Board. His book, *Crossing the Rubicon: The Shaping of India's New Foreign Policy* was published in 2004.

S.D. Muni is Professor at the School of International Studies, Jawaharlal Nehru University, New Delhi. He is also Honorary Director of Research at the Observer Research Foundation, New Delhi and Honorary Fellow of the Monash Asia Institute, Monash University, Melbourne, Australia. He served as India's Ambassador in Lao P.D.R. (1997–99). He has edited and authored 17 books and more than 70 research papers. Some of his latest books include *India's Energy Security: Prospects of Cooperation with Extended Neighbourhood* (2005), *The Maoist Insurgency in Nepal* (2003) and *China's Strategic Engagement with the New ASEAN* (2002).

Girijesh Pant is Professor in Centre of West Asian and African Studies at Jawaharlal Nehru University. He has authored and edited seven books. Published more than 50 articles in various journals. He has attended national and international seminars and traveled extensively. His specialisation includes Political Economy of Development, West Asian Economies and Hydrocarbon Economics. He has also been the Vice-Chancellor, GGD University, Bilaspur and Vice President, Indian Academy of Social Sciences.

Ajay Patnaik is Professor and Chairperson at the Centre for Russian and Central Asian Studies, School of International Studies, Jawaharlal Nehru University, New Delhi. A PhD from JNU (1988), Patnaik was a Visiting Scholar at the Faculty of Social and Political Sciences, University of Cambridge (1992–93) and ICSSR Exchange Scholar at the Institute of Ethnography, Moscow (1999). He has contributed numerous articles to national and international journals and edited volumes. His recent article on 'Education, Press and Public Health in Central Asia, 1950–1990', is part of the forthcoming Volume VI of *History of Civilizations of Central Asia* brought out by UNESCO. Author of three books—*Nations and Minorities in Post-Soviet Central Asia* (2003), *Central Asia between Modernity and Tradition* (1996), *Perestroika and Women Labour Force in Soviet Central Asia* (1989)—Patnaik is the Executive Editor of the journal *Contemporary Central Asia*, brought out by the Central Asian Studies Foundation, New Delhi. His current research interests include geopolitics and the security scenario, social impact of globalisation and identity issues in Central Asia.

Rajesh Rajagopalan is Associate Professor in International Politics at the Centre for International Politics, Organisation and Disarmament, School of International Studies, Jawaharlal Nehru University, New Delhi. He has a PhD from the City University of New York (1998). Before joining the Centre, he was Senior Fellow at the Observer Research Foundation, New Delhi (2002–2004), Research Fellow at the Institute for Defence Studies and Analyses, New Delhi (1998–2002) and Senior Research Aide at the Ralph Bunche Institute on the United Nations, now the Ralph Bunche Institute for International Studies (1997). He also served as Deputy Secretary in the National Security Council Secretariat, Government of India (2000–2001). He has taught at Hunter College, Brooklyn College, and Queens College of the City University of New York. His areas of research interest are international relations theory, military doctrines, and nuclear weapons and disarmament.

Gulshan Sachdeva is Associate Professor at the School of International Studies, JNU, New Delhi. He has also taught and researched at the Centre for Policy Research, New Delhi, University of Delhi and KOPINT DATORG Institute, Budapest. His research work has been published in scholarly journals in the UK, USA, Germany, Hungary, Australia, and India along with about 15 articles in edited books. He is also author of *The Economy of North-East: Policy, Present Conditions and Future Possibilities* (2000). His major areas of research are transition economies, regional economic arrangements, and Northeast India.

Varun Sahni is Professor in International Politics at Jawaharlal Nehru University (JNU), New Delhi. He is also the Editor of *South Asian Survey*, an academic journal on the region published by Sage. He lectures regularly to foreign diplomats and officer trainees of the Indian Foreign Service at the Foreign Service Institute in New Delhi. Professor Sahni teaches international relations theory and writes on issues of international and regional security. His research articles have been published in the *Journal of Latin American Studies*, *Contemporary South Asia* and *International Studies*. He is currently writing a textbook on world politics for graduate students.

INDEX

11 September 2001, 37, 117, 191, 210
1996 Outline, principles of the, 235
1996 US-Japan joint statement, 243
ABC (Arab Business Council),
  establishment of, 187
advisory council of experts,
  recommendations of, 243
Afghan jihad by Pakistan, 113
Afghanistan and India: bilateral
  agreement between, 222; transit
  trade between, 67
Afghanistan and Indian subcontinent,
  economic integration between, 69
Afghanistan: developments in, 49;
  economic and developmental
  assistance to, 223; importance of
  road connection with, 69; India's
  enhanced presence and role in, 66;
  India's policy towards, 65; land
  barrier in the form of, 68; obstacles
  to India's involvement in, 66;
  Pakistan's expanded presence in,
  69; Pakistan's policies in, 106;
  preference trade agreement with, 67
Agha, Ayesha Siddiqa, Pakistani
  defence analyst, 111, 113, 117, 125
AHDRs (Arab Human Development
  Reports), 188; criticism of, 189
Ahmed, Qazi Hussain, influence of, 113
Air Self-defence Force (see ASDF)
Aiyar, Mani Shankar, petroleum
  minister, 102–03
Al Qaeda, 19, 44

American pursuit of national interests, 40
American arms aid to Pakistan, 110, 166
American: focus on Southwest Asia,
  shifting of, 159; forces on Okinawa,
  88; globalisation, 37; military
  presence in Asia, 82; power,
  preponderance of, 81; strategy of
  muscular dominance, 82;
  unilateralism, anxieties about, 56
Anjuman-e-Sipah-e-Sahaba, founding
  of, 114
anti-state movements, features of, 252
anti-Taliban Northern Alliance,
  assistance to, 221
APEC (Asia-Pacific Economic
  Cooperation), 63
Arab Business Council (see ABC)
Arab Human Development Report
  (see AHDR)
Arab League, resolution at the summit,
  186
Arab Reform Issues: Vision and
  Implementation, 187
Arab Renaissance, road to, 187
arch of: instability, 47; stability, 47
ARF (ASEAN Regional Forum), 103,
  120, 248; India's strategic objective
  in, 63; membership of, 63
armed conflicts in Asia, 26;
  analysis of, 257
armed forces, special rights of, 252
Armitage, Richard, US Deputy
  Secretary of State, 240